BAD MOON
RISING

★★★★★

*"Derek Gilbert is one of the most
thorough researchers and original thinkers
in the world of prophecy writers."*

— Joel Richardson, *New York Times* bestselling author of *Mystery Babylon* and *Mideast Beast*

BAD MOON
RISING

*Islam, Armageddon, and the Most
Diabolical Double-Cross in History*

DEREK P. GILBERT

Bestselling author of *The Great Inception*

DEFENDER

CRANE, MO

Bad Moon Rising: Islam, Armageddon, and the Most Diabolical Double-Cross in History
Derek P. Gilbert

Defender Publishing
Crane, MO 65633
©2019 by Derek Gilbert

A CIP catalog record of this book is available from the Library of Congress.

Cover design by Jeffrey Mardis.

Unless otherwise noted, all Scripture from ESV.

For Sharon.
Each day is an adventure.
I can't imagine sharing it with anyone else.

Contents

Acknowledgments

A s always, top credit is due our Lord and Savior for choosing to work in some small way through the gifts with which He's blessed me. Anything that's correct in this book is His; whatever misses the mark is mine.

My gratitude to Tom and Nita Horn for offering Sharon and me the opportunity to be a part of SkyWatch TV and support the incredible work at Whispering Ponies Ranch.

Thanks to Dr. Michael Heiser for his tireless work to make his research and teachings available and accessible to us here in Christian Middle-earth. If you haven't read *The Unseen Realm* or *Reversing Hermon*, do it soon.

Chris White, author of *False Christ, Mystery Babylon: When Jerusalem Embraces the Antichrist, The Islamic Antichrist Debunked*, and a great commentary on the Book of Daniel, deserves credit for leading me to think outside of the end-times prophecy box.

I owe an unpayable debt to my parents, Paul and Shirley Gilbert:

Dad for a curiosity about the way things work, and Mom for a lifelong love of reading and learning.

To our daughter, Nicole, sincere thanks for inspiring me to find the foundation for my life. A man cannot teach his child right from wrong when his worldview is built on sand.

Most of all, thanks and love to my best friend and co-host of my life, Sharon. Her unwavering love and encouragement make me believe I can slay dragons. Our adventure together is still new after twenty-one years.

Introduction

The moon-god has been getting away with murder for more than five thousand years.

Ask a Christian today why the world is such a mess and we may blame Satan. Or maybe not; recent research reveals that about 60 percent of American Christians don't believe the devil is real, so we may put the blame on Hollywood, lack of jobs, or the opposing political party.

If we're aware of the deep state or hold a conspiracist view of history, we might hold secret societies such as the Freemasons, Jesuits, or Illuminati accountable. We might blame occult systems based on the Roman sun-god Sol Invictus or the dark god Saturn.

Sometimes we blame Nimrod. Sometimes we conflate Nimrod with the sun-god or the storm-god, Baal. Sometimes we *really* confuse things and mix them all together.

The Bible makes it clear that the gods of the ancient world are real. The prophets and apostles knew it, and what they wrote makes a lot more sense when we view the world through their eyes.

"But there is only one God!" you say. Yes, only one capital-*G* god.

There are, however, a boatload of small-*G* gods—at least seventy, according to the Bible, and a couple hundred more if you accept the testimony of the pseudepigraphal Book of 1 Enoch.

Where are those seventy gods in the Bible? Start at Deuteronomy 32:

When the Most High gave to the nations their inheritance, when he divided mankind, he fixed the borders of the peoples according to the number of the sons of God. (Deuteronomy 32:8)

Your English translation may read "sons of Israel" instead of "sons of God." This is based on the reading in the Masoretic Hebrew text, which was compiled between the seventh and tenth centuries AD. The ESV and several other newer English Bibles follow older Hebrew texts—copies of Deuteronomy found among the Dead Sea Scrolls and the Septuagint translation of the Old Testament, which was completed about 200 BC. The original sense of the passage was rendered out of the Masoretic text, which is what most English translators have used until the last half-century or so.

The bottom line: When God divided the nations after the Tower of Babel incident, He assigned to those nations *bənê hā'ĕlōhîm* ("sons of God") as divine intermediaries, or small-*G* gods.[1] Count the number of names in the Table of Nations in Genesis 10, and you find seventy.

Not coincidentally, the Canaanites who lived alongside the ancient Hebrews believed that their creator-god El held court on his "mount of assembly," which was almost certainly Mount Hermon[2] at the northernmost point in Israel, with his consort Asherah and their seventy sons. Similarly, a ritual performed at the ancient city of Emar, in what is now northern Syria, sacrificed seventy lambs for the chief god Dagan and all the gods of the city.[3]

It shouldn't be a surprise to learn that the number of bulls slaughtered at the annual Feast of Tabernacles, or Sukkot, was exactly seventy.[4]

Does this mean that precisely seventy angels abused their authority to rule the world since the days of Nimrod? Not necessarily. In the ancient Near East, seventy wasn't always a literal number. It represented a full set, the complete amount, not one left out.[5] The sacrifice of seventy bulls at Sukkot represented Yahweh's promise to deliver Israel from the gods of all of the nations, regardless of the precise number. In other words, the festival is a commemoration of "Yahweh's victory on behalf of his people over the totality of the powers of darkness—every other supernatural being."[6]

Now, if you were brought up in a typical Christian church, the use of the word "gods" probably makes you a bit uncomfortable. But God calls them "gods," so we're on solid theological ground here. In fact, our traditional understanding of pagan gods as nonexistent makes the First Commandment kind of silly, if you think about it. God did not say, "Thou shalt have no imaginary friends before Me." No, He said, "Thou shalt have no other *gods* before Me."

There are other gods, but only one capital-*G* God, and He is Yahweh, Creator of heaven and earth. He created the other gods and placed them over the nations, and they rebelled—for which they have been judged and sentenced.

> God has taken his place in the divine council; in the midst of the gods he holds judgment: "How long will you judge unjustly and show partiality to the wicked? *Selah*...."
>
> I said, "You are gods, sons of the Most High, all of you; nevertheless, like men you shall die, and fall like any prince." (Psalm 82:1–2, 6–7)

The day that their sentence is carried out is still in the future. We have some difficult roads to walk between now and then, and that's partly because those small-*g* gods are still at work.

In this book, you'll learn how the moon-god of the ancient world has influenced human history far more than you ever imagined. We'll profile the moon-god and his colleagues from ancient Mesopotamia to show you how God responded to the religious system established by the moon-god's followers—a system so wicked that the Hebrew prophets used it as a symbol of the false religion of the fearsome end-times enemy of God and Israel.

To be clear: This book is not intended to bash Muslims. "We wrestle not against flesh and blood."[7] Our enemy is not mortal, it's supernatural. It's hard to remember that when our spiritual nemesis hides behind a human face. But Jesus died for Muslims, too. If we allow ourselves to be baited into responding with anger, we build the stumbling block between them and the gospel even higher than it already is.

Previous analyses have tended to identify one spiritual source behind the teachings of Muhammad—Satan, usually, or the moon-god, because of the crescent moon that overshadows Islam's holiest space. However, it's generally assumed that the moon-god isn't real, which is, to be blunt, unbiblical.

We'll examine Islam and its teachings to show you why it's the supernatural equivalent of a corporate merger, a partnership formed by the old gods who were caught off-guard at Calvary. As Paul wrote, if "the rulers of this age, who are doomed to pass away" had understood what was happening, "they would not have crucified the Lord of glory."[8]

While the crescent symbol of the moon-god looks down on the Ka'ba in Mecca, the moon-god is not alone. The Fallen have joined forces to create a bloody religion that could become the largest on earth before the end of the twenty-first century.

But this army of darkness won't be enough to save the rebel gods from their fate on the great and terrible Day of the Lord.

Part 1

Moon over Mesopotamia

1

The Amorites

God made a puzzling statement to Abraham while establishing His covenant with the patriarch, linking the time that Israel would sojourn in Egypt to the behavior of one particular group of people.

> Then the LORD said to Abram, "Know for certain that your offspring will be sojourners in a land that is not theirs and will be servants there, and they will be afflicted for four hundred years. But I will bring judgment on the nation that they serve, and afterward they shall come out with great possessions. As for you, you shall go to your fathers in peace; you shall be buried in a good old age. And they shall come back here in the fourth generation, for the iniquity of the Amorites is not yet complete." (Genesis 15:13–16)

Iniquity is easy enough to understand; it means sin, vice, or immorality. But what did the Amorites do that God found so offensive? Who were these people and where did they come from?

The Amorites first stepped onto the world stage in the middle of the third millennium BC. The earliest known reference to an Amorite was from the ancient city of Shuruppak, dated to about 2600 BC. According to the Sumerian King List, Shuruppak, about halfway between modern Baghdad and the Persian Gulf, was the home city of the last Sumerian king before the Flood. That king was either the unfortunately named Ubara-Tutu or his son, the hero of the Sumerian flood myth, Ziusudra, the Mesopotamian Noah.

Scholars disagree on the location of the Amorite homeland. There are two main candidates: One is Jebel Bishri, a low mountain range along the west side of the Euphrates River in central Syria. The other is the Diyala River Valley, which descends from the Hamrin mountains toward modern Baghdad. This is the traditional border between Iraq and Iran, and between Arab lands to the south and Kurdish territory to the north.

There is evidence for both theories. One of the peaks in the Jebel Bishri range, Jebel Diddi, may be named for an ancient Amorite tribe, the Didanu (or Tidanu, or Tidnum, depending on when and in what language it was written).[9] Or it may be that the tribe was named for the mountain. Either way, the name is important.

Estonian scholar Amar Annus has demonstrated that the name of this ancient Amorite tribe was probably the origin of the name of the old Greek gods, the Titans.[10] That's significant, because it links the Amorites and their worship of gods connected to the netherworld, such as Molech, Dagan, Baal-Hammon, and the Rephaim to the sinful angels mentioned by Peter[11] and Jude[12]—the "sons of God" of Genesis 6:1–4, called "Watchers" in Jewish texts of the Second Temple period such as the Book of the Watchers, or what we know now as the first thirty-six chapters of the Book of First Enoch.

Annus also showed that the Watchers were known as *apkallu* in ancient Mesopotamia long before the Second Temple period. They were considered sages who brought the gifts of civilization to humanity on behalf of Enki, the god of wisdom.[13] That's similar to the description of the Watchers in Enoch, although the Jewish and early Christian view of "gifts" like weapons, witchcraft, and mating with human women to produce giants was considerably less favorable than in, say, Babylon.

How do Watchers differ from run-of-the-mill angels? Unfortunately for us English speakers, our language lacks the richness of some others. The word "angel," borrowed from the Greek *angelos* ("messenger"), hides the fact that there are a number of classes or categories of angel, such as *malakim* ("messenger"), *cherubim, seraphim, ophanim* (the wheels of Ezekiel's vision), and others. Based on the use of the term in Enoch, it's clear that Watchers were especially powerful and exercised free will. Their decision to commit what they knew was a sin[14] suggests that they also had knowledge of good and evil.

Not coincidentally, the Bible tells us that these rebellious angels were cast into Tartarus, just like the Titans of the Greeks. Although your Bible probably reads "hell" in 2 Peter 2:4, the original Greek names Tartarus as the prison of these spirits. Tartarus is a separate place from Hades, a sort of maximum-security hell reserved for supernatural threats to the divine order. Yet the Amorites (and their descendants, the Phoenicians), Greeks, and Romans continued to worship the old gods, especially the king of the Titans, Kronos (Saturn to the Romans, Baal-Hammon to the Phoenicians). Their offspring, the demigod heroes such as Perseus and Hercules, were, by definition, Nephilim.

By 2000 BC, the Tidanu tribe had developed a reputation across the ancient Near East of being mad, bad, and dangerous to know—so dangerous, in fact, that the last Sumerian kings of Mesopotamia ordered a massive public-works project directed at these savage Amorites. The kings of the Third Dynasty of Ur, a mighty city-state in what is now southeastern Iraq, built a wall north of modern Baghdad 175 miles long, from the Euphrates across the Tigris to the Diyala. This wall, which one smart-aleck scholar recently suggested was intended to "make Sumer great again," was built specifically to keep the Tidanu away. We know this because the Sumerian name of the wall literally translates into English as "Amorite Wall That Keeps Tidanu Away."

The problem for Ur was that it *didn't* keep Tidanu away. More on that later.

So, the big question for scholars is this: Did the Amorites come from the middle of Syria or did they come from northeastern Iraq/northwestern Iran? The answer may be "yes" to both.

Some scholars believe that Amorites, specifically the Tidanu/Ditanu, began migrating east from around Jebel Bishri sometime in the middle of the third millennium BC, moving through northern Mesopotamia and northwest Iran before descending the Diyala Valley and entering Sumer from the north. Evidence suggests that Amorites lived farther east into what is now Iran than previously thought, possibly following their flocks through the mountains or setting up trading posts along routes that connected Sumer to people living east of Mesopotamia. Lapis lazuli, a blue stone prized in the ancient world, is still found mainly in northeast Afghanistan, and it was used in art and jewelry in Egypt as far back as 3700 BC. Merchants hauling cargo through the mountains needed places to eat, sleep, and care for their donkeys, and it appears that some of those ancient caravan stops on the eastern edge of Mesopotamia may have been staffed by Amorites by the time of Abraham in the early second millennium BC.

We're limited in how far back we can trace the Amorites. While it's clear that the Amorites had their own language, most of what we know about it comes from deciphering Amorite names. Almost all of the early written records from the places they lived are in Sumerian or Akkadian. For example, while the moon-god was called Nanna by Sumerians and Sîn by Akkadians, he was Yarikh to the Amorites. But when Amorites came to power across the Near East after 2000 BC, government documents were still written in Sumerian or Akkadian, even in diplomatic messages sent to faraway countries like Hatti (the Hittites, who controlled most of modern Turkey) and Egypt. So, piecing together Amorite culture and history from tablets written in Amorite will probably never happen. Tracing their movements is only possible by identifying Amorite names in Akkadian and Sumerian records.

While it can't be proved beyond a shadow of a doubt, evidence suggests that the cult of Kronos, king of the Titans, began where the Amorites were first identified. Stories of the old god did not originate in Greece. Instead, evidence firmly documents the earliest worship of Kronos in northern Mesopotamia (southern Turkey or northern Syria), and older circumstantial evidence points specifically to Jebel Bishri,[15] exactly where the earliest Mesopotamian records place the Amorites.

At the risk of sounding like a television presenter (oh, wait—I am one), I have to ask: Is it possible that the Titans, called Watchers by the Hebrews, made an infernal bargain with the early Amorites? Was this why the Amorite kings who ruled nearly all the lands of the Bible in the days of Abraham, Isaac, and Jacob traced their ancestry back to one Ditana, the legendary founder of the Tidanu/Ditanu tribe? Could this explain the pride of the Amorites who founded Babylon, whose magicians considered themselves masters of occult knowledge received from the spirit realm before the Flood? Is this why Amorite kings as late as the time of the judges in Israel summoned "the council of the Ditanu" from the netherworld through necromancy rituals?

More important: Is the child sacrifice demanded by the old god, Kronos (and his other identities, Saturn and Baal-Hammon), the reason the practice continues even today?

Almost five thousand years after they emerged onto the world stage, the iniquity of the Amorites is *still* not complete. The bad news is the Watchers/Titans were not the only gods they served.

Two hundred years after their existence was confirmed by clay tablets found in Mesopotamia, the history of the Amorites is still debated by scholars. We don't really know the details of their rise and fall, even though it was pretty spectacular. The truth is the Amorites set the cultural and religious tone of Mesopotamia, including Canaan/Israel, for about two thousand years, all the way down to the time of Jesus. So, it's worth summarizing the history of the Amorites, but I'll keep it brief—a detailed history would be way too long, mostly irrelevant, and probably boring.

As mentioned in the previous section, the earliest reference found so far is from about 2600 BC in the ancient city of Shuruppak, in what is Iraq today. The next mentions show up in the archives of Ebla, a city near modern Aleppo that dominated northern Syria from about 3000 BC until about 2250 BC, when it was destroyed either by Sargon the Great of Akkad or by Ebla's main rival, the kingdom of Mari in southeastern Syria. The discovery of the ruins of Ebla in 1964, confirmed in 1968, included about eighteen hundred complete clay tablets and thousands of fragments covering a period from about 2500 BC to about 2250 BC.

One of the last rulers of Ebla, a vizier named Ebrium, married his daughter to an Amorite named Tidinu, "chief of the mercenaries."[16] Because you're observant, you've noticed the similarity between the name of this soldier and that of the legendary Amorite tribe. Apparently, since Ebla depended on foreign soldiers, a marriage to secure the relationship between the government of Ebla and its Amorite contractors was good politics.

This highlights an important point: Even though they weren't mentioned often in the texts from the third millennium BC, it appears that even at that early date, Amorites in general and the Tidanu/Ditanu in particular had earned a warlike reputation.

This is reflected in a number of texts found in southeastern Iraq, the heart of ancient Sumer. The "Tidnumites" are among the barbarians blamed for the destruction of Sumerian civilization:

Below, the Elamites are in charge, slaughter follows in their wake, Above, the Halma-people, the "men of the mountains," took captives, The Tidnumites daily fastened the mace to their loins.[17]

Incursions by Amorites, who apparently found a way around the "Amorite Wall That Keeps Tidanu Away," had weakened the kingdom of Ur by making travel between the cities of Sumer too dangerous for the cheap transport of goods. Imagine the price of a loaf of bread if armed guards had to protect farmers, crops, bakers, and truckers at every step of the process before the bread even reached your local grocery store.

That may have been a picture of the situation in Sumer in the last years before Ur collapsed. Records from the seventh and eighth years of the reign of Ur's last king, Ibbi-Sin, show that the price of grain skyrocketed to sixty times normal! Finally, weakened by the breakdown in communications between the capital and the edges of its empire, Ur was overrun by invaders from Elam, a kingdom along the coast of the Persian Gulf in what is now western Iran. Around 2004 BC, Ibbi-Sin, the last Sumerian king of Mesopotamia, was carried off to Elam, where he was imprisoned and presumably killed.

This led to a dark age of about a hundred years in Mesopotamia. Despite the many tablets found at major archaeological sites like Ur, Babylon, Mari, and Ebla, scholars really don't know what happened in the twentieth century BC. All that can be said for sure is that when the dust settled around 1900 BC, Amorite dynasties controlled every major political entity in what is now Iraq, Syria, southern Turkey, Lebanon, and Israel. It was the dawn of the Age of the Amorites.

Until the mid 1800s, the Amorites were known only from a handful of mentions early in the Old Testament. When scholars began pulling clay tablets out of the Mesopotamian sand in the nineteenth and early twentieth centuries, the many references to Amorites they found convinced some that the Amorites had ruled a vast empire across the Near East around the time of Abraham.[18] That wasn't quite true; divisions between the Amorites, like the rivalries among the tribes of Israel, prevented any of the various Amorite kingdoms from ruling the Near East for very long.

The first Amorite kingdoms to emerge after the collapse of the Third

Dynasty of Ur were the city-states of Isin and Larsa. Both were located on the Euphrates in what is southern Iraq today—Larsa, a little north of Ur, with Isin farther northwest, about halfway between the Persian Gulf and Babylon.

These two cities gave their names to the Isin-Larsa period of Mesopotamian history, which covers the time from the fall of Ur in 2004 BC until the defeat of Larsa by Hammurabi of Babylon in 1763 BC.

The first kings of Isin and Larsa were named Ishbi-Erra and Naplanum, respectively. Ishbi-Erra may have been an Amorite. He was described by king Ibbi-Sin of Ur as "a monkey from the mountains," a "man of Mari with the mind of a beast" who was "not of Sumerian seed."[19] This suggests that Ishbi-Erra was either an Amorite or an Akkadian from a city that had frequent contact with Amorite nomads. Ishbi-Erra may have put those Amorites to use as mercenaries in support of his ambition to set up his own royal dynasty. (It also tells us something about the attitude of Sumerians toward people from the Amorite homeland in Syria.)

For his part, Naplanum of Larsa was definitely an Amorite.[20] Both were clearly men of power during the last years of Ur. Ishbi-Erra had been made a governor of the territory around Isin and Nippur by king Ibbi-Sin of Ur, but Ishbi-Erra either had more ambition than the king realized, or he took matters into his own hands when it became obvious that the government of Ur was no longer powerful enough to enforce the king's will. The fact that Ishbi-Erra was either an Amorite or had friendly dealings with the Amorites, the bandits who'd made it too dangerous for most travel and trade in the kingdom, is probably relevant. Ishbi-Erra may have encouraged the turmoil that led to the downfall of Ur, which led to his own rise to power.

Whatever his reasons, Ishbi-Erra became a king in his own right around 2017 BC, and he survived the Elamite sack of Ur in 2004 BC by about twenty years. In fact, Ishbi-Erra eventually marched downriver, drove the Elamites back out of Sumer, and recaptured Ur along with the important cities of Uruk and Lagash.

Meanwhile, Naplanum established a dynasty that ruled Larsa, only about twenty miles from Ur, as an independent city-state for nearly 250 years. Records of grain sales found at Ur mention a wealthy merchant named Naplanum, who may be one and the same, although some scholars believe Naplanum was head of the royal bodyguard for the last two kings of Ur. That could explain how he was able to establish an independent kingdom so close to the throne of his former boss. It also explains the title of *rabium amurrim*, "chief [or "great one"] of the Amorites," which was used by the kings of Larsa for generations.

Over time, Naplanum's successors realized that their location between Isin and the Persian Gulf gave them a strategic advantage over their northern rival. By blocking Isin's access to the Gulf, the kings of Larsa controlled the lucrative trade route to the Indus River valley (now southern Pakistan), which was home to the prosperous Harappan civilization that reached into India and Afghanistan for nearly two thousand years. The Harappans traded with Mesopotamia and Egypt via the Persian Gulf throughout the second millennium BC, and for the first half of the millennium, that trade was controlled by Amorites.

A pattern that began with Nimrod has continued down to this day in the Near East (and, sadly, around the world): Cycles of war based on strong, charismatic leaders who rise to power, dominate a region and elevate his tribe, culture, or civilization for a time until another leader emerges, the kingdom collapses, and the cycle starts again. It's like a pot of stew simmering on the stove: Bubbles form, rise to the surface, and burst—over and over. Some bubbles are bigger than others, but all of them collapse in the end. The Amorites didn't invent the game, but they were very good at it.

During the lifetime of Abraham—who was born around 1950 BC, entered Canaan from the north around 1876 BC, and died in the Holy Land around 1776 BC—Amorite kingdoms emerged to dominate the entire Near East, from the Persian Gulf to the Mediterranean. By the time of Isaac's birth around 1850 BC, all of modern-day Iraq, Syria,

Jordan, Lebanon, Israel, and even northern Egypt were ruled by Amorite kings and chiefs. Regional powers included Isin and Larsa, already mentioned; Mari; Yamkhad, based at Aleppo; Qatna, near modern Homs in west-central Syria; the kingdom of Northern Mesopotamia, centered on what later became Assyria; smaller Amorite kingdoms in Canaan, with Hazor near the Sea of Galilee the largest of those; and, of course, Babylon.

As noted, the Isin-Larsa period came to a sudden end around 1763 BC when Hammurabi of Babylon defeated Larsa's powerful king, Rim-Sin. At its peak, Hammurabi's kingdom dominated the land between the Tigris and the Euphrates from the Persian Gulf in the south to Mari in the north, which was on the Euphrates near the present border between Syria and Iraq. You've guessed by now that Hammurabi was an Amorite; he was the sixth-generation ruler of a kingdom that grew out of an insignificant village that wasn't an independent state until 1894 BC.[21]

Babylon was founded by an Amorite chief named Sumu-Abum of the Amnanum tribe, who got the party started by grabbing land from a neighboring town, Kazallu. Babylon was so unimportant that the first four kings of the dynasty didn't even call themselves "king of Babylon." It wasn't until Hammurabi put it on the map in the eighteenth century BC that the city became Babylon as we think of it. Beginning around 1792 BC, he conquered all of Sumer, Akkad, and the Euphrates Valley as far as Mari, where Hammurabi not only defeated his "old friend" and "brother," the Amorite king Zimri-Lim, but he apparently ordered the ritual destruction of the palace and main temple there.[22]

That points us back toward the theme of the book, which is identifying the spirits behind geopolitics—"theopolitics," as it were.

Scholars typically define the name of Babylon's greatest king as meaning "my kinsman is a healer," from the Amorite term 'Ammurāpi, derived from 'Ammu ("paternal kinsman") and Rāpi ("healer"). But rāpi is from the same root as the biblical word "Rephaim." There isn't a single

16

example in Canaanite texts where the *rapha* are healers. It's more likely his name means "my kinsmen are Rapha," or more simply, "my fathers are the Rephaim."[23]

A genealogy of the dynasty of Hammurabi, compiled about a hundred years after he died, names one of the ancestors of the Amorite kings of Babylon as Ditanu,[24] which, you've noticed, is the name of the ancient Amorite tribe that gave its name to the Greek Titans. That same Ditanu was claimed as an ancestor by the ruling houses of at least two other powerful Amorite kingdoms between the eighteenth and thirteenth centuries BC. Ditanu was one of "seventeen kings who lived in tents" named as ancestors of Shamshi-Adad, an Amorite king who ruled northern Mesopotamia around the time of Hammurabi.[25]

About five hundred years later, the Amorite kingdom of Ugarit summoned a group called "the council of the Ditanu" from the netherworld during necromancy rituals,[26] and a temple to the Ditanu confirms that they were believed to be among the gods.[27]

The kingdom established by the Amorite dynasty that produced Hammurabi has cast a long shadow across history. It built on earlier religious and cultural traditions established by the Sumerians and Akkadians, but God called out Babylon and the Amorites specifically for their wickedness. The occult religious system of Babylon was so vile it became a symbol of evil from the time of Moses through the end of the apostolic age. John the Revelator used Babylon to represent the corrupt end-times church of the Antichrist.

Of course, the kingdom of Hammurabi's Babylon was doomed to collapse almost as soon as he established it. After the great lawgiver's death around 1750 BC, his successors kept the kingdom intact for a while, but Elamites from the east, Assyrians from the north, and people in the far south broke away, so that by about 1600 BC, the Amorite dynasty in Babylon once again controlled only the land around the city. Still, the power of Hammurabi was such that southern Mesopotamia has been called Babylonia ever since the time of Abraham.

In 1595 BC, an army from the new Hittite kingdom in central Anatolia (modern Turkey), led by king Ḫattušili I, conducted a long raid down the Euphrates. Bypassing the Assyrians in northern Mesopotamia, the Hittites sacked Mari and then ejected the Amorites from Babylon. The Hittite withdrawal back into Anatolia left a vacuum that was filled about twenty-five years later by the Kassites, a mountain people from western Iran who captured Babylon and controlled it and much of the territory once ruled by Hammurabi for the next four hundred years.

This makes the Kassites, not the Amorites or Chaldeans, the people who ruled Babylonia the longest, and the Kassite kingdom extended from the time of Jacob until the period of the judges in Israel.

Meanwhile, Amorites slowly assumed power in northern Egypt. During the time of the Hebrew sojourn, the rulers of Egypt—at least the part where the Israelites settled, the Nile delta—were Amorites. They were called "Hyksos" by native Egyptians, a word that roughly translates as "rulers of foreign lands." Egyptologists refer to it as the Second Intermediate Period, which lasted from about 1750 BC to 1550 BC. It appears that after a series of weak rulers, Egypt was divided between a native kingdom in the south based at Thebes and the foreign Hyksos in Lower (northern) Egypt, whose capital city was Avaris in the northeastern Nile delta. The Hyksos brought with them their art, their architecture, their weapons, and their gods.

This helps make sense out of the greatest miracle that God performed during the Exodus. You see, even though the Hyksos were run out of Egypt by the Egyptians about a hundred years before Moses led Israel to Mount Sinai, the chief god of the Hyksos, Baal, was worshiped in Egypt for several centuries more. Ramesses the Great, who ruled Egypt about two hundred years after the Exodus, was a Baal worshiper. He set up a stela at Pi-ramesses, near the site of the abandoned Hyksos capital Avaris. The engraved memorial stone commemorated Set's four hundredth anniversary of ruling at Tanis,[28] but the god was depicted exactly like the images of Baal found in Syria, with a tasseled Canaanite kilt and conical headdress with a streamer. The gods of the Amorites influenced Egypt far more than we've been taught; the Amorite Hyksos and the Egyptian pharaohs who came after them worshiped Baal-Set as a single entity.[29]

That's the key to understanding the parting of the Red Sea: In Canaanite religion, Baal became king of the gods by fighting and beating the sea-god, Yamm. Amorite, Canaanite, and Phoenician sailors worshiped Baal as their patron and protector for more than a thousand years.

So, the parting of the Red Sea, which happened right in front of a place called Baal-zephon, named for Mount Zaphon, the home of Baal's palace in Amorite religion, was a demonstration of Yahweh's mastery over the chief god of Israel's oppressors.

Have you ever noticed that God told Moses to turn the Israelites around and camp in front of Baal-zephon to wait for the Egyptian cavalry to catch up?[30] God didn't just deliver Israel from the hand of Pharaoh; He delivered Israel from the hand of Baal!

In short, the social and religious culture of the Amorites was the world from which God called the patriarchs and prophets to establish His chosen people in the land where His Name would dwell,[31] Canaan. The language, customs, and, most of all, the gods of the Amorites dominated the world of the ancient Hebrews.

The Amorites faded from history after the conquest of Canaan, at least under the name "Amorite." But their descendants continued to play important roles in ancient Israel. The Arameans, whom scholars generally agree were descended from the Amorites,[32] set up kingdoms in Damascus and elsewhere in Syria after the so-called Bronze Age collapse, a period of violence and chaos in the eastern Mediterranean around 1200 BC. They were a thorn in the side of Israel (and Judah, after Solomon's death) for hundreds of years. The Chaldeans, who established the Neo-Babylonian Empire in the seventh century BC, likely emerged from nomadic Amorite tribes who migrated from the west into southeastern Mesopotamia sometime around 900 BC.[33]

The greatest Chaldean king, Nebuchadnezzar, is generally who comes to mind when we think of Babylon, but that city was around for a long, long time before the Chaldeans took it over. Think about the time scale—Hammurabi the Great died more than eleven hundred years before Nebuchadnezzar was born. Now, who was president of the United States in AD 919?

Trick question. How about the king of England?[34]

Exactly. Eleven hundred years is a very long time. Yet the gods of Mesopotamia were the same, with few exceptions.

Meanwhile, the Phoenicians, descendants of the Amorites who occupied the Mediterranean coast of Syria and Lebanon, brought their culture and religion into Israel from the time of the judges to the time of Jesus and beyond. For example, Jezebel, the infamous wife of Israel's king Ahab, was from Tyre, which competed with the Greeks and Romans for control of trade on the Mediterranean for centuries. Carthage, a colony in north Africa established by Tyre around the time of Jehoash, king of Judah (circa 814 BC), nearly destroyed Rome in the late third century BC. Temples to Phoenician gods like Melqart, Baal-Hammon, and Tanit have been found as far away as Spain.

And tophets, ritual places of burial for infants and children sacrificed to Baal-Hammon, similar to the Tophet near Jerusalem where children were burned as offerings to Molech, have been excavated at Carthage and multiple sites on Sicily and Sardinia.

Here's the point of this brief history: The iniquity of the Amorites still affects the world today. And the gods behind it are pushing the world toward Armageddon.

2

The Moon-god

The Apostle Paul told us that our contest in this life is not against human opponents, but against "cosmic powers over this present darkness" and "spiritual forces of evil in the heavenly places."[35] The prophets and apostles knew this. Their writings reflect this spiritual war, although it's been downplayed in our churches to the point that most American Christians view Jesus as more of a life coach than as the commander of an invincible heavenly army.

This chapter dials in on one of the gods worshiped by an important group of people. He's been overlooked by most Christians, even those of us who recognize that the pagan gods of the world aren't make-believe.

Given the space we've devoted thus far to the Amorites and the fact that an Amorite tribe was responsible for founding Babylon, you might think that I'm referring to the chief god of that city, Marduk. That would be a logical guess. It's not quite right, but we'll spend a few minutes on him anyway.

We know quite a bit about Marduk from ancient texts discovered in Iraq. Around the time of the patriarchs, he was elevated from his status as the patron god of Babylon, which, remember, had been an unimportant river village for centuries. When the Amorite dynasty of Babylon fought their way to become the most powerful city-state in Mesopotamia, Marduk came along for the ride and became king of the Mesopotamian pantheon. It wasn't a coincidence that this happened at the same time Hammurabi elevated Babylon to the most powerful state in the Near East. As Babylon grew in power, it surpassed Nippur, home city of the former chief god, Enlil, and Eridu, the oldest city in Sumer and home of Enki, god of the *abzu*—the abyss.

Marduk was described as the son of Enki, and he appears to have taken on some of the characteristics of the elder god. Marduk more or less absorbed the identity of one of the gods of Eridu, Asarluhi, who passed on to Marduk his role as a god of magic. Likewise, as Babylon eclipsed Nippur politically, the role and authority of Enlil was handed off to Marduk.

This pattern of succession was repeated across the Near East as older gods were replaced or overthrown by younger generations. In Mesopotamia, the sky-god Anu was replaced as head of the pantheon by Enlil, who in turn was replaced by Marduk. By the time of the Greeks and Romans, the names had changed—Ouranos/Caelus to Kronos/Saturn to Zeus/Jupiter—but the outline of the story was the same. Other cultures, including the Hittites, Hurrians, and Amorites, had similar stories about their gods. In most cases, the storm-god emerged as king of the pantheon, but not in Babylon. Sumer, which is southeastern Iraq today, was mainly desert. The Sumerian storm-god, Ishkur, was a third-tier deity, much less important than the gods of sky, sun, moon, and magic, or the goddess of sex and war. Maybe a weather-god just wasn't relevant in a place that depended on irrigation to grow crops.

All of that said, the focus of this book is not Marduk, nor is it the storm-god under any of his names, although he is a major player in the last days, as you'll see.

It's not the sun-god, either. Contrary to what you've heard about the solar deity, another member of the Mesopotamian pantheon was far more important, and he still influences the world today spiritually and geopolitically.

Even though Babylon's political power lifted Marduk to the position of chief god in the pantheon, the personal god of the Amorite chiefs who founded Babylon was not Marduk. It was the moon-god, Sîn (pronounced "seen").

The first king of Babylon, Sumu-Abum, swore oaths by Sîn, not Marduk. The year-names of Sumu-Abum's reign, which is how scribes marked time back in the day, honored the moon-god.[36] Marduk was essentially a figurehead, with the moon-god the real power behind the throne of Babylon. Even the great Hammurabi, five generations later, credited Sîn in his famous law code with establishing his dynasty and creating him personally.

The moon-god, personal god of the founders of Babylon, inspired or encouraged the occult system that became a biblical symbol for evil and the pattern of the prophesied one-world religion of the Antichrist.

So, who was this moon-god? Why was he important to that particular band of Amorites, and why does it matter to us today? Let's start with his biography.

The moon-god went by several different names. To the Sumerians, he was Nanna. Akkadians called him Suen, or Sîn, which is the name we'll use most of the time. The Amorites called him Erah, or Yarikh. Remember that, because it's relevant in an upcoming chapter.

The moon-god was the first-born son of Enlil, who was king of the gods before the rise of Marduk. In Sumer, Sîn was one of the "seven gods who decree," with Anu, the sky-god; Enlil, the king; Ninhursag, mother of the gods; Enki, the god of wisdom; Shamash, the sun-god; and Ishtar, the goddess of sex and war.

Interestingly, not only was the moon-god more important than the sun-god to the Amorites who founded Babylon, Sîn was the *father* of the sun-god. The wild, violent, gender-fluid goddess Ishtar was also a child of Sîn, and in some accounts, the moon-god also fathered the storm-god, Ishkur.

The moon-god cult began at least five thousand years ago. The oldest example of the god's Sumerian name, Nanna, was found at Uruk, dated to the Jemdet-Nasr period (3100–2900 BC).[37] For context, the Jemdet-Nasr period immediately followed the Uruk period, a run of about nine hundred years when the city of Nimrod and Gilgamesh dominated the Near East. So, let's speculate: If the power of Uruk collapsed after the language of the people was confused at Babel, then evidence of the moon-god turning up in Nimrod's hometown shortly thereafter suggests that Nanna/Sîn may have been one of the Watcher-class angels who persuaded Nimrod, whom I believe was the Sumerian king Enmerkar, to build Babel (at Eridu—Babylon wouldn't be founded for at least another thousand years) as "the great abode, the abode of the gods."[38]

The Sumerians apparently considered Nanna to be just slightly less important than Anu, Enlil, Enki, and Inanna (Ishtar). We'll see, however, that the powerful influence of the lunar deity on the Amorites, who inherited the land and religious traditions of Sumer, is evident by how often Yahweh contended with the moon-god and his followers in the Bible.

Nanna/Sîn was depicted in Mesopotamian art, not surprisingly, by a crescent moon, often as part of a "cosmic triad" that included the sun-god Shamash, and Ishtar, who was represented by the planet Venus. Those three symbols are found together in many ancient inscriptions and cylinder seals.

Another common symbol of the moon-god was the bull. One of the moon-god's epithets was the "frisky calf of Enlil" or "frisky calf of heaven."[39] Not only does the crescent moon resemble the horns of a bull, but the moon's link to fertility probably began with his role as the patron god of herds. The obvious connection between the regular phases of the moon and the menstrual cycle may have had something to do with that as well.

Mesopotamia ran on a lunar calendar long before Moses received the Law. So, each month began with the new moon, the sighting of the first sliver of the lunar disc after it spent a few days in darkness. Regular festivals were held monthly for Nanna/Sîn on the first, seventh, and fifteenth of each month, which corresponded to the new, first-quarter, and full moons in the lunar cycle.[40]

A more important festival, often attributed to Marduk and Babylon, was the *akitu*. It's usually described as a new year celebration, because the festival at Babylon was held near the spring equinox, on the first of Nisan, the first month of the year. Even today, Nisan 1 is the first day of the religious year on the Hebrew calendar. But, like the Tower of Babel, the *akitu* began long before Babylon was founded, probably originating around 2500 BC at the great city of the moon-god, Ur.[41]

Akiti, the Sumerian form of the word, refers both to the festival and the special building where it was held.[42] Unlike the festival for Marduk in Babylon, which was held only in the spring, the *akiti* celebrated for Nanna at Ur was also held in the seventh month, around the time of the autumn equinox. The celebration involved the image representing the god traveling by boat from the city to the *akiti*-house and then returning to the city with great fanfare.[43]

The autumn festival was the more important of the two. Why? Nanna was the patron god of Ur, and the fall *akiti*, which lasted at least eleven days into the month,[44] took place as the waxing moon grew larger and larger, symbolizing the god's reentry into his city just as the days were getting visibly shorter and the moon asserted his dominance in the sky over Utu, the sun-god.[45]

Similar festivals were held in many cities for their patron gods, from Ur to Babylon to Harran in northern Mesopotamia. The question is why the ritual required the patron god to travel from his or her city to the *akiti*-house and back. Scholars who have studied this festival report that "nothing unusually significant occurred" at the *akiti*-house.[46] So, why bother?

The solution is the obvious. Perhaps the best-known children's riddle is, "Why did the chicken cross the road?" The answer to this riddle is the obvious: "to get to the other side." Why then was the *akitu*-house built outside the city? The answer: "so that the gods could march back into the city."[47]

Well, maybe. But why? We may never know for sure, but there's a fascinating tidbit buried just beneath the surface of the historical record. It appears the *akiti* rites at Ur included a ritual procession around the fields outside the walls, presumably to call for divine protection of the crops. This circular march, or circumambulation, was combined with offerings to Nanna, a ritual purification of the gate to the moon-god's temple, and—of course—tithing by merchants to the temple.[48]

The significance of the circumambulation ritual will become obvious later in the book. And it may be much, much older than the city of Ur.

In September of 1869, the British military engineer and explorer Sir Charles Warren climbed to the summit of Mount Hermon on behalf of the Palestine Exploration Fund (PEF). The PEF was founded in 1865 under the patronage of Queen Victoria. The society included some of the giants in the field of archaeology, such as Sir William Flinders Petrie, T. E. Lawrence ("of Arabia"), Kathleen Kenyon, and Sir Leonard Woolley,[49] who excavated Ur in the 1920s. But it's no coincidence that many of those sent into the field had military training; by the second half of the nineteenth century, the Ottoman Empire was crumbling and the great powers of Europe had their knives out, ready to carve up the carcass. While we've learned a lot about the ancient world from the work of men like Warren, Petrie, and Lawrence, the British government collected useful intelligence at the same time.

Anyway, on top of Hermon, more than nine thousand feet above sea level, Warren visited an ancient temple called Qasr Antar, the highest man-made place of worship on the planet. It was probably built during the Greek or Roman period, so it only dates back to about the second or third century BC at the earliest.

But inside the temple, Warren found an artifact that had been overlooked by visitors for nearly two thousand years—a stela, a slab of limestone about four feet high, eighteen inches wide, and twelve inches thick, inscribed in archaic Greek:

According to the command of the greatest a(nd) Holy God, those who take an oath (proceed) from here.[50]

Because the inscription is Greek rather than a Semitic language like Aramaic, Hebrew, Canaanite, or Akkadian, the stela can't be dated earlier than Alexander the Great's invasion of the Levant in the late fourth century BC. But it still connects Mount Hermon to the Watchers of Genesis 6, whose mutual pact on the summit is described in 1 Enoch:

Shemihazah, their chief, said to them, "I fear that you will not want to do this deed, and I alone shall be guilty of a great sin." And they all answered him and said, "Let us all swear an oath, and let us all bind one another with a curse, that none of us turn back from this counsel until we fulfill it and do this deed." Then they all swore together and bound one another with a curse. And they were, all of them, two hundred, who descended in the days of Jared onto the peak of Mount Hermon.[51]

Since the "greatest and holy god" on Warren's stela is linked to the Watchers, it probably refers to the Canaanite creator-god, El. The summit of Hermon has been scooped out like a giant bowl, probably to receive a drink offering, something scholars call "the rite of hydrophory."[52] This ritual was called *yarid* in Hebrew, based on a root that means "to come down," which it shares with the names Jared and Jordan (since the river "comes down" into the Galilee from Mount Hermon). This suggests that the Watchers did not descend to Mount Hermon in the "days of Jared," but rather in the days when *yarid* was performed on the summit of Hermon.

The point is this: Warren noted that those bringing the *yarid* had to approach the summit in a specific way:

> On the southern peak there is a hole scooped out of the apex, the foot is surrounded by an oval of hewn stones, and at its southern end is a Sacellum, or temple, nearly destroyed: the latter appears to be of more recent date than the stone oval....
>
> The oval is formed of well-dressed stones, from two to eight feet in length, two and a-half feet in breadth, and two feet thick; they are laid in a curved line on the uneven ground, their breadth being their height, and their ends touching each other.[53]

In other words, to reach the summit of Mount Hermon in ancient times, one had to circumambulate the peak, walking in a spiral with the summit always on the left. Is there a link between religious rituals on Mount Hermon and the oldest *akiti* rites for the moon-god at Ur?

Admittedly, this is speculation, another bit of circumstantial evidence as we build our case. There is smoke, but not exactly a smoking gun.

One more note, a hint at the importance of the moon-god in the ancient Near East: During the time of the patriarchs, which scholars call the Old Babylonian period, the moon-god Nanna/Sîn was, at least for some, the most important god in the pantheon.

Even though Enlil was still king of the gods at that point in history, a text fragment from Nippur written during the Old Babylonian period, translated in 2011, explicitly describes the moon-god as ruling over the Mesopotamian divine assembly, which was called the Ubšu-ukkina. Anu and Enlil, whom we'd expect to be the presiding deities, are described as advisors, along with the other "gods who decree."[54]

> You, who stand before him to sit in the Ubšu-ukkina
> An, Enlil, Enki, Ninhursag, Utu, and Inanna sat in assembly for the king
> They advised him there.
> Nanna sets the holy…in order.…
> The great gods were paying attention to.…
> Suen (Sîn), his assembly's decision, his speech of goodness, abundance.…
> for Suen, they implement abundance in heaven and earth properly(?)
> The king suitable for holy heaven, the barge in the midst of heaven.[55]

"The barge in the midst of heaven" is the crescent moon. Besides resembling the horns of a bull, it also looks like a reed boat sailing across the night sky. Even though bits of the tablet are missing, it's clear that Sîn was "the king" in the Mesopotamian divine assembly, with the other "great gods" in subordinate roles. Marduk isn't even mentioned. This supports the theory that the Amorite founders of Babylon, even though they hailed from the city of Marduk, considered the moon-god, Sîn, their patron.

It's also important to remember that to Mesopotamians, the Ubšu-ukkina was a physical place. The assembly of the gods took place in Nippur, inside Enlil's temple complex the *E-kur*, or "House of the Mountain."

That's important, too. From Eden to Armageddon, this long spiritual war is all about the mountain where the gods assemble. The prize is Yahweh's *har mô'ēd* ("mount of assembly")—Zion.

3

City of the Moon-god

Ur was not the only center of the moon-god cult in the ancient world, but it was the most important. As we noted earlier, the *akiti* festival, which was eventually celebrated for gods at cities all over Mesopotamia, probably originated at Ur sometime between 3000 and 2500 BC.

Throughout most of that millennium, other cities dominated the Fertile Crescent. After the decline of Uruk around 3100 BC (in our view, probably due to the confusion of language at Babel), "kingship" alternated between cities in Mesopotamia, including Uruk, Kish, Lagash, Mari, and Ur, down to the time of Sargon the Great.

Around 2334 BC, Sargon of Akkad established the first pan-Mesopotamian empire since the days of Nimrod, conquering and controlling an area that stretched from the Persian Gulf to the modern border between Syria and Turkey. The great king attributed his success mainly to the elder gods of the pantheon (except for Inanna/Ishtar, goddess of sex and war):

Sargon, king of Akkad, overseer (*mashkim*) of Inanna, king of Kish, anointed (*guda*) of Anu, king of the land, governor (*ensi*) of Enlil.[56]

But as with all kingdoms, the Akkadian Empire eventually collapsed. It was overrun by the Gutians, barbarians from the mountains of western Iran, around 2154 BC. Fifty years later, Ur-Nammu came to power in Ur. He ran the Gutians out of the land and then defeated the city-states of Uruk and Lagash. Ur-Nammu and his descendants, the Third Dynasty of Ur, controlled the entire Fertile Crescent for the next 150 years, apparently collecting tribute from as far away as Canaan.

Ur-Nammu was a builder credited with the construction of a number of buildings in Sumer, most notably the Great Ziggurat of Ur for Nanna/Sîn, the moon-god. You've probably seen pictures of American soldiers visiting the reconstructed step pyramid after the invasion of Iraq in 2003. Saddam Hussein rebuilt the facade and the enormous staircase of the crumbling temple in the 1980s.

Before the Gulf War erupted with "shock and awe" in 1990, it was widely reported that Saddam was rebuilding Babylon, perhaps seeing himself as a modern Nebuchadnezzar.[57] It wasn't as well known that he also spent a lot of money reconstructing the ancient temple of Sîn. No wonder; as we've seen (pardon the pun), the spirit behind Babylon wasn't Marduk—it was the moon-god.

The ziggurat of Ur was immense, measuring 210 feet long, about 150 feet wide, and at least 100 feet high. Imagine that—a ten-story building made entirely of mud brick, still standing (though in disrepair) four thousand years after it was built. The temple was called *Ekishnugal*, the "House of Thirty, the Great Seed," an obvious reference to the fertility aspect of the moon-god. The massive platform that formed the base of the temple was the *E-temen-nì-gùru*, which means "House-foundation That Is Clad in Terror."

Unintentionally prophetic.

The brief renaissance of Ur came to an end around 2004 BC when the Amorites, probably with help from the Elamites and Gutians, stamped out the last Sumerian kingdom in Mesopotamia. After that, for our purposes, the important centers of the moon-god shifted north and west, to the heart of Amorite country.

One of the reasons the moon-god is a focus of study in this book is the biblical connection between Ur and ancient Mesopotamia's other major center of moon-god worship, Harran. That link is Abraham.

Until about a hundred years ago, when the famed archaeologist Sir Leonard Woolley excavated the fabulous Royal Tombs of Ur in the early 1920s, Bible scholars generally believed the patriarch of Jews, Muslims, and Christians had come from southern Turkey. That's exactly where we find ancient Harran (spelled with a single *r* in the Bible), on the Balikh River about ten miles north of the Syrian border. In the early second millennium BC, after the collapse of the Third Dynasty of Ur, Harran was an important trading center on the caravan route between the Mediterranean coast and Assyria, in what was probably in a border zone between the Assyrians to the southeast, the Hurrians to the northeast, an emerging Amorite kingdom at Halab (Aleppo) to the southwest, and the Hittites, who were arriving in Anatolia to the northwest around that time.

Close by Harran was Ura, a town known as a home base for traveling merchants,[58] as well as cities bearing the names of Abraham's father, grandfather, great-grandfather, and brother—namely Serug (Sarugi), Nahor (Nahur), Terah, and, of course, Haran, the father of Lot.[59] Those cities are older than the time frame of the Bible. Working backwards from the Exodus, Abraham was born around 1950 BC. That puts the births of Terah, Nahor, and Serug around 2020 BC, 2049 BC, and 2079 BC, respectively. It's probable that Abraham's relatives were named for those cities instead of the other way around. At the very least, their names suggest a much stronger connection between Abraham and northern Mesopotamia than with Ur in Sumer, about six hundred miles to the southeast.

Likewise, Abraham's lifestyle as a tent-dwelling nomad is more consistent with the Amorite culture of the Levant than with Sumer. He was not a city-dweller, and neither were Isaac and Jacob. Based on Sumerian writings about the Amorites of the Syrian steppe, such a lifestyle would have been completely alien to someone raised in the sophisticated urban culture of Sumer.

And this must be said: If Abraham's father, Terah, really meant to go from Ur in Sumer to Canaan, he wouldn't have ended up in Harran, not even by mistake. A map of the caravan trails of the ancient Near East makes it obvious. After following the Euphrates northward from Ur, Terah would have had to miss a left turn at Mari, near the modern border between Iraq and Syria. A well-known caravan trail there crossed the steppe to Tadmor (Palmyra) and Damascus before descending into Canaan by way of Bashan, the modern Golan Heights.

Harran isn't just a little out of the way; it's *ridiculously* out of the way. Going from Ur to Canaan by way of Harran is like driving from Atlanta to Dallas by way of Chicago. It would not have happened like that.

Most important, the Bible supports this theory. When Joshua called on the tribes of Israel to remember their origins, he said:

Thus says the LORD, the God of Israel, "Long ago, your fathers lived beyond the Euphrates, Terah, the father of Abraham and of Nahor; and they served other gods. Then I took your father Abraham from beyond the River and led him through all the land of Canaan, and made his offspring many." (Joshua 24:2–3)

The key phrase there is "beyond the River." Ur in Sumer is on the west bank of the Euphrates River. Abraham would not have crossed it to get to Canaan. Harran, however, is on the far side of the river. As scholar Cyrus H. Gordon argued in 1958, "it is now clear that Abraham was a merchant prince…from the Hittite realm."[60]

Abraham was not from Sumer. He came from northern Mesopotamia and the pastoralist Amorite culture.

The moon-god's importance in Harran is no mystery; the city was founded as a trading outpost by the kings of Ur, city of the moon-god.[61] Harran, where the deity was mainly called by his Akkadian name Sîn, sat on the main east-west route between Antioch and Nineveh. From there, traders could follow the Tigris River south to Babylon, which, as we noted above, was just beginning its rise to power in the days of Abraham.

The temple of Sîn in Harran was an important religious and political site for the Amorites of northern Mesopotamia. For example, Amorite tribes would meet at the temple of Sîn and sacrifice a donkey to ratify treaties.[62]

That wouldn't have been weird in Syria four thousand years ago. Donkeys were sacred animals to the Amorites, and they've been found buried after ritual slaughter at sites all over the Near East, like Mari, Jericho, and Avaris in northern Egypt.[63] In fact, Amorite kings rode donkeys, not horses. That tradition was still alive when Jesus made His triumphal entry into Jerusalem, a point not lost on the people or the local authorities.[64]

It's important to remember that there was no separation of church and state back then. As we'll see, that hasn't changed in that part of the world over the last five thousand years.

Farther west, another moon-god center is famous for being the first city conquered by Joshua west of the Jordan River. You see, the Amorite name for the moon-god was Yarikh, which is similar to the Hebrew form, *yareakh*. (That's where *yerakh*, the old Hebrew word for "month," comes from.) Transliterating from Semitic into English turns the *y* into a *j*, and Yarikh becomes Jericho. We'll have more to say about Jericho in a bit.

Another site at the north end of the Jordan River Valley was also home to worshipers of the moon-god. At the southwest corner of the

Sea of Galilee is Bet Yerah ("House of Yarikh" or "Temple of Yarikh"), an important center for pottery production throughout the Early Bronze Age, from about 3500 to 2300 BC.[65] Artifacts at the site and at Abydos, an ancient city on the Nile in central Egypt, confirm that Bet Yerah traded with the First Dynasty of Egypt between about 3100 and 2850 BC.[66] However, after 2850 BC, following an unidentified crisis that resulted in the abandonment of a number of sites in the Jordan Valley, Bet Yerah was resettled by migrants from the area of modern Armenia, Georgia, and Azerbaijan.[67]

Around that time, a megalithic, crescent-shaped stone structure longer than one and a half football fields was built eighteen miles (about a day's journey) from Bet Yerah. Known locally as Rujum en-Nabi Shu'ayb, or "Jethro's Cairn," it was finally identified in 2014 as a monument to the moon-god.[68]

So, during the Early Bronze Age, both ends of the Jordan River Valley, the Sea of Galilee and the Dead Sea, were anchored by sites occupied by worshipers of the moon-god. Although Bet Yerah had fallen on hard times by Abraham's day, with nothing left other than a small potter's workshop, it points to the popularity of Sîn/Yarikh among the people who lived in the region for more than a thousand years by the time the patriarch entered Canaan.

And, as we'll see, the fallen *elohim* who passed himself off as the moon-god was a target of God's wrath very early in the history of Israel.

4

Mountain of the Moon-god

All of this would be nothing more than an exercise in history if God hadn't taken a personal interest in the moon-god and his worshipers—namely, the Amorites. Remember, God called them out specifically when He made his covenant with Abraham.

The moon-god, under various names, was of supreme importance to Amorites in general, and especially to those of Babylon and Canaan.

It shouldn't be a surprise that the Amorites and their gods tried to interfere with God's plan for His people right from the Book of Genesis. After God divided the nations at Babel "according to the number of the sons of God,"[69] He chose Abraham to establish a new people as "His allotted heritage."[70]

So, the principalities and powers, who were no doubt watching Yahweh's every move, took note when He directed Abraham to Canaan and miraculously intervened on behalf of his nephew, Lot—especially after Abraham and his 318 retainers successfully raided the army of the kings of the east who'd just defeated the Rephaim tribes living in the Transjordan.

They must have been *very* interested when God miraculously blessed the aged Abraham and Sarah with Isaac. Suddenly, now, the promise of offspring who would be "as the stars of heaven"[71] was a real possibility.

Then things took a strange turn: God told Abraham to take Isaac to the land of Moriah and sacrifice him as a burnt offering.

You have to wonder what was in the minds of the Fallen at this point—after all, human sacrifice was *their* turf. The detestable rite has been practiced on every continent except Antarctica, but Yahweh had made it clear to Noah that shedding human blood was forbidden.[72] Sacrificing and burning children as an offering to the gods was even more offensive to God.[73] Yet there was Abraham, with Isaac tied up on a pile of wood, ready to plunge a knife into his only son.

It was a test, shocking to us modern Christians. Why would Abraham even *listen* to a God who demanded such a thing? Well, the world was a lot different then. Human sacrifice was a reality in the world of the Amorites. Archaeologists have found children ritually slaughtered at a number of Amorite sites during the time of Abraham.[74]

Their Sumerian and Egyptian predecessors likewise practiced it; "retainer sacrifice," the ritual murder of the servants of kings and nobles who'd died, is well documented in the tombs of ancient Ur and the kings of Egypt's First Dynasty. So, it wouldn't have been unusual for a god to demand the sacrifice of a loved one in Abraham's day.

Here's another significant part of the story: Some scholars believe "the land of Moriah" was "the land of the Amorites," with the name *Amurru* losing its first syllable over time the way English-speakers shorten "until" to "till," a phenomenon called "aphesis." Connecting Moriah to the Amorites was apparently in the minds of the Jewish translators of the Septuagint, who rendered it from Hebrew into Greek in 2 Chronicles 3:1 as Ἀμωρία—*Amōriā*.

Why does this matter? Because Mount Moriah, the Mountain of the Amorites, is where David bought the threshing floor of Araunah, upon which Solomon built the Temple. In other words, Mount Moriah is the Temple Mount—Zion.

Have you ever noticed that it was on the third day when Abraham saw the place God had appointed for His message to the rebel spirits?[75] No Christian can miss the symbolic significance of that detail.

That's where Armageddon will be fought. God staked His claim to that mountain in the nineteenth century BC when He stopped Abraham from harming Isaac in the heartland of the Amorites.

Yahweh telegraphed the coming battle for the land occupied by the moon-god's followers sometime between 1840 and 1830 BC. Isaac was born around 1851 BC, but since Abraham asked his son to carry the wood up to Mount Moriah, Isaac wasn't a small child when they traveled to the land of the Amorites.

Four hundred years later, when the Israelites were freed from their oppressors in Egypt, the battle was officially on.

They set out from Elim, and all the congregation of the people of Israel came to the wilderness of Sin, which is between Elim and Sinai, on the fifteenth day of the second month after they had departed from the land of Egypt. (Exodus 16:1)

It's important to remember that there are no throwaway details in the Bible. The prophets and apostles didn't add things for just for color, drama, or word count. So, what do we take away from this passage?

Elim is probably in the Wadi Gharandel, a normally dry riverbed in the western Sinai. The Wilderness of Sîn must have been the desert that covers the center of the Sinai Peninsula. Now, why would Moses record the specific day of the month when the people entered this wilderness? And what's the significance of the fifteenth day?

In the ancient Near East, the calendar was based on the cycles of the moon. The fifteenth day was the time the moon was full—meaning the moon-god was at full strength.

Does the name of the desert suddenly make sense?

Yes, the Wilderness of Sîn. *That* Sîn. The Wilderness of the Moon-god.[76]

The reasons behind the name of the desert should be apparent. In a land where daytime temperatures in the summer average 97 degrees Fahrenheit (36 Celsius), one travels at night whenever possible. Since the moon's predictable changes coincide with fertility cycles, which were important to both humans and herds, the moon-god's movement through the sky guided the lives of the pastoral nomads who traveled through the wilderness of Sîn.

Just as He did at the Red Sea, Yahweh led Israel on a specific route—in this case, at a specific time—to confront the small-*g* gods who'd rebelled against His authority.

Not surprisingly, the people complained.

And the whole congregation of the people of Israel grumbled against Moses and Aaron in the wilderness, and the people of Israel said to them, "Would that we had died by the hand of the LORD in the land of Egypt, when we sat by the meat pots and ate bread to the full, for you have brought us out into this wilderness to kill this whole assembly with hunger." (Exodus 16:2–3)

Is it any wonder they grumbled? Moses led them into a land named for one of the most powerful gods of the Amorites on a day when the god was at full strength! They'd already learned how difficult it was to find water in this land; they were three days out from the Red Sea before they found the waters of Marah—and even then, divine intervention was required to make the water drinkable.

How did God respond? The morning after Israel entered the Wilderness of Sîn, when the moon-god was believed to be at full power, Yahweh caused bread to rain down from heaven.[77]

Coincidence? No. It was another demonstration of His power over the supernatural realm, especially over the *bene elohim* who'd dared to set themselves up as gods. The manna fell from heaven for Israel until the day they crossed the Jordan forty years later.

Here's another paradigm-shifter: Have you ever considered that Sinai, "the mountain of God" where Moses saw the burning bush, was named for the moon-god? Neither did I. But this isn't a new idea; scholars have believed that the Mesopotamian moon-god was the origin of the name "Sinai" for more than a hundred years.[78] So, this showdown between Yahweh and Sîn in the middle of the Sinai was more than forty years in the making.

Think about this: It was on the mountain of the moon-god where Yahweh revealed Himself to Moses and where He shared with Moses that His Name was Yahweh.

> Then Moses said to God, "If I come to the people of Israel and say to them, 'The God of your fathers has sent me to you,' and they ask me, 'What is his name?' what shall I say to them?" God said to Moses, "I AM WHO I AM." And he said, "Say this to the people of Israel: 'I AM has sent me to you.'" God also said to Moses, "Say this to the people of Israel: 'The LORD, the God of your fathers, the God of Abraham, the God of Isaac, and the God of Jacob, has sent me to you.' This is my name forever, and thus I am to be remembered throughout all generations." (Exodus 3:13–15)

> God spoke to Moses and said to him, "I am the LORD. I appeared to Abraham, to Isaac, and to Jacob, as God Almighty, but by my name the LORD I did not make myself known to them." (Exodus 6:2–3)

In other words, "I am Yahweh. I appeared to Abraham, to Isaac, and to Jacob, as *El Shaddai*, but by my name Yahweh I did not make myself known to them."

So, what does El Shaddai mean? Most probably, "God of the mountains."[79] Some scholars have assumed that this title was originally applied to the Canaanite creator-god, El. After all, his mount of assembly was Mount Hermon,[80] the most impressive peak in the Near East.

The Amorites, who were considered uncultured mountaineers by the city-dwelling Sumerians, were represented in the Mesopotamian pantheon by an uncivilized god called Amurru. One of the epithets of Amurru was Bêl Šadê, which is Akkadian for "lord of the mountains."[81] Because you're observant, you probably noticed the similarity between Bêl Šadê and El Shaddai right off. (The funny-looking š is pronounced "sh.") Because of this, some scholars believe Amurru was the Amorite original on which the later Hebrews modeled Yahweh.

Of course, that requires believing Moses more or less invented Hebrew religion, an idea we reject. If Jesus—who healed the sick, cast out demons by His own authority, walked on water, and prophesied His own Resurrection—was wrong about Moses, then you and I are in a world of trouble.

But there's another possibility, and it supports our theory that the moon-god was far more important in the ancient world than we realize. Amurru, which refers to the Amorites as well as to the god of that name, may have been an epithet rather than a proper name.

Instead of Amurru being a god who shared the name of the Amorite people, it may have been a title of the moon-god: "Sîn, god of the Amurru-land."

There is substantial evidence to support the identification of *Bêl Šadê*, the god of the Amurru-land, with a lunar deity, specifically with Sîn. (1) Harran, from at least the Middle Bronze period until the late Middle Ages, was regarded as a major sanctuary of the moon-god Sîn. And we know in particular that the Amurru-peoples concluded treaties in his temple during the Mari period. (2) There are a number of seal cylinders on which the god Amurru, recognizable by inscription, curved staff, and sacred gazelle, is shown standing under a lunar crescent. If this is felt insufficient to establish his lunar nature, the fact that he sometimes holds or stands before a cult standard atop which is a crescent certainly strongly suggests it. (3) Once we find the sacred staff of the god Amurru on the seal of a devotee of the god Sîn. The inscription reads: *E-til-pi₄-Ištar...arad^{d}Sîn.* (4) Several individuals with theophoric names of the Sîn-type describe themselves on their seals as servants of the god Amurru.

We may reasonably conclude, therefore, that the god worshiped by the nomadic Amurru-peoples in the Balikh-Harran region by the epithets "Amurru" and "Bêl Šadê," at the time of the Mari and Old Babylonian texts, was a lunar deity. Sometimes he is specifically named (or at least identified with) Sîn.[82]

The Balikh-Harran region is precisely where Abraham began his journey to Canaan. Abraham came from a land where the moon-god was called "lord of the mountains." Is it surprising, then, that Yahweh revealed Himself to the patriarchs as the *true* God of the mountains, El Shaddai, and that Moses would have his first encounter with Yahweh at *har hā'ĕlōhîm*, the "mountain of God"?

But which god? *Elohim* is a designation of place, not a proper name. Based on the name Sinai and its location in the middle of the Wilderness of Sin, it's reasonable to conclude that in Moses' day, this mountain was considered the abode of the moon-god.

Yahweh brought Moses to Mount Sinai during his sojourn with Jethro and the Midianites for a reason. And He brought the Israelites there right after springing them from Egypt for a reason. What could that reason be?

Evidence suggests that from the last days of Sumerian rule over Mesopotamia through the rise of Babylon, the moon-god, Sîn, was the most important deity of the Amorites. It wasn't Marduk, although he was the patron god of Babylon, or the elder god, who went by different names across the Near East (Enlil in the east, Dagan along the Euphrates River, and El in the west). All across Mesopotamia, Amorites served the moon-god, whether they hailed from Babylon, which preserved the traditions of Ur, the ancient city of the moon-god; the north, where Harran was a major moon-god cult center; or Canaan, where the oldest city known to man, Jericho, bore the Amorite name for the moon-god, Yarikh.

Although God's first supernatural showdown on the way out of Egypt targeted the king of the Canaanite pantheon, the storm-god Baal, it was to the mountain of the moon-god that Yahweh led Moses and the Israelites. Imagine what must have been going through the minds of the people when they realized where they were!

Yet that was where God led the Israelites immediately after their escape from Egypt. And it was there He called Moses to receive the Law.

Then, God did something even more remarkable. He directed Moses to bring some guests up the mountain.

> Then Moses and Aaron, Nadab, and Abihu, and seventy of the elders of Israel went up, **and they saw the God of Israel**. There was under his feet as it were a pavement of sapphire stone, like the very heaven for clearness. And he did not lay his hand on the chief men of the people of Israel; **they beheld God, and ate and drank.** (Exodus 24:9–11, emphasis added)

It's impossible to overstate the importance of this brief passage. All of history is about God's plan to restore humanity to His divine council. The council originally met in Eden on "the holy mountain of God."[83] We've been barred from the council because of the sin of Adam and Eve, but the sacrifice of the Messiah, Jesus, paid the price for our sins and bought back the right for us to enter the garden someday.

The point is this: The long war between God and the gods is for control of the holy mountain—the *har mô ʿēd*, the "mount of assembly" or "mount of the congregation." There at Mount Sinai, Moses, Aaron, and the seventy elders of Israel became the first humans since Adam and Eve to see God face to face on His holy mountain!

This was a message aimed right at the rebel gods: "My people are free. And someday, they will take your place in My council."

Remember—When God divided the nations after Babel, "He fixed the borders of the peoples according to the number of the sons of God"[84]—angelic beings that He "allotted to all the peoples under the whole heaven" as the gods of the nations.[85] Remember, too, that the Table of Nations in Genesis 10 names seventy clans descended from Noah, representing all the people of the earth.

Seventy nations. Seventy elders of Israel.

Coincidence? No way.

By the way, there's a chance you're thinking that the story of dinner on Sinai must be a weird translation. Haven't we been taught that it's impossible for humans to see the face of God and live?

Yes, that's in the Bible. Moses was in that story, too. That was different. We'll get to that in a minute.

Well, the moon-god didn't just surrender. While Moses was up on the mountain for forty days, the people coerced Aaron into creating an idol—the golden calf.

"Up, make us gods who shall go before us. As for this Moses, the man who brought us up out of the land of Egypt, we do not know what has become of him." So Aaron said to them, "Take off the rings of gold that are in the ears of your wives, your sons, and your daughters, and bring them to me." So all the people took off the rings of gold that were in their ears and brought them to Aaron. And he received the gold from their hand and fashioned it with a graving tool and made a golden calf. And they said, "These are your gods, O Israel, who brought you up out of the land of Egypt!"

When Aaron saw this, he built an altar before it. And Aaron made a proclamation and said, "Tomorrow shall be a feast to the LORD." And they rose up early the next day and offered burnt offerings and brought peace offerings. And the people sat down to eat and drink and rose up to play. (Exodus 32:1–6)

We should note that the Hebrew word rendered "play" here, *tsachaq*, is used in other contexts as a euphemism for sexual activity—for example, Genesis 39:14 and 17, the encounter between Joseph and Potiphar's wife. This wasn't a day of celebrating the holiness of God. This was a pagan party of carnal indulgence.

Now, it's easy to empathize with Aaron to a point. It's hard to stand up to pushy people, especially in groups, and particularly when they're motivated by the fear that they alone among the nations were without the protection of a national deity. But, come on—Aaron had personally witnessed Yahweh supernaturally smack around the two most popular gods in the Amorite pantheon. (Not that you or I would have done better in his place.)

The excuse Aaron gave to Moses when he came down from Sinai is comical:

Let not the anger of my lord burn hot. You know the people, that they are set on evil. For they said to me, "Make us gods who shall go before us. As for this Moses, the man who brought us up out of the land of Egypt, we do not know what has become of him." So I said to them, "Let any who have gold take it off." So they gave it to me, and I threw it into the fire, and out came this calf. (Exodus 32:22–24)

"Out came this calf"?! Most parents have heard better excuses from seven-year-olds.

Some scholars interpret the golden calf as evidence that Yahweh was a bull-god, or at least represented by a bull. To be fair, there are passages in Scripture that liken the power of God to a bull, which was a common theme among gods in the ancient Near East.[86] But that's not what this was about.

Several years ago, I speculated that the golden calf represented the storm-god, Baal, who was sometimes described as a bull. But that wasn't typical; Baal was usually depicted as a human in a smiting pose, with a mace in one hand and thunderbolts in the other. No, it's far more likely that the golden idol represented "the frisky calf of heaven," patron god of shepherds and pastoralists, the god whose mountain the Israelites were camped in front of—the moon-god, Sîn.

Needless to say, God was not amused. His reaction was similar to His response after Babel: Yahweh told Moses that Israel had better repent, and then, they could forget about God traveling with them into the Promised Land because, as stubborn as they were, He'd probably smite them before they got there and start over with just Moses.

Well, the people mourned, like children caught doing something they shouldn't. Based on future actions, the regret was more about being punished than about disappointing the Creator of the Universe. (Again, not that you and I would have done any better.) Moses, while pleading for the people, asked Yahweh for a favor:

> Moses said, "Please show me your glory." And he said, "I will make all my goodness pass before you and will proclaim before you my name 'The LORD.' And I will be gracious to whom I will be gracious, and will show mercy on whom I will show mercy. **But," he said, "you cannot see my face, for man shall not see me and live."** And the LORD said, "Behold, there is a place by me where you shall stand on the rock, and while my glory passes by

I will put you in a cleft of the rock, and I will cover you with my hand until I have passed by. Then I will take away my hand, and you shall see my back, but my face shall not be seen." (Exodus 33:18–23, emphasis added)

Why the change since the meal on Mount Sinai? What about those verses that describe Yahweh talking things over with Moses "face to face"?[87] These are hints of the Trinity in the Old Testament. The personal encounters of the patriarchs—remember, Abraham ate a meal with God and bargained with Him to try to save Sodom—was with a visible, *physical* presence, a form that concealed His true, overwhelming glory. In a sense, Moses asked for a peek behind the mask. That's something Yahweh couldn't do, not even for Moses.

In any case, God did send His "presence" (*pānîm*) with Israel to the Promised Land. This is a concept that's hard to wrap your head around. What's the difference between Yahweh, His angel, and His presence? In some verses, none at all. Sometimes, the Angel of Yahweh is obviously Yahweh, because He takes credit for things that Yahweh did and promised.[88]

His "presence," however, is a little different. The clearest example may be in the priestly blessing that God taught Aaron:

The LORD bless you and keep you; the LORD make his face [*pānāy*] to shine upon you and be gracious to you; the LORD lift up his countenance [*pānāy*] upon you and give you peace. (Numbers 6:24–26)

It may be of interest that in Ezekiel 38:20, God promises that His presence will be on the battlefield during the war of Gog and Magog, which concludes with the Battle of Armageddon. We'll dig into that in more depth later, but it's safe to say that the one time you do not want the Lord to lift up His countenance upon you is when He's leading the army you're about to attack.

Armageddon won't be the first time somebody's made that bad choice. That's exactly what happened about thirty-four hundred years ago in Canaan. And the forces lined up against the host of Yahweh were devotees of the moon-god.

5

YHWH vs. the Moon-god

As this book is concerned more with the importance of the moon-god through biblical history than the specifics of the Exodus and the conquest of Canaan, we'll skip over the forty years of wandering in the desert to the beginning of hostilities in the war for the Holy Land.

After a skirmish in the Negev with the Canaanite king of Arad, Moses led the Israelites northward, around the edges of the lands controlled by Edom and Moab. Their kings, suspicious of their long-lost cousins, refused to allow the Israelites passage.

The first battle was against the Amorite king, Sihon, who ruled a small territory east of the Jordan between Moab and Ammon. He must have been a tough dude; the Book of Numbers preserves a song about Sihon that was apparently a hit back in the day:

Come to Heshbon, let it be built;
let the city of Sihon be established.
For fire came out from Heshbon,
flame from the city of Sihon.

It devoured Ar of Moab,
and swallowed the heights of the Arnon.
Woe to you, O Moab!
You are undone, O people of Chemosh!
He has made his sons fugitives,
and his daughters captives,
to an Amorite king, Sihon.
So we overthrew them;
Heshbon, as far as Dibon, perished;
and we laid waste as far as Nophah;
fire spread as far as Medeba. (Numbers 21:27–30)

Why did Sihon fight instead of letting the Israelites pass? We can only speculate. The king of Heshbon couldn't have had much hope of winning a battle on his own. Numbers 1:46 tells us that Israel counted more than six hundred thousand men who were able to go to war. United Nations statistics show that there are only about a million men between the ages of twenty and forty-five—fighting age—in the entire country of Jordan today![89] The kingdom of Sihon was much smaller and entirely agrarian, unlike present-day Jordan. In other words, Sihon's forces were probably outnumbered by the host of Israel, and not by a little bit.

Maybe Sihon counted on help from his ally to the north, Og of Bashan, or from the Amorites west of the Jordan River in Canaan. It's not like Israel's arrival was a secret; moving a couple million people, along with their flocks and herds, about six miles a day ruled out *blitzkrieg* from the list of tactics available to Moses and Joshua. It's clear from what Rahab of Jericho told the Israelite spies that the people of the land had been dreading the coming of Yahweh and His people for forty years.

Maybe that's why help never came for Sihon.

Sihon may have been induced to attack Israel by his god. If he served the moon-god, the "god of the Amurru-land," could Sîn/Yarikh have been looking for payback? After all, Yahweh had used Sinai, his mountain, to deliver the Law to Moses and prepare Israel for the conquest of Canaan, which was occupied by moon-god worshipers. What an insult to the *elohim* who was called "Father of Wisdom," "Lord of Destinies," and "Originator of Life" by his followers!

Remember that this is just speculation on the little we know about Sihon. It's also possible that the king of Heshbon saw Israel's arrival on his border as an existential threat and figured he had nothing to lose, even though Moses had sent messengers asking for peaceful passage through his territory.[90] Or maybe the prospect of looting and enslaving a couple million people was just too tempting to pass up. After all, the Amorites spawned the Bedouin culture that elevated caravan raiding to the status of holy war when Muhammad arrived on the scene about two thousand years later.

Whatever the reason, Sihon attacked, and his army was utterly destroyed. His fellow Amorite king to the north, Og, was next.

Og appears to have been the Israelites' first target all along. The obvious question: Why? Bashan wasn't on the direct route to the Holy Land. It's a long walk from the Dead Sea to the Golan Heights, especially with infants, old people, and cattle along for the trip—probably two to three weeks, at best. Maybe after forty years, that didn't seem like a big deal, but since the plan was to cross the Jordan near the Dead Sea, at Jericho, the attack on Og meant walking to the north end of the Jordan Valley, fighting a battle, and then marching south again. That was at least an extra month of travel, not including the time to fight the army of Og, plunder the cities of Bashan, and take possession of Og's territory.

God probably directed Moses and the Israelites to take out Og before crossing into Canaan because Bashan was a site of special supernatural significance. It was believed to be the home of pagan gods of the underworld: Rapiu, "King of Eternity,"[91] whose name is the singular form of *rapiuma* (Rephaim), who may be the same deity as Molech,[92] the god to whom the Judahite kings Ahaz and Manasseh sacrificed their children.

Even the name "Bashan" in the Canaanite dialect of Ugarit meant "place of the serpent."[93]

In short, the kingdom of Og was believed to be the entrance to the netherworld. It's not a coincidence that Bashan was just below the southern slopes of Mount Hermon.

Veneration of the dead and gods of the underworld was a snare to the Israelites for centuries. Worship of Baal-Peor, another god connected to the netherworld, caused God to send a plague among the people in the plains of Moab.[94] But while targeting Bashan first may have been due to Og being the last of "the remnant of the Rephaim,"[95] it may also be that he represented the occult system of Babylon.

> Behold, his bed was a bed of iron. Is it not in Rabbah of the Ammonites? Nine cubits was its length, and four cubits its breadth, according to the common cubit. (Deuteronomy 3:11)

Why did Moses bother to write down that odd detail? Was Og really a giant thirteen feet, six inches tall?

Not necessarily. Here's why: The dimensions of Og's bed match *exactly* the cultic bed in the temple of Marduk in Babylon,[96] where every spring, during the annual *akitu* festival, Marduk and his consort Sarpanitu were believed to have ritual sex.

So, Og's height wasn't as important as the spiritual power behind his throne. Moses used the size of Og's bed to explicitly link Bashan, the "place of the serpent," to Babylon and the occult religious system established by Amorite kings who worshiped the moon-god, Sîn.

Having dispatched the Amorite kings in the Transjordan, it was time for Israel to finally turn its attention to the Holy Land.

As noted earlier, one of the other major cult centers of the moon-god in the ancient Near East was Jericho. The Amorite name for the moon-god was Yarikh, but by transliterating the *Y* to a *J*, you see that the city was named for the Amorite moon-god. It was also the name of an Amorite tribe, the Yarikhu, who are mentioned in texts found in the ruins of Mari. A city called Yarikh, located north of Mount Hermon in Lebanon's Bekaa Valley, was called a "ruin" in a letter to the Mariote king, Yasmah-Addu. The scholar who translated the letter identified the city as a settlement of the Yarikhu tribe.[97]

This means that at the time of the patriarchs, a city and tribe named for the moon-god anchored the northeastern end of the Great Rift Valley that extends from the Lebanese border with Syria down to the Red Sea. Jericho sits at the south end, near the Dead Sea, and in the middle, near the Sea of Galilee, was another city called "House of the Moon-god," Bet Yerah, just a day's walk from a huge stone monument shaped like the crescent moon. In other words, there were moon-god worshipers all along the Jordan Rift Valley from about 3000 BC until the time of the conquest of Canaan.

The Yarikhu were one of five tribes in a confederation called the *Binu Yamina*, a name that means "sons of the right hand." Since Mesopotamians oriented themselves by facing east, the direction of the rising sun, the Binu Yamina were considered "southerners," while the *Binu Sim'al* ("sons of the left hand") were "northerners."[98] This was more or less how the tribes' pastureland was distributed in western Mesopotamia.[99]

As a side note, "Binu Yamina" was just the Amorite way of saying "Benjamin." That doesn't mean there was any connection to the Israelite tribe of Benjamin, but it confirms that the culture described in the Bible is consistent with what archaeologists have been digging out of the ground for the last two hundred years.

The presence of cities and a tribe bearing the Amorite name of the moon-god suggests that Yarikh/Sîn was one of the more prominent gods of Canaan. God knew it. It's no coincidence that Jericho, the city of the moon-god, was the first objective in the Holy Land. Let's examine the record and consider the evidence.

First of all, pay attention to dates in the Bible. They're included when they're important.

While the people of Israel were encamped at Gilgal, they kept the Passover on the fourteenth day of the month in the evening on the plains of Jericho. And the day after the Passover, on that very day, they ate of the produce of the land, unleavened cakes and parched grain. And the manna ceased the day after they ate of the produce of the land. And there was no longer manna for the people of Israel, but they ate of the fruit of the land of Canaan that year. (Joshua 5:10–12)

God started those daily deliveries of manna (except on the Sabbath) forty years earlier on the very day the Israelites entered the Wilderness of Sîn, the fifteenth day of the second month after leaving Egypt. Passover is always in the month of Nisan, the first month of the year in the Hebrew calendar. So, the attack on Jericho, which began shortly thereafter, occurred on or about the fifteenth of Nisan. Not only was this the anniversary of the night in Egypt when God had convinced the oppressors of Israel to let His people go, it means Joshua's attack on the city of the moon-god was during the first full moon of the new year!

But it's even cooler than that. Have you ever wondered why God told Joshua and the Israelites to march around Jericho for seven days?

Think back to our previous discussion of the *akitu* festival. This celebration of a city's patron deity was held at least once a year. The ritual originated at Ur, the city of the moon-god, more than a thousand years before the Exodus. It was celebrated in spring and fall, on the first day of the first month, Nisan, and the seventh month, Tishrei.

Based on what scholars have pieced together from texts from Ur and nearby Sumerian cities like Uruk and Nippur, the *akitu* festival lasted for eleven days. Rituals during the first seven days of the festival took place outside the city, and the idol representing the god was carried from its temple in the city to the *akitu*-house outside the walls. The last three days of the festival were held at the temple inside the city.

Needless to say, this involved a lot of traveling from the city to the *akitu*-house and back for rituals and festivities. One of those rituals, remember, was circumambulating of the fields to raise a spiritual hedge of protection against wind demons and other evil forces that might destroy the city's crops.[100]

Hmm. Marching in a circle around a place to earn the favor of the city's patron god. Does that sound familiar?

> You shall march around the city, all the men of war going around the city once. Thus shall you do for six days. Seven priests shall bear seven trumpets of rams' horns before the ark. On the seventh day you shall march around the city seven times, and the priests shall blow the trumpets. And when they make a long blast with the ram's horn, when you hear the sound of the trumpet, then all the people shall shout with a great shout, and the wall of the city will fall down flat, and the people shall go up, everyone straight before him. (Joshua 6:3–5)

The big difference between the ancient festival at Ur and the march around the Amorite city of the moon-god was that there was no idol representing Yahweh leading the Israelites. It was better—Joshua 5:13–15 tells us that the Angel of Yahweh, "the commander of the army of YHWH," was there in person. That was a Christophany. The Messiah—God—was there in person to fight for Israel at Jericho.

The Israelites camped outside the walls spoiled the moon-god's party that year. "Jericho was shut up inside and outside because of the people of Israel. None went out, and none came in."[101] While stopping the usual flow of goods into the city was bad enough, there was a spiritual element at work. Remember, when dates are recorded in the Bible, they're important. The dates recorded in chapter 5 of Joshua match the dates of the *akitu* festival at the moon-god's cult centers, Harran and Ur.

Now, get this: Texts about various *akitu* celebrations in ancient Mesopotamia suggest that a god's triumphal return to his or her city took place on day seven of the festival.[102]

Day seven. The day the walls of Jericho came tumbling down, and in a reversal of a festival more than a thousand years old, Yahweh symbolically entered the city of the moon-god.

Boom. Mic drop.

In the interest of accuracy, even though there are plenty of records documenting the *akitu* at Ur and Harran, we don't have any direct evidence that the *akitu* was celebrated at Jericho. Secular scholars don't even agree on when the city was destroyed and whether the Israelites were responsible. (For the record, I have no problem with the biblical account.)

But the evidence fits our theory: Not only did Yahweh time the attack to begin on the anniversary of Israel's release from Egypt *and* immediately after the spring *akitu* festival, when the moon-god was supposed to be at full strength, but He also apparently directed the Israelites to reverse an ancient ritual created to honor the moon-god.

Coincidence?

Let's add another nugget: Think back to the story of the discovery of the stela at the temple on Mount Hermon. In addition to the stela, Sir Charles Warren discovered an ancient stone wall that forced people climbing to the summit of the mountain to pour out drink offerings to approach in a circular path with the summit always on the left—a counterclockwise circumambulation.

Again, it's worth asking, as Warren did in his 1870 report for the Palestine Exploration Fund: Did the pagan ritual of circumambulating a place or thing to gain favor with the gods originate on the summit of Mount Hermon?

Even those of us who didn't really pay attention in church know that the destruction of Jericho was just the beginning of Israel's war with the natives of Canaan. The collapse of Jericho's walls was an unmistakable message to the moon-god and his colleagues, but the fighting was far from over.

After Israel destroyed Jericho and Ai, an Amorite coalition led by Adoni-zedek of Jerusalem marched on Gibeon to punish that city for making a treaty with Israel. With Yahweh's help, Joshua and the Israelites routed the Amorites.

You probably remember the story from Sunday school. This is another one of the tales that's so cool it's become a favorite with Christian pastors and teachers. Sadly, some interpret it the wrong way, using a method of Bible study that pastor and radio broadcaster Chris Roseborough calls "narcigesis." That's a combination of "narcissism" and "exegesis," a disturbing trend of Christians to read themselves into every story in the Bible.

In this case, the victory over the Amorite army was so complete that Joshua prayed and asked God to stop the sun from setting so Israel could complete the victory in daylight. "Narcigesis" would have us believe that by praying the same way Joshua prayed, God will do miraculous things—stopping the sun in the sky, as it were—so we can have everything we want. No. God is not obligated to respond to our wishes if we speak the right words in the right way. That's the definition of witchcraft.

Interpreting Joshua's prayer in the Valley of Aijalon as the key to personal success completely misses the point of that battle. It's so much *bigger* than finding the magic words to get God to do what we want. At the Valley of Aijalon, God literally fought against the small-*g* gods of Israel's pagan enemies.

> At that time Joshua spoke to the LORD in the day when the LORD gave the Amorites over to the sons of Israel, and he said in the sight of Israel,
>
> "Sun, stand still at Gibeon, and moon, in the Valley of Aijalon."

And the sun stood still, and the moon stopped, until the nation took vengeance on their enemies.

Is this not written in the Book of Jashar? The sun stopped in the midst of heaven and did not hurry to set for about a whole day. There has been no day like it before or since, when the LORD obeyed the voice of a man, for the LORD fought for Israel. (Joshua 10:12–14)

Did you catch that? The sun stopped and kept the moon(-god) out of the sky for "about a whole day."

Just as He did at the Red Sea, God sent a message not just to the human enemies of His people, but to their gods. In Egypt, Yahweh parted the waters to humiliate the storm-god, Baal, who claimed credit for taming the chaos-god of the sea. At the Valley of Aijalon, Yahweh literally kept the moon-god out of the sky for a whole day while Israel obliterated an army of the moon-god's followers. This was a message to the patron god of the Amorites who'd founded Babylon and dominated the Near East for four hundred years.

The prophet Habakkuk later suggested this battle was more real than we've been taught:

The sun and moon stood still in their place at the light of your arrows as they sped, at the flash of your glittering spear. (Habakkuk 3:11)

Using the Hebrew for "sun" and "moon," the first line reads, "Shemesh (the sun-god) and Yarikh stood still in their place." "Glittering spear" is *baraq chaniyth*, which literally means "lightning spear"—a thunderbolt, the favorite weapon of the storm-god, Baal.

Yes, God has a sense of humor.

While the Amorites were unknown outside the Bible until about two hundred years ago, their influence on the world continues to the present day. God called them out for their wickedness; they're responsible for the occult system of Babylon, the symbol of the end-times church of the Antichrist; and the most prominent god of their pantheon in the days of the patriarchs, the moon-god, was an early target in God's war against the supernatural rebels who wanted to destroy His people.

The moon-god was down, but he wasn't out. Meanwhile, another rebel god was ready to take his shot at Israel.

Part II

The Infernal Council

6

A Change in the Weather

There was a shift in the direction of the supernatural wind about the time of the judges in Israel. Followers of the moon-god faded into the background as worshipers of Baal became more of a problem for Israel.

What caused this change in the supernatural threat? Was it simply a swing in demographics, an example of diversity in action? Maybe. The Amorites from the east, who occupied lands that were mainly mountains, steppe, and desert, lived very differently than their city-dwelling cousins along the Mediterranean coast. From a naturalistic view, you can understand why the moon-god was more important than the storm-god where rainfall was rare. Amorites in the east lived where rain-fed agriculture wasn't possible. Sure, the storm-god was a violent, dangerous deity who could flatten your crops in a single day, but he just didn't visit the desert all that often. So, in ancient Sumer (southern Iraq today), the storm-god, called Ishkur, was a junior member of the pantheon. The storm-god, under the name Addu or Hadad (Baal in the Bible), only rose to kingship in the west—modern Syria, Turkey, Lebanon, and Israel (and later, Greece and Rome as Zeus/Jupiter)—where people could farm without irrigation canals.

Did this apparent transfer of power from the moon-god to the storm-god reflect a political change in the natural realm, the rising power of Baal-worshiping Arameans after the Bronze Age Collapse around 1200 BC? Or was this a supernatural conflict between the Fallen?

There is some evidence that these rebel gods don't always get along. In chapter 10 of the Book of Daniel, the prophet is told by an angelic messenger that he'd been delayed for twenty-one days by "the prince of the kingdom of Persia."[103] The angel only broke free to deliver his message when the archangel Michael arrived to take up the fight with the prince *and* the "kings of Persia." In that context, the angel can only have been referring to supernatural entities, what the people in Daniel's day would have called the gods of Persia, and rightly so.

The point is this: A number of nations that were enemies of Israel—Egypt, Babylon, Assyria, Persia, Greece, and Rome—fought more with each other than they did with God's chosen people. Why would they do that if the principalities and powers behind those kingdoms were hell-bent on destroying the bloodline that would someday produce the Messiah?

First of all, God wouldn't have allowed it, of course. But consider this: If the Fallen had hubris enough to rebel against the Creator of the Universe, why *wouldn't* they fight one another to become the supreme ruler? It's like the premise of the supernatural television series *Highlander*—there can be only one. That is precisely the goal of the rebellious sons of God.

> How you are fallen from heaven, O Day Star [KJV: "Lucifer"], son of Dawn! How you are cut down to the ground, you who laid the nations low! You said in your heart, "I will ascend to heaven; above the stars of God I will set my throne on high; I will sit on the mount of assembly in the far reaches of the north;

I will ascend above the heights of the clouds; I will make myself like the Most High." (Isaiah 14:12–14)

Lucifer, the divine rebel from Eden, doesn't just want to knock Yahweh off His throne, he hopes to elevate himself and his "mount of assembly" above the stars of God—a poetic way of saying that Lucifer wants to be supreme above everything and everyone.

So, the Book of Judges appears to mark a change in the main supernatural threat to Israel. Prior to the conquest, it was the moon-god, chief deity of the founders of Babylon and the occupants of Canaan. After the Israelites settled in the land, the forces arrayed against the people of Yahweh were more often than not worshipers of Baal and the other major gods of the western Amorites, such as El, his consort Asherah, and Astarte, better known as Ishtar (and later as Aphrodite and Venus). This seems to reflect division or competition between the rebel gods in the spirit realm. Imagine the power wielded by the fallen *elohim* who could claim victory over the people of Yahweh!

The story of Gideon and his three hundred is a perfect example of the changing times.

Calendar check: It was about 1200 BC. The Mediterranean world was in turmoil. The Trojan War had probably been fought about fifty years earlier on the west coast of what is now Turkey. For reasons scholars still haven't untangled, a wave of warlike peoples swept across the eastern Mediterranean, destroying the Hittite Empire and smaller Amorite kingdoms like Ugarit and Amurru in Syria. They even threatened Egypt itself, then ruled by Ramesses III, son of Ramesses the Great.

Scholars call this coalition the Sea Peoples for lack of a better term; the members of the league haven't been positively identified, although it's generally accepted that the Philistines were one of them. Other groups may have included remnants of the Minoan civilization from Crete, Mycenaean Greeks, Etruscans, Sicilians, Sardinians, or displaced Hittites fleeing the destruction of their civilization.

Whoever they were and whatever prompted the mass movement, evidence points to a tsunami of social upheaval around the eastern Mediterranean around 1200 BC, and Canaan was no exception.

This is the period of the Book of Judges. Conflicts between the tribes of Israel and their neighbors are set against a backdrop of war and destruction from Greece to Babylon, where the Kassites, who'd ruled that kingdom for four hundred years, were routed and sent into obscurity by Elam, a kingdom in northwestern Persia.

Things weren't easy for the tribes of Israel. Although they had been in the Promised Land for two centuries, they weren't exactly its masters. By the time we get to chapter 6 of Judges, the Israelites had already been oppressed by Aram, Moab, the Philistines, and Jabin, the Amorite king of Hazor, whose general Sisera appears to have been from the group of Sea Peoples called the Sherden or Shardana—possibly Sardinians who built the mysterious stone towers called *nuraghe* on that island.[104]

So, by the time of Gideon, two hundred years after Joshua led the people against Jericho, Israelites must have been growing weary of this cycle of oppression. For seven years, Israel had been dominated by the Midianites, Amalekites, and "the people of the East." They'd arrive every spring, so numerous that they and their camels couldn't be counted, and they would devour or steal all the crops. Things got so bad, the Israelites were forced to hide out in caves.[105]

They couldn't say God didn't warn them.

When the people of Israel cried out to the LORD on account of the Midianites, the LORD sent a prophet to the people of Israel. And he said to them, "Thus says the LORD, the God of Israel: I led you up from Egypt and brought you out of the house of slavery. And I delivered you from the hand of the Egyptians and from the hand of all who oppressed you, and drove them out before you and gave you their land. And I said to you, 'I am the LORD your God; you shall not fear the gods of the Amorites in whose land you dwell.' But you have not obeyed my voice." (Judges 6:7–10)

Catch that: "I am Yahweh your God; you shall not fear the gods of the Amorites in whose land you dwell." Apparently, the people of Israel had failed to understand that Canaan now belonged to *their* God, Yahweh. It was no longer the possession of the gods of the Amorite pantheon.

We need to detour for a moment to explain the concept of "holy ground." This was more than just the place where God was physically present, such as when Moses encountered the burning bush at Sinai or when the captain of Yahweh's host met Joshua at Jericho. Canaan was now Israel, ground holy and sacred to Yahweh, and belonging to Him alone among the *elohim*. Unfortunately, His people hadn't learned that yet. Maybe that's why they had drifted away from God despite the miracles they'd seen in the recent past.

Dr. Michael Heiser points out that belief in the rights of gods to specific geography was the norm in Old Testament days.[106] For example, when David was on the run from King Saul, he lamented that being chased from the land of Israel meant he would be separated from Yahweh:

> Saul recognized David's voice and said, "Is this your voice, my son David?" And David said, "It is my voice, my lord, O king." And he said, "Why does my lord pursue after his servant? For what have I done? What evil is on my hands? Now therefore let my lord the king hear the words of his servant. If it is the LORD who has stirred you up against me, may he accept an offering, but if it is men, may they be cursed before the LORD, for they have driven me out this day that I should have no share in the heritage of the LORD, saying, 'Go, serve other gods.'" (1 Samuel 26:17–19)

Another incident illustrates this point. Naaman of Damascus, the commander of the Aramean army, was healed of leprosy after following the instructions of the prophet Elisha. So, he made a strange request:

Then he returned to the man of God, he and all his company, and he came and stood before him. And he said, "Behold, I know that there is no God in all the earth but in Israel; so accept now a present from your servant." But he said, "As the LORD lives, before whom I stand, I will receive none." And he urged him to take it, but he refused. Then Naaman said, "If not, please let there be given to your servant two mule loads of earth, for from now on your servant will not offer burnt offering or sacrifice to any god but the LORD. In this matter may the LORD pardon your servant: when my master goes into the house of Rimmon to worship there, leaning on my arm, and I bow myself in the house of Rimmon, when I bow myself in the house of Rimmon, the LORD pardon your servant in this matter." (2 Kings 5:15–18)

As with David, Naaman understood that worshiping Yahweh required being on holy ground—Israel. Since Naaman lived in Damascus, this was a problem. His solution was to haul some holy ground with him back to Aram. (By the way, Rimmon was an epithet of the storm-god, Baal. It means "thunderer.")

Do you see now why Jesus devoted so much of His ministry to casting out demons? Yes, Jesus was relieving the misery of those possessed by the evil spirits, but in the supernatural realm He was doing battle with the sons of the Watchers who dared to occupy ground sacred to Yahweh. Jesus was kicking them off of His property!

Back to Gideon's day: The people of Israel apparently still felt they needed to appease the gods of the Amorites, which included the two main deities God had specifically attacked during the Exodus and conquest of Canaan—Baal, the storm-god, and Sîn/Yarikh, the moon-god.

This time, with Gideon, God would teach them, and Israel, a lesson.

Gideon was the son of a Baal worshiper. His father, Joash of the tribe of Manasseh, had his own altar to the storm-god and an Asherah pole to boot. Scholars aren't sure what those poles were, exactly, but since Asherah was considered a fertility goddess, you can guess what it may have represented.[107]

The Angel of Yahweh directed Gideon to destroy the altar and the Asherah, raise an army, and, to prove to Israel that this victory was not the work of a superior human general, send almost all of it home again.

Over the previous two hundred years, God had delivered Israel through Caleb's son-in-law Othniel, Ehud, Shamgar, and Deborah (who practically had to shame Barak into leading the army). Still, the people turned from Yahweh to the gods of the Amorites. So, this time, God would make it obvious to everyone that the victory was His.

> The LORD said to Gideon, "The people with you are too many for me to give the Midianites into their hand, lest Israel boast over me, saying, 'My own hand has saved me.'" (Judges 7:2)

Thirty-two thousand men answered the messengers Gideon sent throughout the territories of Manasseh, Asher, Zebulon, and Naphtali, the northern tribes. But even with thirty-two thousand soldiers, victory was no sure thing. The enemy army was four times bigger—about one hundred thirty-five thousand men were camped in the Valley of Jezreel.

Well, God was going to make it *obvious* that this victory was not the work of human hands. Through a series of tests, He reduced the size of Gideon's army from thirty-two thousand to three hundred.

Then He lowered the boom.

You've heard the story, no doubt, so I won't repeat it. Besides, aside from the miraculous deliverance from an army that vastly outnumbered the small Israelite force, the supernatural significance is what matters. It's hidden in a small detail at the end of the account.

Zebah and Zalmunna said, "Rise yourself and fall upon us, for as the man is, so is his strength." And Gideon arose and killed Zebah and Zalmunna, and he took the crescent ornaments that were on the necks of their camels. (Judges 8:21)

The kings of Midian decorated their camels with crescent ornaments—the symbol of the moon-god. They came from the desert of northwestern Arabia—southeast of Israel, south of Edom (and possibly overlapping Edom) and just east of the Red Sea. During the time of Moses, two hundred years earlier, their territory included the "mountain of God," Sinai, in the middle of the Wilderness of Sîn. Devotion to the moon-god wouldn't be surprising, and as we'll see, people living in the land of Midian continued to worship the moon-god under various names well into the Christian era.

But for the time being, the moon-god was no longer a clear and present danger to Israel. The next major showdown between Yahweh and Sîn would be more than six hundred years in the making.

7

The Fall of Babylon

Reading the Old Testament, one can wonder what was going on in the minds of the ancient Israelites. They'd been miraculously rescued from the Egyptians, Amorites, Amalekites, Midianites, Edomites, Moabites, Ammonites, Arameans, Philistines, and Assyrians (the southern kingdom of Judah, anyway) over a period of more than six hundred years. The Israelites fell into a pattern that was repeated again and again: A neighboring people would oppress Israel until they cried out to God, He'd send a deliverer to free them from bondage, and a short time later, the people would be back to whoring after Baal, Asherah, Astarte and her cult prostitutes, worshiping golden calves, and sacrificing children to Molech.

Eventually, God ran out of patience. The wickedness of Manasseh, king of Judah, was even worse than that of the Amorites, according to the chronicler,[108] worshiping the whole host of heaven, which includes the moon-god, and burning his son as an offering. Manasseh, who reigned between 709 and 643 BC, even defiled the Temple, setting up pagan altars and a carved Asherah inside the house of the Lord.

God delivered the bad news through His prophets: The kingdom of Judah was toast.

> Behold, I am bringing upon Jerusalem and Judah such disaster that the ears of everyone who hears of it will tingle. And I will stretch over Jerusalem the measuring line of Samaria, and the plumb line of the house of Ahab, and I will wipe Jerusalem as one wipes a dish, wiping it and turning it upside down. (2 Kings 21:12–13)

It took a while, in human terms. Manasseh died in 643 BC. Forty-six years later, Nebuchadnezzar of Babylon captured Jerusalem, deposed king Jehoiakim, and put Zedekiah on the throne in his place.

Now, imagine similar circumstances here in the United States. Suppose prophets began declaring God's judgment of doom on the United States because of, say, Richard Nixon. Do you think anybody today would believe that doom was still imminent after forty-six years of hearing that message? People being what we are—no, probably not.

But suddenly, there was the army of Chaldeans from Babylon outside the walls of Jerusalem. And even *that* wasn't enough to wake up the people. Ten years later, despite the warnings of Jeremiah, who was imprisoned and then thrown into a cistern for speaking truth to power, the Judean kingdom rebelled against Babylon again. God's message couldn't have been clearer:

> Thus says the LORD, God of Israel: "Thus shall you say to the king of Judah who sent you to me to inquire of me, 'Behold, Pharaoh's army that came to help you is about to return to Egypt, to its own land. And the Chaldeans shall come back and fight against this city. They shall capture it and burn it with fire. Thus says the LORD, Do not deceive yourselves, saying, "The Chaldeans will surely go away from us," for they will not go

away. For even if you should defeat the whole army of Chaldeans who are fighting against you, and there remained of them only wounded men, every man in his tent, they would rise up and burn this city with fire.'" (Jeremiah 37:7–10)

Pharaoh Hophra sent a relief army into Judah in 587 BC. The Egyptian king wanted to keep Judah as a client kingdom for himself. It didn't work; Hophra either decided saving Jerusalem wasn't possible or was not worth a major showdown with Nebuchadnezzar, and he retreated into Egypt. When the Chaldean army returned to Jerusalem, it did exactly as Jeremiah foretold—the city and the Temple were looted and destroyed.

Fast forward to 539 BC. Exiles from Judah had been in Babylonia for more than fifty years, ever since Nebuchadnezzar's first siege of Jerusalem in 597 BC. For reference, this includes most of the life of Ezekiel, who was in the first wave of exiles after that siege and likely died around 570 BC.[109]

By 539 BC, Nebuchadnezzar had been dead for more than twenty years. Nabonidus had been king since about 556 BC, when he led a coup against Nebuchadnezzar's young grandson, Labashi-Marduk, who was apparently deemed unfit to rule. Nabonidus is an interesting character who might have been remembered as one of the great pagan kings of the ancient world if he hadn't been caught on the wrong side of a supernatural war.

Nabonidus, whose name means "Nabu is praised" (Nabu being the Mesopotamian god of wisdom, literacy, and scribes), wasn't a Chaldean like Nebuchadnezzar. His background is somewhat fuzzy. He may have been Assyrian based on his origin in Harran, where his mother served at the great temple of the moon-god, Sîn.

Nabonidus might be history's first archaeologist.[110] It's possible he tried to ingratiate himself to the home crowd by aligning himself with Babylon's past glory, or maybe he genuinely loved history, but Nabonidus dug up artifacts all over Babylon and displayed them in museums. He also located and restored ancient temples of Shamash, the sun-god, and Ishtar, the goddess of sex and war, in the city of Sippar. He no doubt pleased his mother by doing the same for the sanctuary of Sîn at Harran that had been built more than fifteen hundred years earlier by the great Akkadian king Naram-Sîn.

The most interesting aspect of Nabonidus' life, for our purposes, is his devotion to the moon-god. That's probably not a surprise, considering his mother's lifetime commitment to Sîn. What's unusual is the degree to which Nabonidus took it. While scholars aren't completely agreed about this, evidence suggests he tried to replace Marduk at the top of the Babylonian pantheon with the moon-god. In addition, Nabonidus spent most of his seventeen-year reign outside of Babylon, living for ten years at Tayma,[111] an oasis in the Arabian desert probably named for one of the sons of Ishmael.[112]

And, surprise—Tayma was a center of moon-god worship.[113]

What was Nabonidus doing there? Some scholars suggest he was mainly after wealth. Tayma was situated on a trade route, the easternmost branch of the ancient incense road.[114] Like any king needing creative ways to balance his royal budget, Nabonidus may have felt that his presence was necessary to control the lucrative trade routes from south Arabia to Mesopotamia, especially as it became clear that the Medes and Persians to the north and east were becoming an existential threat.

There may be another explanation. A prayer attributed to Nabonidus found among the Dead Sea scrolls, an Aramaic text called 4Q242, suggests that his long stay at Tayma was for his health.

1. The words of the p[ra]yer which Nabonidus, king of [Ba]bylon, the great king, pray[ed] when he was stricken]
2. with an evil disease by the decree of G[o]d in Teman. [I Nabonidus] was stricken with [an evil disease]
3. for seven years, and from [that] (time) I was like [unto a beast and I prayed to the Most High]
4. and, as for my sin, he forgave it.[115]

The similarity of this account with the story of Nebuchadnezzar's madness in chapter 4 of the Book of Daniel is obvious. Some scholars believe the biblical account may have inspired the text at Qumran.

On the other hand, there is evidence that Nabonidus' time at Tayma was a spiritual quest. The oasis is believed to have been a center of moon-god worship as far back as the Bronze Age,[116] at least five hundred years before Nabonidus.

This oasis was in the heart of what had been Midian six hundred years earlier, in the days of Gideon. As we'll see in a later chapter, worship of the moon-god continued in Arabia long after Babylon became a sand-covered ruin.

So, it appears that Nabonidus, born in Harran, the city of the moon-god in northern Mesopotamia, settled in the Arabian city of the moon-god for reasons beyond its strategic importance. It may be that he was waiting for a message from the moon-god—a prophecy or sign of some sort. While he stayed at Tayma, his son ruled as regent in Babylon. That was Belshazzar, the king we know from the Book of Daniel.

Belshazzar was in a delicate situation. There were certain religious duties that the king of Babylon was expected to perform. He played a key role in the annual spring *akitu* festival with the god Marduk. If the king wasn't in Babylon to "take the hand of Bel" (Marduk), the rites couldn't be performed, and the city, it was believed, wouldn't receive the blessing of its patron god. Remember, Nabonidus was out of Babylon for ten years, living at Tayma in the Arabian desert.

Nabonidus didn't seem to feel that this was a problem, lending credence to the belief that his goal was to replace Marduk as the chief god of Babylon with Sîn, the moon-god. That plan couldn't have been popular with the ancient priesthood of Marduk or religious conservatives in Babylon.

On that fateful night in 539 BC, recorded in chapter 5 of the Book of Daniel, Belshazzar, the son and co-regent of Babylon's king Nabonidus, hosted a drunken party at the palace. During the festivities, he ordered his servants to bring out the gold and silver vessels that had been plundered from the Temple in Jerusalem more than half a century earlier, and he used them to serve wine to the Chaldean nobles and his wives and concubines.

Then:

Immediately the fingers of a human hand appeared and wrote on the plaster of the wall of the king's palace, opposite the lampstand. And the king saw the hand as it wrote. Then the king's color changed, and his thoughts alarmed him; his limbs gave way, and his knees knocked together. (Daniel 5:5–6)

Daniel was summoned to interpret the sign. Bad news for Belshazzar.

You have lifted up yourself against the Lord of heaven. And the vessels of his house have been brought in before you, and you and your lords, your wives, and your concubines have drunk wine from them. And you have praised the gods of silver and gold, of bronze, iron, wood, and stone, which do not see or hear or know, but the God in whose hand is your breath, and whose are all your ways, you have not honored.

Then from his presence the hand was sent, and this writing was inscribed. And this is the writing that was inscribed: MENE, MENE, TEKEL, and PARSIN. This is the interpretation of the matter: MENE, God has numbered the days of your kingdom and brought it to an end; TEKEL, you have been weighed in the balances and found wanting; PERES, your kingdom is divided and given to the Medes and Persians. (Daniel 5:23–28)

All this you probably know. The story is popular with all ages, from Sunday school kids to grownups. It's an easy moral for a Sunday sermon:

Don't get too big for your britches. But there's a lot more to it just under the surface.

The timing of the fall of Babylon is key. The festival hosted by Belshazzar wasn't random event, some excuse for Belshazzar to show off in front of his friends. This party had spiritual significance.

> The tradition of the festivities might reflect historical fact. According to the chronicle, Babylon was taken on the sixteenth of Tašritu. Accepting that Nabonidus imposed new features of the cult of Sîn in the capital after his return from Teima, it is conceivable that festivals linked with the cult of Sîn at Harran were transplanted to Babylon, perhaps even the *akitu* festival. This festival started on the seventeenth of Tašritu. As Babylon was captured on the eve of the seventeenth, the festivities mentioned by Herodotus and the Book of Daniel may have been those of the Harran *akitu* festival, as celebrated in the capital by the supporters of Nabonidus.[117]

Not to put too fine a point on it, but the Babylonian calendar was tweaked so that the fall *akitu* festival for the moon-god was specifically timed to coincide with either the Harvest Moon or the Hunter's Moon:

> The seventeenth of Tašritu always fell during one of the two periods of the year that the moon had an unusually prominent place at night. It should also be remembered that the Harvest Moon and Hunter's Moon, by a curious trick of perception, are popularly believed to be unusually large and luminous. It is therefore singularly appropriate that the *akitu* festival in honor of the moon god Sîn should take place on the seventeenth of Tašritu, when the lunar deity, several days after full moon, retained its sway throughout the night.[118]

Because most of us Christians, including this author, are not very familiar with the festivals of Yahweh, let me point out that the last feast of the year, Sukkot (the Feast of Tabernacles), begins on the fifteenth of Tašritu/Tishrei.

So, here's the situation on the night of Belshazzar's party: Babylon was ruled by a king so devoted to the moon-god that he tried to overturn more than a thousand years of religious tradition to elevate Sîn above Marduk in the pantheon. His son, the co-regent, had just kicked off the *akitu* festival to honor the moon-god, an annual rite in Mesopotamia at least two thousand years old. Meanwhile, the most important annual festival of Yahweh, Sukkot, had begun two days earlier. Then Belshazzar, for reasons unknown, decided to liven up the party for his god, Sîn, by ordering the wine served in sacred utensils consecrated for use in the Temple of Yahweh.

Why did Belshazzar do it? What inspired him? (And why was he partying while the enemy Medes and Persians were right outside the city walls?)

It's impossible to say. Accounts of the last night of Babylon are somewhat contradictory. Some say Nabonidus was at the battle; others say he wasn't. It seems unlikely that Cyrus could have marched an army into Babylonia without word reaching the king. If the account in Daniel is accurate, and I assume it is, then maybe the *akitu* feast for Sîn was too important to postpone, even for an invasion. Maybe Belshazzar's decision to bring out the Temple utensils was to demonstrate the power of the moon-god over the God of the exiles from Judah.

Big mistake.

Lights out. Babylon was done.

And that was the last time the moon-god threatened the people of Yahweh for more than a thousand years.

8

"The" God

As noted in the introduction to this book, God took the rebel gods by surprise with His act of self-sacrifice at Calvary. Paul put it this way: "None of the rulers of this age understood this, for if they had, they would not have crucified the Lord of glory."[119]

The Greek word translated "rulers," *archontōn*, could refer to the Jewish and Roman officials who sent Jesus to the cross, but in context, it's more likely that Paul meant principalities and powers—the supernatural sons of God who'd been in a state of rebellion against their Creator for more than three thousand years.

The beauty of this spiritual jujitsu move is that Jesus telegraphed it with the Parable of the Tenants:

And he began to speak to them in parables. "A man planted a vineyard and put a fence around it and dug a pit for the winepress and built a tower, and leased it to tenants and went into another country. When the season came, he sent a servant to the tenants to get from them some of the fruit of the vineyard. And they took him and beat him and sent him away empty-handed. Again he sent to them another servant, and they struck him on the head and treated him shamefully. And he sent another, and him they killed. And so with many others: some they beat, and some they killed. He had still one other, a beloved son. Finally he sent him to them, saying, 'They will respect my son.' But those tenants said to one another, 'This is the heir. Come, let us kill him, and the inheritance will be ours.' And they took him and killed him and threw him out of the vineyard. What will the owner of the vineyard do? He will come and destroy the tenants and give the vineyard to others." (Mark 12:1–9)

The priests, scribes, and elders assumed that Jesus was talking to them. He was, of course, but on a deeper level, the parable was directed at the spirits *behind* the Jewish religious authorities. The tenants in Jesus' story were the *bene elohim* placed over the nations after the Tower of Babel incident. The servants sent by the vineyard's owner were the prophets, none of whom lived easy lives. The son and heir, of course, was the Messiah, Jesus.

Even though He told them exactly what would happen, the "cosmic powers over this present darkness" could not resist sending Him to the cross.

Things didn't go the way they planned. Jesus took the opportunity of His physical death to explain a few things to the first generation of rebels, the Watchers who'd been locked up in Tartarus for the Mount Hermon rebellion.

He went and proclaimed to the spirits in prison, because they formerly did not obey, when God's patience waited in the days of Noah. (1 Peter 3:19b–20a)

The Greek word translated "proclaimed" is sometimes rendered "preached" in English Bibles, but the sense of the verse is more forceful than just preaching. In a nutshell, Jesus visited the Watchers in the abyss to explain what had just taken place in Jerusalem: He was dead in the flesh, *and that was exactly what He wanted to happen.*

In other words, to paraphrase Dr. Michael Heiser: "Thank your minions for helping me complete that part of my mission. By the way, I'm getting out of here at dawn of the third day—and you're still dead."

World history suggests that the gods of the nations have been at war as much with each other as they've been with their Creator. The shock of the Resurrection and the improbable survival of the early church despite efforts by Rome and Jerusalem to stamp it out forced the pagan gods to admit they'd been completely outplayed. The clock was ticking and their backs were against the wall. It was time to try something desperate—setting aside differences for a joint effort to build a counter-religion to the growing faith in Jesus Christ.

Let's meet the colleagues of the moon-god as they were described in the texts left behind by their followers, from the time writing was invented through the period of the early Christian church.

One of the oldest gods in the Mesopotamian pantheon has a name that's led to a lot of confusion over the years about who he is and where his cult began. That's because the name of this deity became a generic word for "god" in multiple languages, including some still spoken today. I'm referring to "the" god, variously known as El, Ilu, and Enlil in the ancient Near East.

Among the earliest Amorites who came into contact with the Akkadians and Sumerians, the two most popular deities were the moon-god and "the" god. This is easy to document; we just need to look at the Amorite names that appear in records archaeologists have found and translated from ancient Sumer and Akkad.

If we then take a look at the 43 most popular Amorite names (in this case: Amorite names occurring three times or more). We can see immediately the moon-god Erah [Note: alternate spelling of *Yarikh*] and El ('God') are the two most popular (and only) theophoric elements in these early OB Amorite personal names. This is a striking parallel with the Akkadian personal names. This parallel pleads against the "Amorites" as newcomers, because such a phenomenon is typically the result of long-term contact and/or acculturation.[120]

The period covered in that study is the time of Abraham and Isaac, texts dated to between 1900 BC and 1791 BC.[121] Considering the number of gods in the Mesopotamian pantheon, it's significant that Amorites in Akkad and Sumer during the lifetime of Abraham only honored *two* of them.

Why these two? Since we've already discussed the moon-god in some detail, let's deal with his father, "the" god.

First of all, just like the moon-god, the deity called El was known by a number of different names over the centuries. A trilingual god list from the Amorite kingdom of Ugarit, which comes from the time of the judges, offered this handy equation: Enlil = Kumarbi = El.[122]

Kumarbi was a god of the Hurrians, an Indo-European people who lived in eastern Anatolia and northern Mesopotamia, roughly the area occupied today by the Kurds in Iraq, Syria, and Turkey, extending as far north as modern Armenia. His name may derive from an ancient town in northern Syria, meaning "he of Kumar," a site identified with modern Kīmār about twenty-five miles northwest of Aleppo.[123]

The Hurrian myth also locates Kumarbi in the western part of the Khabur River triangle, near the river along the border between Turkey and Syria, and the ancient city of Tuttul, which was near the modern city of Raqqa. Tuttul was a major cult center of Dagan,[124] providing evidence that the first-generation gods of the ancient Near East, from east to west, were one and the same: Enlil = Dagan = Kumarbi = El.

This is an important link in our chain, because connecting El to Enlil helps untangle the etymology of the Enlil's name.

84

Scholars used to believe "Enlil" was a combination of the Sumerian words *en* ("lord") and *lil* ("air/wind" or "storm").[125] That's too simple. Analyzing texts about Enlil doesn't yield any of the characteristics you'd expect from a wind- or storm-god.[126] Based on his identification with El, Kumarbi, and Dagan, Enlil should be understood as "a universal god who controls different spheres and domains, different areas without any defined specialization"[127]—in other words, Enlil was "the" god.

That makes the etymology of Enlil's name easier to grasp. Rather than Sumerian *en* + *lil*, it's more likely derived from a Semitic (i.e., non-Sumerian) language, *il-ilī*, meaning "god of all the gods."[128]

That certainly fits the character of Enlil, El, Dagan, and Kumarbi in their respective pantheons. All of them were considered creators of the world, described by epithets like "father of the gods," "great mountain," "ancient one," and so on.

All of them, to people in the ancient world, bridged the gap between time immemorial and the present day. In each case, "the" god had assumed kingship over the pantheon by replacing a primordial deity who represented the sky or heaven. El, Kumarbi, and Dagan supplanted Anu, while El took the place of Šamêm ("Heaven").[129] In the case of Kumarbi, the confrontation with his father, Anu, was particularly violent; in the fight for control of the universe, Kumarbi castrated Anu—with his teeth.

This detail links Kumarbi to Kronos of Greek mythology, who likewise castrated his father, Ouranos, although Kronos used an adamantine sickle. In turn, the king of the Titans was identified by Greek and Roman historians with Saturn and the Phoenician god Baal-Hammon, who was infamous for the tophet at Carthage, a burial site for very young children sacrificed and burned as offerings to the god—which suggests a connection to another Semitic god, Molech.

Before we get ahead of ourselves, let's recap: It appears that the same entity, called by different names, occupied the same slot in the pantheons of multiple civilizations. Specifically, Enlil (Sumer/Akkad), Dagan

85

(Amorites of Syria), El (Canaan), Kumarbi (Hurrians and Hittites), Kronos (Greece), Saturn (Rome), and Baal-Hammon (Phoenicians) were essentially one and the same.

Recent discoveries point to northern Syria, especially the region near Aleppo, Antioch (modern Antakya), and the mountains and valleys around them as key to the history of "the" god. Baal-Hammon, Saturn, and Kronos were the names of this god in the western Mediterranean, and they emerged in the first millennium BC after the time of David. The older names are found farther east.

Kumarbi of the Hurrians was linked to a town between Aleppo and Antioch; El was probably worshiped at Mount Zaphon before it became Baal's mount of assembly;[130] the name of their Phoenician equivalent, Baal-Hammon, means "lord of the Amanus,"[131] which are the mountains just north of Zaphon; Dagan was the chief deity along the middle Euphrates in what is now Syria; and since the name "Enlil" appears to be Semitic rather than Sumerian, it's possible that he, too, began his career in this part of northern Mesopotamia.

In other words, rather than emerging from Sumer in the south as Mesopotamian civilization is assumed to have done, "the" god Enlil may have been imported *to* Sumer from lands far to the northwest. In a very broad sense, that includes Jebel Bishri, the origin point of the Amorites (and Jebel Diddi, apparently named for the Ditanu tribe that gave its name to the Titans), Mount Hermon, Mount Zaphon, and the Amanus range—all mountains connected to the rebel gods.

Why? What made that area a hot spot for two of the most important rebel gods, Enlil/El/Dagan ("the" god) and Hadad (Baal), the storm-god? We can only guess.

Speaking of Dagan, who was Enlil/El by a different name: By now, you've likely wondered about the connection between this god and Dagon, the chief god of the Philistines. Good catch! You're right, they're one and the same. Over the thousand-plus years between the oldest texts to mention Dagan in Syria and the story of Samson in the Book of

Judges, the pronunciation changed a little. The last "a" sound shifted to an "o," not an unusual change.

But since the worship of Dagan isn't recorded anywhere in ancient Lebanon or Israel (maybe because the pagans there called him El), you may also be wondering how and when the Philistines transplanted a god from the north of Syria to the Gaza strip. Good question.

Archaeologists digging in the Amuq River valley in southern Turkey since the early 2000s have discovered evidence of a powerful early Iron Age state called Palistin (or Walistin), which was based at a city called Kunalua about fifteen miles southeast of Antioch. This may be the Calneh or Calno mentioned twice in the Bible (Amos 6:2, Isaiah 10:9).[132] Palistin emerged after the Bronze Age collapse around 1200 BC, when the Hittite Empire in Anatolia was destroyed along with most of the kingdoms in the eastern Mediterranean. This new state survived from the eleventh century BC down to about 700 BC, roughly from the time of Samuel and Saul to the time of Isaiah and Hezekiah.

Scholars first assumed that the eleventh century BC pottery they found at Kunalua was Aegean—the Greeks or their cousins. However, some are rethinking that theory and concluding that the pots were actually local copies of styles "not of Greece but rather of Cyprus and south-west Asia Minor."[133] That means these people weren't invaders, but descendants of the survivors of the chaos and destruction of the Bronze Age collapse. In other words, the kingdom of Palistin was probably founded by people who probably knew and worshiped Dagan all along.

You've surely noticed the similarity between "Palistin," "Philistine," and "Palestine." Scholars are pretty certain it's the same name. So, how did they get from around the border between Turkey and Syria down to Gaza, on the boundary with Egypt?

Egyptian records document several battles with the Sea Peoples between about 1200 and 1150 BC. This coalition included groups the Egyptians called Ekwesh, Denyen, Sherden (probably Sardinians),

Weshesh, and Peleset, who were almost certainly the Philistines. Scholars have assumed that these battles took place near the Egyptian homeland and that the defeated Philistine invaders were settled along the coast in Canaan in the cities that became infamous in the Old Testament—Gaza, Gath, Ashdod, Ekron, and Ashkelon. But some scholars have been rethinking this, placing those battles in what is now Syria rather than in Egypt.

1. The land battles between Egypt and the "Sea-Peoples" occurred along the northern frontiers of the Egyptian empire in the Levant.
2. The naval clashes were most likely raids on the prosperous Egyptian cities of the Nile Delta.
3. The "Sea-Peoples" were essentially north Levantine (including western Anatolian) populations known as former allies of the Hittites.
4. There is no textual or archaeological evidence that Philistines were ever settled by the Egyptians in Canaan. There is, however, evidence of their settlement in Egypt and in Syria soon after the battles.
5. Some of those "Sea-Peoples" established the kingdom of Palistin in the 'Amuq Plain. Others reached Philistia, probably by sea, as Egyptian rule over the Levant deteriorated.[134]

Not only does this explain how worshipers of Dagan got from northern Syria to the territory of the Philistines on the border of Egypt, it also IDs the kingdom of Palistin as the mostly likely place where the Hittite and Hurrian myths of Kumarbi, "he of Kumar" (the city near Aleppo, which was part of the territory ruled by Palistin), were transmitted to Cyprus and western Asia Minor, where, over the course of several hundred years, they were transformed into stories of the Greek Titan, Kronos.[135]

It's important to remember that there is little we can know for sure about the entity who wore all of these names. In fact, it's possible that more than one interacted with our distant ancestors under one or more of these identities. We humans do not see clearly into the spirit realm, and besides, these entities have been lying to us since the beginning. The best we can do is try to discern patterns without getting hung up on fine details. That way madness lies.

Utter disregard for human life and a connection to the underworld are recurring themes with Enlil/El/Dagan, etc. In ancient Sumer, Enlil was the one who decided that creating humankind was a mistake because our noise kept him awake at night. His solution was the global flood, which the Sumerians recorded in their king lists. According to the *Epic of Atrahasis*, named for the Sumerian Noah, humanity was saved by the intervention of the crafty god Enki, lord of the *abzu* ("abyss"), who disobeyed the command of Enlil and warned his faithful worshiper, Atrahasis, of the genocide decreed by Enlil.[136]

Make sure you register that deception: The ancient Mesopotamians believed that the lord of the abyss saved humanity from the Flood.

In general, "the" god was considered a cold, distant entity who had to be appeased through sacrifice—often the human variety. This is a well-documented aspect of Baal-Hammon and Kronos. The tophets excavated at Carthage and other Phoenician sites around the Mediterranean have yielded the remains of literally thousands of infants and young children who did not die of natural causes.

Saturn is best known as the god behind the Roman winter festival called Saturnalia, which featured role reversals and a loosening of social norms. For example, masters would wait on slaves, who were allowed to disrespect their owners; courts and schools were closed; people wore clothing normally considered gauche; and most work was suspended for the duration of the holiday.

But Saturn, like his counterparts, had a dark side. The fourth-century Roman poet Ausonius suggested that Saturn received dead gladiators as offerings during his festival,[137] a claim echoed by Macrobius, writing two generations later, in his *Saturnalia*.[138]

Because you're a logical thinker, you won't be surprised to learn that the Saturnalia was based on an earlier Greek holiday called the Kronia, which was celebrated in mid to late summer. Sacrifices of adult humans to Kronos are attested on the islands of Crete and Rhodes,[139] and he was identified as the Greek equivalent of the Phoenician god Baal-Hammon. As we noted earlier, his name probably means "lord of the Amanus (mountains),"[140] referring to a range in southern Turkey near Mount Zaphon (today called Jebel al-Aqra), the mountain sacred to Baal. This and evidence from southern Turkey of a festival that appears to be a forerunner of the Kronia[141] are solid evidence that the veneration of Kronos began closer to Mesopotamia than to Greece.

The similarity of "the" god's struggles with his father, Ouranos/Anu, and son Zeus/Teshub (the Hurrian storm-god), make the equation Kronos = Kumarbi a sure thing. Here we come full circle, as the Hurrian god Kumarbi was identified in the ancient world as Dagan, chief god of the middle Euphrates region, and Enlil, king of the pantheon in ancient Sumer.[142] Nippur, the city sacred to Enlil in Sumerian religion, is named as Kumarbi's home in the Hittite myth called *Kingship in Heaven* or *Song of Emergence*.[143]

Thus, Enlil was Kumarbi, Dagan, El, Kronos, Saturn, and Baal-Hammon.

Archaeologists have not documented human sacrifice in the worship of El, Dagan, and Kumarbi, but there are definite underworld connections for all three. For example, Dagan, chief god of the lands along the Euphrates River in Syria, was called *bēl pagrê*, which has been variously translated as "lord of corpse offerings, lord of corpses (a netherworld god), lord of funerary offerings, and lord of human sacrifices."[144] Kumarbi was one of the "primeval gods" of the Hurrians, deities who'd once ruled the world but who, like the Titans of Greek myth, had been banished to the netherworld by the storm-god.[145]

Texts from the Amorite kingdom of Ugarit point to Mount Hermon as the abode of El, and the connections between that mountain and the netherworld are well documented, as we've already noted. Amorites in western Mesopotamia and the Levant believed El and his consort Asherah held court on Mount Hermon along with their seventy sons.

Hermon is the northernmost point in Israel today, the border between the Jewish state, Lebanon, and Syria. Below its southeastern slopes was Bashan, the kingdom of Og, called the last of the remnant of the Rephaim.[146] Veneration of the Rephaim was a key element of Canaanite religion, whose depiction in Ugaritic texts is consistent with their portrayal in the Bible as the spirits of mighty kings of old. Careful reading of certain passages of the Bible, especially Isaiah 14:9–21, Ezekiel 32:27, and Ezekiel 39:11 shows that the prophets surely knew of the Rephaim. Their condemnation of those spirits and the veneration thereof is clear.

As mentioned earlier, a god named Rapiu, the singular form of "Rephaim," was believed to rule at Ashtaroth and Edrei, the same two cities named in the Bible as the seats of Og's kingdom. Ugaritic religious texts also connect Ashtaroth to the god Molech, further supporting the identity of Bashan as an evil place.

This also gives new meaning to the phrase "bulls of Bashan" in Psalm 22:12, a prophecy of the Messiah suffering on the cross. Dr. Robert D. Miller II correctly observes that the term is "not about famous cattle but about cultic practice." In his 2014 paper, Miller used archaeology and climatology to show that Bashan, contrary to what you may have heard, was a lousy place to raise cattle three thousand years ago, concluding that "Bulls of Bashan refers not to the bovine but to the divine."[147]

So, those bulls were not cattle but the spirits of the Rephaim and their masters, the fallen angels who masqueraded as gods. It's not a coincidence that bull imagery is connected to them in the Bible: The Canaanite creator-god was called Bull El; the root word behind the name Kronos likely means "horned one";[148] and the name Titan, derived from the tribe named Ditanu or Tidanu, probably originates with the Amorite *ditanum*, meaning "bison" or "aurochs."[149]

Then, on the southwest side of Hermon, we find Banias, better known as the Grotto of Pan. This is the cave from which the waters of the Jordan emerged in ancient times. Pagans venerated the site for centuries, and ancient historians wrote that sacrifices were tossed into the waters of the cave where they were accepted by the god therein if the offerings sank.

Not to belabor the point, but the bottom line is that Hermon, El's mount of assembly, towered over the entrance to the underworld.

Alone among these entities, El of the Canaanite pantheon seemed to deal with humanity in a positive way. In the *Legend of Keret*, a text from Ugarit dated to about the period of the judges in Israel, El personally intervened on behalf of a king who was distressed over the lack of an heir. Interestingly, King Keret's domain in the tale is called Hubur, which was the name of a river that played a role in older Sumerian and Akkadian myths similar to that of the River Styx in Greek cosmology—the border between the land of the living and the netherworld.

On the other hand, we have to consider El's favorites to take his place as king of the gods: Yamm, the chaos-god of the sea, and Mot, the god of death. The storm-god Baal had to defeat both in brutal combat to assume kingship. Since life-giving rain for crops, livestock, and our own survival is far more welcome among us mortals than chaos or death, El's favorites among the gods reveal an inconsistent level of concern for his human creations, at the very least.

To summarize: "The" god of the ancient world was, for the most part, a distant, uncaring entity, often linked to the underworld. At his worst, he demanded the sacrifice of humans, including children, and, in the case of Enlil, was prepared to obliterate the entire human race just for a good night's sleep. His home, at various points in his career, was the Sumerian city Nippur, the Amorite town Tuttul (near Raqqa in northern Syria), the Amanus mountains, Mount Hermon on the northern border of Israel.

Finally, in the guise of Saturn, considered the founder of the Latin race, he settled in west-central Italy, where Rome would eventually rise under the divine kingship of his son, the storm-god, Jupiter.

9

The Storm-god

Probably the most important bit of evidence that links the religions of the ancient world is the way the storm-god consistently emerged at the head of the pantheons. From Sumer to Rome and beyond, a pattern was repeated in which a first generation of primordial gods was replaced by anthropomorphic deities, who in turn were replaced, often violently, by a younger group headed up by a god of weather. These transfers of power were sometimes violent and usually resulted in the second-gen gods confined to the underworld.

To the Amorites near ancient Israel, the storm-god was called Baal, a title ("lord") that eventually replaced his original name, Hadad or Addu. As we noted earlier, Baal became king of the gods by defeating the favorites of El, the sea-god Yamm and Mot, the god of death.

The Hurrians, Hittites, and others in northern Mesopotamia (the lands now in northern Iraq, Turkey, Armenia, Georgia, and Azerbaijan) called the storm-god Tarhunz, Teshub, and Teisheba. He became king by defeating his father, the grain-god Kumarbi and a couple of his monstrous sidekicks.

This story was passed on to the Greeks as the conflict between Zeus and Kronos, the Titanomachy, a ten-year war in which the Olympians, led by the storm-god, rebelled against the Titans. They eventually prevailed and exiled most of the old gods to Tartarus, a place as far below Hades as the earth is below heaven, a special prison reserved for gods.

A version of this was handed down to the Romans, although they believed Saturn managed to escape his underworld prison after losing the war with Jupiter, settling in western Italy where Rome would be founded centuries later.

The only place in the ancient world where the storm-god didn't emerge on top of the pantheon was Babylonia. There, Enlil was replaced by Marduk, the city-god of Babylon, rather than by the storm-god, Ishkur. Although there are clear parallels between the Babylonian creation myth, the *Enuma Elish*, and the Ugaritic account of Baal's battle with Yamm, Marduk was not a weather-god. His origins are so humble that scholars just don't know much about him before Babylon emerged as a political power during the reign of Hammurabi. Then most of Marduk's attributes appear to have been borrowed from deities that had been worshiped in Mesopotamia for centuries, including the storm-god.[150]

Like Baal, Marduk is portrayed as a warrior, but that description also applies to other popular gods, such as the Canaanite plague-god Resheph (who was identified with the Babylonian god Nergal) and the Akkadian deity Ninurta. Marduk's symbol, the spade, suggests that he was originally associated with agriculture, possibly in connection with the construction and maintenance of irrigation canals.[151]

Outside of the Bible, most of what we know about the storm-god comes from the texts discovered in 1928 at Ras Shamra in Syria, the Amorite kingdom of Ugarit destroyed around 1200 BC. As you would expect of a god of weather, he was believed to be the one responsible for the conditions necessary for agriculture.[152] Not coincidentally, his battles with the gods of death and the sea are similar to the tensions between Zeus, Hades, and Poseidon in Greek mythology.

On another level, and more relevant to our study here, Baal was believed to be the lord of the Rephaim, who are called "warriors of Baal" in the Rephaim texts found at Ugarit. Some scholars believe that the *Legend of Aqhat*, the text designated KTU 1.17, indicates that Baal was believed to have the power to restore life to the dead.[153]

Interestingly, the abode of Baal was very near sites identified with his "father." Baal's palace was on Mount Zaphon, today called Jebel al-Aqra. It's an impressive peak on the Turkish coast just north of the border with Syria, rising more than fifty-two hundred feet from the Mediterranean Sea. According to the Baal Cycle, Zaphon is where the storm-god built his royal home with gold, silver, and fire.[154] It's very near the Amanus mountain range, identified with the Phoenician god Baal-Hammon ("lord of the Amanus"), and the ancient city of Kumar, identified as a home of his Hurro-Hittite equivalent, Kumarbi. And, as we noted earlier, El was probably venerated at Zaphon before it was associated with Baal.[155]

Because ancient Israel had a lot of contact with Baal-worshipers, the name of Baal's mountain was burned into the Hebrew psyche. The word for the compass point north in other ancient Semitic languages was *sim'al*, but it's *tsaphon* in Hebrew to this day. This is a clue that helps explain why God chose to part the Red Sea on Israel's way out of Egypt.

> Then the LORD said to Moses, "Tell the people of Israel to turn back and encamp in front of Pi-hahiroth, between Migdol and the sea, in front of Baal-zephon; you shall encamp facing it, by the sea. For Pharaoh will say of the people of Israel, 'They are wandering in the land; the wilderness has shut them in.' And I will harden Pharaoh's heart, and he will pursue them, and I will get glory over Pharaoh and all his host, and the Egyptians shall know that I am the LORD." And they did so. (Exodus 14:1–4)

Have you ever wondered why God told Moses to turn around? The Israelites were getting away! Why the about face? Why camp in front of a place called Baal-zephon—which, you've noticed, is named for Baal ("lord of Zaphon")?

More important, what is a place named for the mountain of the king of the Canaanite gods doing on the shore of the Red Sea in Egypt?

These are easy questions to answer if we apply a little history. First, Egyptologists know very well that migrants from Canaan, Amorites called Hyksos ("rulers of foreign lands") by the Egyptians, controlled northern Egypt for roughly two hundred years between about 1750 and 1550 BC. They brought their art, their architecture, and their gods with them, including Baal. Remember, Baal fought a battle with the sea-god, Yamm, to become king of the gods. Archaeologists have found plenty of evidence at the capital city of the Hyksos, Avaris, to confirm that Baal was not only worshiped there, he was also the patron god of sailors.[156]

The showdown at the Red Sea was specifically engineered by Yahweh. He didn't part the sea because it was Israel's only route of escape; He told Moses to *turn around* and camp in front of a place sacred to Baal.

Now, why would God take the Canaanite storm-god so seriously? The prophet Isaiah has the answer.

How art thou fallen from heaven, O Lucifer, son of the morning!
How art thou cut down to the ground, which didst weaken the nations!
For thou hast said in thine heart, I will ascend into heaven,
I will exalt my throne above the stars of God:
I will sit also upon the mount of the congregation, in the sides of the north:
I will ascend above the heights of the clouds; I will be like the most High. (Isaiah 14:12–13, KJV)

The identity of the divine rebel from Eden is revealed by these verses. Lucifer's "mount of the congregation," or "mount of assembly," is named by the Hebrew phrase translated "sides of the north," *yarkete tsaphon*—Mount Zaphon, the mountain sacred to Baal.

Surprise! Lucifer is the storm-god. Confirming this ID, Jesus twice linked the storm-god to Satan—once when confronted by Pharisees who accused Him of casting out demons by the power of Beelzebul ("Baal the prince"), and again when He dictated a letter to John the Revelator for the church at Pergamum, "where Satan's throne is."[157]

The hubris of Baal is evident from the five "I wills" in the verses above from Isaiah. It also shines through in religious texts from Ugarit.

> For I have a word that I would say to you,
> a message that I would repeat to you:
> a word of tree and whisper of stone,
> the sighing of the heavens to the earth,
> of the deep to the stars,
> I understand the thunder
> which the heavens do not know,
> a word unknown to men,
> and which the multitudes of the earth do not understand.
> Come,
> and I shall reveal it
> in the midst of my divine mountain, Saphon,
> in the sanctuary,
> on the mountain of my inheritance,
> in Paradise, on the height of victory.[158]

It's beautiful poetry underscored by an undeniable arrogance. It wouldn't be worth mentioning, however, if Baal wasn't a threat to God's chosen people.

The smackdown at the Red Sea was only one of several confrontations in the Bible between the Hebrew prophets and the storm-god. The most obvious, of course, was the challenge on Mount Carmel between

Elijah and the prophets of Baal. There is more back story to this show-down than we usually hear in church.

For one thing, God sent a drought that lasted three and a half years before the confrontation, then He consumed the sacrifice with the storm-god's favorite weapon, the thunderbolt. Ahab's victories over larger Aramean armies in 1 Kings 20, in spite of his rebellious spirit, were victories of God over forces loyal to the storm-god. Note that the king of Aram was named Ben-Hadad ("son of the storm-god"). Letting him go free, a man God had "devoted to destruction," sealed Ahab's doom.[159]

There are numerous examples in the Old Testament where epithets of Baal are applied to Yahweh. It's as though the prophets of God were sending a message to their pagan colleagues: "You think Baal is all that, but he's not. The *real* power in heaven belongs to Yahweh."

For example, Dr. Michael Heiser breaks down how the heavenly scene described in chapter 7 of the Book of Daniel follows the outline of the Baal Cycle:

Ugarit (Baal Cycle)	Bible (Daniel 7)
(A) El, the aged high God, is the ultimate sovereign in the council.	(A) The Ancient of Days, the God of Israel is seated on the fiery, wheeled throne (cf. Ezekiel 1). Like Ugaritic El, he is white haired and aged ("ancient").
(B) El bestows kingship upon the god Baal, the Cloud-Rider, after Baal defeats the god Yamm in battle.	(B) Yahweh-El, the Ancient of Days, bestows kingship upon the Son of Man who rides the clouds after the beast from the sea (yamma) is destroyed.
(C) Baal is king of the gods and El's vizier. His rule is everlasting.	C) The Son of Man is given everlasting dominion over the nations. He rules at the right hand of God. He rules at the right hand of God.[160]

Baal is repeatedly called the "Charioteer of the Clouds" in the Ugaritic texts.[161] Not only was a similar epithet applied to Yahweh in the Bible (Isaiah 19:1, Nahum 1:3, Zechariah 10:1), He literally appeared in a thick cloud to the Israelites during the Exodus,[162] Elijah in the wilderness, Ezekiel,[163] and the apostles at the Transfiguration[164] (which occurred, not coincidentally, on Mount Hermon).[165] And, lest we forget, Jesus Himself announced that when He makes His triumphant return to the earth, He'll be "coming on the clouds of heaven with power and great glory."[166]

Does this mean Yahweh was Baal, or that the Israelites and Canaanites somehow confused the two? No. It's another example of the astonishing pride of the created being who rebelled in Eden and subsequently manifested to the ancient world as the storm-god. Satan/Baal tried to claim titles that rightfully belong to Yahweh.

The ambition of the storm-god was his undoing. Instead of being enthroned above the rest of the stars (i.e., angels) of God, he was thrown down and made lord of the dead.

> Sheol beneath is stirred up to meet you when you come;
> it rouses the shades to greet you, all who were leaders of the
>   earth;
> it raises from their thrones all who were kings of the nations.
> All of them will answer and say to you:
> "You too have become as weak as we! You have become like
>   us!" (Isaiah 14:9–10)

The word translated "shades" in Isaiah 14:9 is the Hebrew *rəpā'îm*—Rephaim. Isaiah described them the way they were remembered by the pagan Amorites of Canaan and Babylon, as "leaders of the earth" and "kings of the nations." The difference is that while the prophet described them as weak, with maggots for beds and worms for covers,[167] the Amorites venerated the Rephaim as the mighty warriors of Baal.

It's hard to overstate the significance of the link between the Rephaim, the pagan neighbors of ancient Israel, and the divine rebel from Eden. As we noted in an earlier chapter, the root behind "Rephaim," *rāpi*, was the theophoric element in some Amorite names, including their most famous king, Hammurabi of Babylon. The Ugaritic Rephaim Texts were necromancy rituals that summoned what were believed to be spirits of the ancestors of the Amorite kings to feasts in their honor at the sanctuary of El on Mount Hermon. The Greek Titans derived their name from an ancient Amorite tribe, the Ditanu/Tidanu, which was closely linked to the Rephaim.[168] The Rephaim were "warriors of Baal," and "Baal is their lord in the realm of the dead, as shown by the circumlocation *zbl b'l arṣ* ('prince, lord of the underworld')."[169]

In short, "the signet of perfection, full of wisdom and perfect in beauty,"[170] was cast out of Eden and thrust down to Sheol, a realm occupied by the spirits of the "mighty men who were of old, the men of renown"—the Nephilim.

Think about that. While Satan/Baal was kicked out of Eden for his rebellion, he was only barred from God's holy mountain. He still had access to the divine council, at least during the Old Testament (see Job 1 and 2). He walked the earth as least as late as Jesus' day, and we see no evidence that he's gone away. But the rebels who came later, the Watchers who descended to Mount Hermon (the Genesis 6:1–4 incident), were banished to the netherworld for their sin. Peter wrote that they were confined in Tartarus, connecting the rebel angels to the Titans. He and Jude both noted that the rebel angels are chained under gloomy darkness until the judgment.[171]

However, according to the Book of Enoch, the spirits of the Nephilim, the children of the Watchers/Titans by human women, called Rephaim by the Canaanites and the Hebrew prophets, became the demons that plague the world to this day.[172] This was the consensus belief among Jews during the Second Temple period and of early church fathers such as Philo, Origen, and Justin Martyr.[173]

Assuming that's correct, then Satan/Baal has inherited a demonic army created by the rebel angels of Genesis 6.

It's clear that the pagan gods of the ancient world were more important to the people around the prophets and apostles than we've been taught. So far, we've discussed several:

- The moon-god, called Sîn and Yarikh, was the patron god of the kings who founded Babylon and the king who ruled Babylon when it was conquered by the Medes and Persians.
- "The" god, variously called Enlil, Dagan, El, Kronos, Saturn, and Baal-Hammon, was connected with death, the underworld, and the horrific practice of child sacrifice.
- The storm-god, mainly known as Baal, Zeus, and Jupiter, had his own links to the underworld, not to mention delusions of grandeur—the idea that he will somehow establish his throne above the angels of God and rule from his mount of assembly in place of the holy mountain of God, Zion.

But there are yet more conspirators in this supernatural plot to steal the throne of the Most High.

10

The Sun-god

Christians digging into the pagan religions of the biblical era may be a little surprised to learn that the sun-god wasn't more important than he was. Well-meaning teachers have taught for generations that pagan worship can be traced to Nimrod and his wife, Semiramis. We're told the two created a solar cult that manifests today in certain traditions of the Roman Catholic Church—including, among other things, the celebration of Christmas.

To be blunt, such teachings are not based on what pagans of the ancient world believed. There is no evidence whatsoever—none at all—that Nimrod was worshiped by anybody, anywhere, at any time. If anything, rabbinic tradition has ascribed to Nimrod attributes of the Mesopotamian god Ninurta, who was not a sun-god,[174] but that doesn't mean anyone alive prior to the modern era worshiped him.

Nimrod *is* venerated by the highest levels of Scottish Rite Freemasonry,[175] but that's a modern cult.

Semiramis, the historic Assyrian queen Shammuramat, lived more than two thousand years after Nimrod. His reign was during the period archaeologists call the Uruk Expansion, when that city at the heart of Nimrod's kingdom controlled the Fertile Crescent. But the Uruk Expansion ended around 3100 BC, and Shammuramat didn't rule Assyria until about 810 BC.

We should also mention that the city of Babylon wasn't founded until about 2300 BC, at least eight hundred years after Babel. Babylon didn't become a regional power until Hammurabi's reign, around 1750 BC, more than a thousand years after Uruk's empire collapsed.

So, Babel had nothing to do with Babylon. Wrong place, wrong millennium. Calling Nimrod a sun-god and blaming him for Babylon has no basis in history. Not that he was a good guy, you understand; you have to be pretty bad for God to personally intervene and put a stop to your pet project.

Other gods have likewise been incorrectly linked to the sun, such as Baal, Osiris, and Apollo, none of whom were sun-gods. Baal was the storm-god, Osiris was god of the dead (hence the green skin), and Apollo was a plague-god. The sun-gods of the ancient world were Utu (Sumer), Shamash (Akkad/Babylon), Ra and Amun (Egypt), Helios (Greece) and Sol (Rome).

Please understand that this is not a defense of Roman Catholicism— or any teaching that comes from outside the Bible, for that matter—but we don't serve God by spreading bad information.

Here's what we *do* know about the ancient sun-god: First of all, in the ancient Near East, he was always subordinate to the moon-god. Called Utu in Sumer, Shamash by the Semitic-speaking Akkadians, and Shemesh by the Hebrews, the sun-god was believed to be the son of the moon-god, Nanna/Sîn. Utu/Shamash was the twin brother of Inanna/ Ishtar. The two had a close relationship in Mesopotamian myth that bordered on incestuous, to be honest.

These three, represented in the sky by the sun, moon, and Venus, were depicted in art as a cosmic triad throughout the ancient Near East. Many stelae and cylinder seals from the Old Babylonian period through the time of Jesus include a crescent moon representing Nanna/Sîn, a radiant solar disc depicting Utu/Shamash, and an eight-pointed star, Venus, representing Inanna/Ishtar. One famous inscription commissioned by the Assyrian king Ashurnasirpal II, who reigned between 883 BC and 859 BC (a contemporary of Omri, Ahab and Elijah in Israel, and Asa and Jehoshaphat in Judah), featured the cosmic triad alongside the symbols of the storm-god Adad (Baal) and Ashur, the Assyrian version of "the" god. In other words, Ashurnasirpal's stela included five of the six deities we're featuring in this section of the book.

The one civilization in the Near East where the sun-god reigned over the pantheon during the time of the patriarchs was Egypt. In the days of Abraham, Isaac, and Jacob, the sun-god Ra was worshiped there as the creator of all things. He emerged as the head of the Egyptian pantheon during the Fifth Dynasty, which roughly coincided with the period covered by the tablets found at Ebla in ancient Syria (ca. 2500 BC–ca. 2350 BC).[176]

Ra's cult center was On, a city in northern Egypt now mostly buried under a suburb of Cairo that is better known by its Greek name, Heliopolis ("Sun City"). If On sounds familiar, it should:

> And Pharaoh called Joseph's name Zaphenath-paneah. And he gave him in marriage Asenath, the daughter of Potiphera priest of On. (Genesis 41:45)

Interesting, isn't it? God not only preserved Joseph through his trials, He elevated him to a position of power and brought him into the family of a priest of the chief god in the land where his family would spend the next two centuries.

Joseph probably arrived in Egypt in the first half of the seventeenth century BC, in the middle of what scholars call the Second Intermediate Period, roughly 1750 BC to 1550 BC. This was when Semitic kings called the Hyksos ruled northern Egypt. Not surprisingly, they brought along their gods—mainly Baal, Astarte, and one we'll meet shortly, Resheph.

However, to legitimize their rule, the Hyksos stuck with Egyptian convention and included Ra in their throne names. The two best-known Hyksos kings, Khyan and Apophis of the Fifteenth Dynasty, were also known as Seuserenre (possibly "the one who Ra has caused to be strong") and Auserre ("the strength of Ra is great").

This is a little weird for a couple of reasons. First, scholars are pretty certain that the Hyksos kings didn't worship Ra, at least not as one of their chief gods. The king of the pantheon for the Semitic Hyksos was Baal, whom they merged with Set, the Egyptian god of storms, the desert, and foreigners.[177] In fact, a Nineteenth Dynasty text called "The Quarrel of Apophis and Seqenenre" attributes to Apophis a radical religious reform that's usually credited to the "heretic" Pharaoh Akhenaten—monotheism. Apparently, Apophis decided to worship Set-Baal and *only* Set-Baal, something that was unheard of back in the day.[178] This was about two hundred years before Akhenaten suppressed the worship of all other gods in favor of Aten, the solar disc.

To make things odder, Apophis was named for the chaos serpent in Egyptian religion. They believed Apophis, a giant, cosmic snake, waited just below the horizon to eat Ra and the solar boat just after sundown. Set-Baal rode with Ra every evening to defend the boat and guarantee another day. How do you think the native Egyptian rulers in the southern city of Thebes reacted when they discovered that the Asiatics in the north had a new king named for the monstrous serpent that tried to destroy their chief god every night?

Here's a clue: Apophis was the next-to-last king of the Hyksos. Their capital city, Avaris, was abandoned around 1550 BC, about a century before the Exodus, and Egyptians regained control over their entire country. Around that time, the sun-god worshiped by the native Egyptians who ruled from the southern city of Thebes, Amun, was merged with Ra into a new and improved sun-god, Amun-Ra. This deity was not only the Egyptian creator-god, but it apparently represented a reunified Egypt.

Although Utu/Shamash was a second-tier god among the Semites below the great deities Anu, Enlil, Enki, Nanna/Sîn, and Inanna/Ishtar, the sun-god was considered the lawgiver of the ancient world, responsible for establishing right and wrong and judging how well humans lived up to those standards. The famous law code of Hammurabi was preserved on a stela that showed the Amorite king receiving the law from the sun-god.

But that wasn't the oldest set of laws from the ancient Near East that's been preserved. Hammurabi's legal code was established at least three hundred years after that of Ur-Nammu, founder of the Third Dynasty of Ur, which was the ancient city of the moon-god. But even there, in the moon-god's city, Ur-Nammu established the law "in accordance with the true word of Utu."[179]

Because of the sun-god's daily travels across the sky, it was assumed that Utu/Shamash visited the underworld each night to judge the dead. This role was expanded in later Amorite religion; at Ugarit, Shapash, the sun-deity (who changed genders from god to goddess at Ugarit, for unknown reasons) accompanied the dead to the underworld—what scholars call a psychopomp, similar to the role played by Charon, the ferryman who carried the dead across the River Styx in Greek mythology.

The other facet of the sun-god in the ancient Near East that's worth mentioning is the role of Utu/Shamash in divination. Perhaps because of the sun's apparent ability to see all things, Utu/Shamash was one of two deities called upon by fortune-tellers in the ancient Near East. Along with the storm-god, Adad/Haddu (i.e., Baal/Satan), Utu/Shamash was the god diviners sought out when they wanted to know what the future held, especially in haruspicy, which is the practice of divining the future by reading patterns in animal entrails. (Before researching this book, I had no clue that there was even a word for that.)

Why the sun-god and storm-god? Maybe it had something to do with calling on the gods responsible for sunshine and rain. Whatever the reason, if you wanted to know your future, you called on a priest and had him read messages hidden in the shapes of animal guts, usually a sacrificed sheep, with the help of the sun-god, Utu/Shamash.

But it's the lawgiver aspect of the sun-god that concerns us. Nearly every religion on earth other than Christianity has this in common with the ancient Near East's sun-god: Salvation comes through following a set of divinely inspired rules. While the laws of Ur-Nammu and Hammurabi dealt with civil government, which is unquestionably important (we are, after all, commanded by Yahweh to pray for those in authority so "we may live a peaceful and quiet life"),[180] our God has freed us from the bondage of rules and laws that must be learned and carefully followed to earn a place in paradise.

While the sun-god wasn't as important in the Mesopotamian pantheons as the others profiled in this section, he clearly influenced the Hebrews. As we noted earlier, God's arrows and glittering spear weren't just directed at the moon-god in the Valley of Aijalon. And though it's not mentioned in the Bible, holding Shemesh/Shamash in place also kept the war-goddess Astarte/Ishtar, represented by the planet Venus, out of sight and out of the battle as far as the pagan Amorites were concerned.

So, that line from a prayer by the prophet Habakkuk confirms that we should take Joshua 10:14 literally: "There has been no day like it before or since, when the LORD heeded the voice of a man, for the LORD fought for Israel."[181] In one shot, Yahweh demonstrated His power and authority over the most prominent deities of the Mesopotamian pantheon—the very beings God warned Israel to avoid.

And beware lest you raise your eyes to heaven, and when you see the sun and the moon and the stars, all the host of heaven, you be drawn away and bow down to them and serve them, things that the LORD your God has allotted to all the peoples under the whole heaven. (Deuteronomy 4:19)

The sun, moon, and "host of heaven" were allotted to the nations as *their* gods, but Israel belonged to Yahweh. Yet, in spite of warnings and the miracle at Aijalon, eight hundred years later, in the days of Ezekiel, the sun-god was being worshiped *in the Temple itself.*

And he brought me into the inner court of the house of the LORD. And behold, at the entrance of the temple of the LORD, between the porch and the altar, were about twenty-five men, with their backs to the temple of the LORD, and their faces toward the east, worshiping the sun toward the east. (Ezekiel 8:16)

Jeremiah, born about thirty years before Ezekiel, apparently witnessed this pagan worship in Jerusalem with his own eyes.

At that time, declares the LORD, the bones of the kings of Judah, the bones of its officials, the bones of the priests, the bones of the prophets, and the bones of the inhabitants of Jerusalem shall be brought out of their tombs. And they shall be spread before the sun and the moon and all the host of heaven, which they have loved and served, which they have gone after, and which they have sought and worshiped. (Jeremiah 8:1–2)

Although the sun-god was clearly more important in Egypt than in Mesopotamia, he (or she, depending on time and place) was obviously on God's radar. And, like the rest of the major deities of Mesopotamia, the sun-god has been hard at work over the last two thousand years to try to frustrate God's plan for humanity.

111

11

The Goddess

It might surprise you to learn that one of the entities we hold responsible for the bloody state of the world today has been worshiped for five thousand years as the goddess of love.

In the Bible, she was called Astarte. Her name in ancient Sumer was Inanna, but we know her better as Ishtar, Aphrodite, and Venus. The brightly shining planet bearing her name represented her in the sky, and she's been called "without a doubt the most important female deity of ancient Mesopotamia in all periods."[182] Her reputation has been cleaned up a lot over the millennia; for one thing, she was indirectly connected to the Tower of Babel, which probably dates to the middle of the fourth millennium BC, sometime around 3500.

Nimrod, usually identified as the builder of the Tower of Babel, was born in the second generation after the Flood. His father was Cush, son of Ham, son of Noah. The heart of Nimrod's kingdom was Babel and Erech, which was the ancient city of Uruk. Its name is preserved today in the modern nation of Iraq. According to the Sumerian King List, the second ruler of Uruk after the Flood was named Enmerkar, son of Mesh-ki-ang-gasher. Interestingly, an epic poem from about 2000 BC called "Enmerkar and the Lord of Aratta" preserves the basic details of the Tower of Babel story.

We don't know the exact location of Aratta, but guesses range from northern Iran to Armenia. Wherever it was, Enmerkar tried to muscle this neighboring kingdom into supplying building materials for a couple of projects that were near and dear to his heart.

Uruk was home to two of the chief gods of the Sumerian pantheon. One, the sky-god Anu, was the primordial deity overthrown by the first-generation cosmic ruler. In Greece, this was Ouranos; in Rome, the sky-god was Caelus, from whom we get the word "celestial."

The other patron deity of Uruk was Anu's granddaughter, Inanna. Here's the thing: She wasn't exactly the goddess of love; her areas of responsibility were actually war and sex. And by sex, we mean the carnal, extramarital kind.

Anu was depicted as more or less retired from direct oversight of humanity, having handed over his duties as head of the pantheon to Enlil. Inanna, on the other hand, played a very active role in Sumerian society. For example, she wasn't just the goddess who assisted forlorn, would-be lovers; scholars have translated ritual texts—magical spells, to be honest—for innkeepers to ask Inanna to guarantee that their bordellos turned a profit.

Apparently, the dispute between Enmerkar and the king of Aratta, whose name, we learn from a separate epic, was Ensuhkeshdanna, was over who was Inanna's favorite. One of the building projects Enmerkar wanted to tackle was a magnificent temple to Inanna, the E-ana ("House of Heaven"), and he wanted Aratta to supply the raw materials. There wasn't much in the way of timber, jewels, or precious metals in Sumer, being mostly desert and marsh, but Enmerkar mainly wanted the lord of Aratta to submit and acknowledge that he was Inanna's chosen one. So Enmerkar prayed to Inanna:

My sister, let Aratta fashion gold and silver skillfully on my behalf for Unug (Uruk). Let them cut the flawless lapis lazuli from the blocks, let them ...... the translucence of the flawless lapis lazuli .... build a holy mountain in Unug. Let Aratta build a temple brought down from heaven - your place of worship, the Shrine E-ana; let Aratta skillfully fashion the interior of the holy *jipar*, your abode; may I, the radiant youth, may I be embraced there by you. Let Aratta submit beneath the yoke for Unug on my behalf.[183]

Notice that Inanna's temple was compared to a holy mountain. Having read this far into the book, you know that the conflict between the rebel gods and the Creator is over control of the mount of assembly, the holy mountain of God, Zion. Even in Sumer, where there aren't any, mountains are sacred. Remember that one of the epithets of the chief god, Enlil, was "great mountain," and his temple at Nippur was the E-kur, the "House of the Mountain."[184]

By the way, given the type of goddess Inanna was, the "embrace" Enmerkar wanted from her was more than just a figure of speech. While scholars still debate whether, and how often, it was performed, the so-called sacred marriage rite between Mesopotamian kings and the high priestess of Inanna/Ishtar, even if it was only play-acted, was a standard part of her cult.[185]

To be honest, some of the messages about Inanna between Enmerkar of Uruk and Ensuhkeshdanna of Aratta were the kind of locker-room talk that got Donald Trump into trouble during the 2016 presidential campaign. But I digress.

Most of the discussion of the rites of Inanna/Ishtar, especially the practice of cult prostitution, cite the work of the Greek historian, Herodotus, who wrote in the fifth century BC:

Surely the most disgusting of all Babylonian customs is the following. Once in her life, every woman of the country must sit down in the sanctuary of Aphrodite and have intercourse with a stranger.... the majority sit in the sacred precinct of Aphrodite wearing wreaths made of cord on their heads.... she may not return home until one of the strangers has tossed silver into her lap and has had intercourse with her outside the sanctuary. When he tosses the silver, he must say, "I call on you in the name of the goddess Mylitta." (The Assyrians call Aphrodite Mylitta.)... the women cannot refuse, and the silver then becomes sacred property.... Then, after they have had intercourse and she has thus discharged her duty to the goddess, she returns home. But after this event, no matter how much you give her, she will refuse you.[186]

However, scholars today generally dismiss this account. It's believed Herodotus was trying to demonize the enemies of Greece. He was born about five years before the epic battle at Thermopylae, where Leonidas and his Spartans made their famous stand against the Persians.[187] Portraying the depravity of Oriental morality would have been popular reading back in the day.

That said, an Old Babylonian text first translated and published in 1997[188] seems to confirm at least some of the Bible's negative characterizations of Inanna's Canaanite counterpart, Astarte, including cult prostitution, "cross-gender activities...and the performance of sexual acts."[189]

Since we'd like to keep this a family-friendly book, we won't dig much deeper into the personality of Inanna, but it's safe to say she definitely was not a girl you'd bring home to meet your mother. In fact, she wasn't always a girl, period.

You see, while Inanna was definitely the goddess with the mostest when it came to sex appeal, she was also androgynous, sometimes depicted with masculine features like a beard. On one tablet from the first millennium BC, probably some three thousand years after Nimrod, Inanna says, "When I sit in the alehouse, I am a woman, and I am an exuberant young man."[190] Her cult followers included eunuchs and transvestites, and she was apparently the first in history to make a practice of sex reassignment:

> She [changes] the right side (male) into the left side (female),
> She [changes] the left side into the right side,
> She [turns] a man into a woman,
> She [turns] a woman into a man
> She ador[ns] a man as a woman,
> She ador[ns] a woman as a man.[191]

It's incredibly ironic. The twenty-first century progressive ideal of gender fluidity was personified five thousand years ago by the Sumerian goddess Inanna. She's celebrated by modern scholars as complex and courageous, transcending traditional gender roles, turning Inanna/Ishtar into an icon of independent man/woman/other-hood.

> (That) a man is like a woman, a maiden is a young man,
> you have put his offspring in the gutter—are yours, Ishtar…
> (That) a m[an goes] the way of a woman,
> a woman [goes] (the way) of a man, [—are yours, Ishtar.]…
> You make men obey (the rules of) garments (and) wigs.
> At night, the women are touched. They are untidy regarding
> the hair-locks.
> The woman, like a man, is equipped with a quiver, she holds
> a bow.
> The man carries a hairpin, a *siBtum*, an *uḫḫu*, a harp.
> The women are carrying bows, slings, sling-stones.[192]

What gender activists don't realize is that Ishtar's act was already old when Moses came down from Mount Sinai with the Law. What God taught the Israelites was new.

A woman shall not wear a man's garment, nor shall a man put on a woman's cloak, for whoever does these things is an abomination to the LORD your God. (Deuteronomy 22:5)

You see, deconstructing God's appointed gender roles isn't progressive. It's regressive. Gender activists are trying to turn back the clock about four thousand years.

A word about that verse in Deuteronomy: It's been misinterpreted by some Christians as God's command that women should not wear pants. That's not what it means.

First, the Hebrew word *kəlî* doesn't necessarily mean "garment." It can mean "piece of equipment," "article" or "object"—basically, "stuff." In this context, the word refers to items that are gender-specific—like quivers, bows, and slings for men, or a hairpin, harp, and *uḫḫu* for women (whatever that is).

In other words, the Law simply says men shouldn't try to be women and vice versa. It's a pretty good bet that the verse cited above was specifically directed at Inanna/Ishtar. Her cult was very old, it extended over the entire biblical world, and shattering God's boundaries for gender was a key element of her cult.

At Inanna's festivals men dressed as women and women dressed as men, and cultic dancers wore outfits that were men's clothes on the right and women's on the left. Some, though not all of, Inanna's priests practiced same-sex behavior.... Therefore, some of Inanna's earliest temple personnel displayed same-sex behavior and took on transgender, non-heteronormative identities.[193]

By emulating their goddess who was both female and male, they shattered the boundary between the sexes.... The cultic personnel of the goddess in their costumes, words, and acts had but one goal: "to delight Ishtar's heart, give themselves up to (otherwise) for[bidden] actions."[194]

We could go deeper into this discussion, but only at the risk of becoming more graphic than necessary to make the point.[195] We can summarize by describing the so-called goddess of love as an androgynous deity of carnal perversion whose followers included cross-dressers, transgenders, homosexuals, and prostitutes.

Worship of Inanna extended well into the biblical era. As the Canaanite goddess Astarte, her cult was spread throughout the Holy Land by the pagan neighbors of Israel. Texts from Ugarit reveal that she was worshiped as both female and male—as Astarte, represented by Venus as the evening star, and as the war-god Attar, who was Venus as the morning star. All too often, the veneration of Astarte was practiced by the Israelites themselves.

Judah, patriarch of the tribe that produced the Messiah, Jesus, had relations with his daughter-in-law, Tamar, while she was dressed up as a cult prostitute, probably for Astarte (see Genesis 38). More than a thousand years later, around 623 BC, King Josiah of Judah "broke down the houses of the male cult prostitutes who were in the house of the LORD."[196]

Think about that: Male cult prostitutes had houses *inside* the Temple! This was less than a century after the kingdom of Judah had been cleaned up by the good King Hezekiah, who followed the Law so closely that "there was none like him among all the kings of Judah after him, nor among those who were before him."[197] This shocking desecration of the Temple is another reminder that the supernatural war is all about control of Zion, God's mount of assembly.

But really, it's not terribly surprising that Inanna/Ishtar/Astarte has had such a long career. It's easy to sell humans on the idea that sex is worship.

With all due respect to the learned scholars who have described this entity as "a complex, multifaceted goddess,"[198] the character of Inanna/Ishtar isn't as complicated as she's made out to be. Frankly, she's a bad screenwriter's idea of a fifteen-year-old boy's fantasy, interested mainly in sex and fighting and better than men at both. She was selfish and violent, ruled by her passions, and incredibly destructive when she didn't get her way.

One of the tales of the Sumerian hero Gilgamesh, who ruled Uruk two generations after Enmerkar (Nimrod), is about his rejection of Ishtar's sexual advances. In the legend, Gilgamesh had the bad manners to point out that every one of the men in the goddess' life had suffered horrible consequences. Take, for example, Dumuzi the Shepherd, king of Bad-Tibara, the second city in Sumer to exercise kingship after Eridu. Even though Ishtar married Dumuzi, she threw him under the bus without hesitation when demons tried to drag her son, Lulal, the patron god of Bad-Tibara, down to the netherworld.

At Ishtar's urging, the demons spared Lulal and took Dumuzi instead. When Dumuzi's grief-stricken sister pleaded for his return, Inanna allowed her to take his place for half the year, thus making Dumuzi the first of many "dying and rising gods" in the ancient Near East. (You probably remember Ezekiel's description of women weeping for Tammuz—Dumuzi—at the north gate of the Temple.)[199]

Well, for daring to remind the goddess about the sad fate of Dumuzi and the other poor idiots who'd succumbed to her charms, she flew up to heaven in a rage and demanded that her grandfather, the sky-god Anu, unleash the Bull of Heaven on Gilgamesh.

That didn't go well for the Bull of Heaven. Although the monstrous bovid tore up Uruk, killing hundreds of people who got in its way, Gilgamesh and his buddy, Enkidu, killed the beast. When Ishtar angrily descended to the walls of the city to curse Gilgamesh, Enkidu mocked the goddess by tearing off the bull's thigh and throwing it in her face.

Sadly for Gilgamesh, however, Enkidu was sentenced to death by the gods as punishment for spoiling Ishtar's revenge.

Bear in mind that, according to *Enmerkar and the Lord of Aratta*, this was who Nimrod wanted to make the patron goddess of his city, Uruk. That says something about the character of Nimrod, who was apparently no stranger to violence. He was the first who tried to build a world empire, evidently by force. That leads to the other aspect of the goddess that we need to explore—her violent side. She was not only the goddess of carnal pleasure, she was a war goddess, too.

Her role in the ancient Near East included that of the heroic warrior. She was often depicted in the art of ancient Sumer with multiple weapons strapped to her back,[200] and the field of battle was described as the "playground of Ishtar."[201] She was also the deity who controlled the masculinity of kings on the battlefield. By rendering rulers impotent, as it were, she directed the outcome of war.[202]

Looking at the values of our modern society, it's no stretch to say that Inanna is the spirit of our age. Gender fluidity is the flavor of the month among Western progressives. The values of Inanna/Ishtar—immediate gratification and sex with whomever, whenever—are considered more open-minded, tolerant, and loving than the virtues of chastity, fidelity, and faithfulness introduced by Yahweh long after Inanna was first worshiped as the Queen of Heaven.

As we'll see, however, the perverse sexual aspects of the goddess have been combined with her mindless rage and bloody violence in a religious system that's been trying to conquer the world for the last fourteen hundred years.

12

The Plague-god

There is a member of the infernal team that's joined forces against God you've probably never heard of—except that you have, you just don't know it.

Chapter 3 of the Book of Habakkuk, a prayer that summarizes God's battles on behalf of Israel, refers to several of the rebellious "sons of God."

> God came from Teman,
> and the Holy One from Mount Paran. Selah
> His splendor covered the heavens,
> and the earth was full of his praise.
> His brightness was like the light;
> rays flashed from his hand;
> and there he veiled his power.
> Before him went pestilence,
> and plague followed at his heels. (Habakkuk 3:3–5)

"Pestilence" (Deber) and "plague" (Resheph) were known as demons or deities by the pagan nations around the Hebrews in the days of the prophets. We should assume that the prophets knew about them, too. Here, the prophet described Deber and Resheph as subservient to Yahweh. They may even have been prisoners of war from an earlier conflict, as God marched off from Mount Sinai (Paran is an alternate name for Sinai) to do battle against the gods of Canaan.

While Deber was a relatively minor character among the gods of the pagans in the ancient Near East, he is mentioned about fifty times in the Bible. Since his name is usually translated "pestilence" or "plague," however, only scholars who spend their lives studying this kind of thing have noticed. The most obvious reference to Deber as an entity, rather than a natural disaster, is the Scripture above, which is Habakkuk's prelude to his account of Joshua's Long Day.

But back in the third millennium BC, Deber was a bigger deal. The texts at Ebla, the ancient city near Aleppo mentioned earlier in this book, Deber was called *dingir-eb-la*^{ki}, the "god of Ebla."[203]

In other words, the demonic creature called "pestilence" was the patron god of the earliest known political power in northern Syria.

At this point you may be asking yourself, why is this relevant? Because Habakkuk named the pestilence-god Deber as a colleague of Resheph, the plague-god, when he told the story of the Exodus and the attack on Canaan, and he described them as servants or prisoners of Yahweh.

How did God convince Pharaoh to let His people go?

Right. *Plagues and pestilence.*

Before the showdown at the Red Sea, which was directed at the king of the Canaanite pantheon, Baal, God subdued two other West Semitic deities, Deber and Resheph. He either overpowered them and compelled them to do His bidding, or He simply demonstrated that they were powerless to protect the people holding Israel captive.

What do we know about Resheph? Even you though may not

have heard his name, Resheph was one of the most popular gods in the ancient Near East for nearly three thousand years.

He was a warrior god, described as a divine archer who spread plague with his arrows. At Ugarit, Resheph served the sun-goddess Shapash as the gatekeeper of the underworld. This identifies Resheph as the Babylonian god Nergal, who was likewise an archer, a plague-god, and gatekeeper of the netherworld.

As Nergal, the god was considered a fierce and terrible warrior. He was sometimes called Erra, who, in this guise, was an agent of chaos and destruction, responsible for periods of political and social instability. He was a "warrior," the "lord of plague and carnage," or "lord of affray and slaughter."[204] Based on the number of copies found by archaeologists, a poem called the *Epic of Erra* must have been one of the most popular pieces of literature in the ancient world, even though it's not nearly as well known as the Gilgamesh epic.[205] It describes how Erra/Nergal ravaged the land with plague after gaining temporary control of the world, nearly destroying mankind in the process.

The root word behind Resheph's name appears to mean "flaming," or "burning," or even "lighting," possibly a metaphorical reference to the fever that accompanies the plague.

One intriguing biblical reference to Resheph comes from the Psalms, where God's punishment of the Egyptians for their treatment of Israel is described.

> He gave over their cattle to the hail
> and their flocks to thunderbolts.
> He let loose on them his burning anger,
> wrath, indignation, and distress,
> a company of destroying angels.
> He made a path for his anger;
> he did not spare them from death,
> but gave their lives over to the plague. (Psalm 78:48–50)

"Plague" in verse 50 is actually the pestilence-god Deber, not Resheph. But here's the interesting part: The thunderbolts in verse 48 are connected to Resheph, rather than to the storm-god, Baal. Even more interesting, the verse literally reads, "He gave over their cattle to the hail and their flocks to the *rəšāpîm*"—the "reshephs."[206]

Consider this: Since the root word behind the type of angelic beings called seraphim, *saraph*, also means "burning," thus making the seraphim "burning ones," is it possible that the *reshephim* are also a class of angel? It's speculation, but possible. An inscription from the Phoenician city of Sidon in the fifth century BC names one of the city's quarters "Land of the Reshephs."[207]

Possibly identifying a previously unknown type of angel is intriguing stuff, but we'll set that aside for another book. The takeaway from Psalm 78 is that the judgments against Egypt were carried out by "a company of destroying angels," which included Deber, Barad ("hail"), and Resheph (or the "reshephs").

The worship of Resheph goes way back, at least to 2500 BC. One of the four city gates of the ancient city of Ebla was named for Resheph. The other three were named for "the" god, Dagan, the storm-god Baal, and Sipish, which was the Eblaite spelling of Shamash, the sun-god.

So, the Big Four among the gods of ancient Ebla were Dagan, Baal, Shamash, and Resheph. The patron god of the city, oddly enough, was the pestilence-god Deber. God dealt with all five of those Eblaite gods in the Old Testament.

If you're having a bad day, just imagine how depressing would it have been to live in a town where the main deities included the god of plague, the god of pestilence, and the "lord of the corpse" (Dagan).

The cult of Resheph extended south into Egypt, probably carried by the Amorites who took over Lower (northern) Egypt as the Hyksos kings in the seventeenth century BC, just about the time Joseph was brought there as a slave. Egyptians continued to worship Resheph for centuries, past the time of Ramesses the Great, who ruled Egypt about two hundred years after the Exodus. Resheph was often depicted in Egyptian art alongside Min, a fertility god, and Qetesh, a goddess of "sacred ecstasy" who may have been an Egyptian form of Astarte/Ishtar.

Now, get this: A native Egyptian king in the fifteenth century BC adopted Resheph as one of his personal gods and his special protector in battle.[208] This was probably because of the deity's warrior aspect as a god of horses and chariots. That king was Amenophis II, also known as Amenhotep II.[209] Scholar Douglas Petrovich has made an excellent case that Amenhotep II, devotee of Resheph, was in fact the pharaoh of the Exodus.[210]

Think about that for a minute. The pharaoh whose special supernatural protector was the plague-god, a divine warrior who was also a god of horses and chariots, was convinced to release the Israelites because his personal god couldn't stop the devastating plagues sent by Yahweh—including the final plague that claimed the life of the pharaoh's first-born son.

Then Pharaoh's elite chariot corps was destroyed, drowned beneath the waves of the Red Sea.

But wait—there's more!

The texts from Ebla reveal some interesting things about these pagan gods. For example, we learn that Dagan, king of the Eblaite pantheon, was called, among other things, "lord of Canaan." Given that he was probably also El of the later Canaanite religion, that makes sense. Resheph, according to one tablet, was the patron god of several cities in the Levant. One of them was Shechem,[211] modern Nablus in Israel. Why is this important?

And Abram took Sarai his wife, and Lot his brother's son, and all their possessions that they had gathered, and the people that they had acquired in Haran, and they set out to go to the land of Canaan. When they came to the land of Canaan, Abram passed through the land to the place at Shechem, to the oak of Moreh.

At that time the Canaanites were in the land. Then the LORD appeared to Abram and said, "To your offspring I will give this land." So he built there an altar to the LORD, who had appeared to him. (Genesis 12:5–7)

Did you catch that? The city of Resheph is where Yahweh appeared to Abraham when he arrived in Canaan to personally confirm that the patriarch was doing the right thing.

It was also where Joshua reconfirmed the covenant with God immediately after Israel destroyed Jericho, the moon-god's city, and nearby Ai.[212] Mount Gerizim and Mount Ebal, where the Israelites recited blessings and curses to celebrate their arrival in the Holy Land according to God's command,[213] bracket Shechem: Gerizim to the south and Ebal to the north.

In 1980, archaeologist Adam Zertal found what appears to be a large altar made of uncut stones on Mount Ebal, the location described in the Bible. While other archaeologists agree that it appears to be a religious site dated to the early Iron Age, not all agree with Zertal's conclusion that this is the altar of Joshua.[214]

It's in the right place, dated to the right time, and there's no evidence of other cultic activity earlier or later at the site. It's Joshua's altar.

And it's on a mountain overlooking a city devoted to the god who just happened to be the personal protector of the pharaoh from whom the Israelites escaped forty years earlier.

Oh, guess where Joseph's brothers were pasturing their flocks when they sold him to Midianite slave traders,[215] which led to Israel's sojourn in Egypt in the first place.

Coincidence?

Does Habakkuk's description of Resheph following at Yahweh's heels like a whipped dog make more sense?

Here's why we've taking this detour into the history of Resheph: Not only was he equated with Nergal, but he was also identified in the ancient world as the divine archer and plague-god of the Greek pantheon, Apollo. As we mentioned in the previous section, the favorite weapon of Resheph/Apollo, the arrow, was employed by Yahweh in the battle on Joshua's Long Day. Even the "glittering spear," the lightning bolt, is described in pagan texts as a weapon of Resheph. The point is that the ancient world saw this entity as a warrior, a death-dealer who could spread plague indiscriminately with his supernatural arrows.

Finally, Resheph/Nergal was a god who opened the gates of the underworld. This, too, is a connection to Apollo. In Revelation 9, terrifying, locust-like beings fly out of the abyss when "a star fallen from heaven" is given its key.

> In appearance the locusts were like horses prepared for battle: on their heads were what looked like crowns of gold; their faces were like human faces, their hair like women's hair, and their teeth like lions' teeth; they had breastplates like breastplates of iron, and the noise of their wings was like the noise of many chariots with horses rushing into battle. They have tails and stings like scorpions, and their power to hurt people for five months is in their tails. They have as king over them the angel of the bottomless pit. His name in Hebrew is Abaddon, and in Greek he is called Apollyon. (Revelation 9:7–11).

The name Apollyon is Greek for "destroyer," and scholars have noted for years that it's an allusion to Apollo, a god of pestilence and destruction, and thus, "Ἀπολλύων can be seen as a demon who brings destruction and whose realm is the underworld."[216]

To step into the realm of speculation here, researcher and author Peter Levenda identified a strange and unexpected connection between the writings of occultist Aleister Crowley, horror fiction author H. P. Lovecraft, and ancient myths about the Babylonian god of the underworld Nergal (i.e., Resheph/Apollo).

In 1907, Crowley claimed he channeled the word *tutulu*, which he included in his book, *Liber Liberi vel Lapidus Lazuli*, even though he didn't know what it meant.[217] Crowley's personal assistant, Kenneth Grant, who later developed Crowley's teachings into a new occult system of his own, suggested that it was "probable" his mentor had misheard the word, mistakenly writing *tutulu* in place of "*kutulu*, in which case it would be identical phonetically, but not qabalistically, with Cthulhu,"[218] the main character in Lovecraft's most famous story, "The Call of Cthulhu."

It's important to note that Lovecraft didn't write "Cthulhu" until 1926, nearly two decades after Crowley's channeling session, and there is no evidence that Lovecraft, who claimed to be an atheist, was familiar with Crowley's writings or beliefs.[219]

Why is this significant?

Cthulhu can be rendered in the Sumerian language as *kutu lu* or "the man from Kutu" or "the man from the Underworld." Kutu—the Biblical Gudua, sometimes rendered Kutu or Kuta—was the ancient city of Cutha, sacred to Nergal and the entrance to the Underworld in Sumerian religion.[220]

In other words, the same supernatural source may have inspired and guided both Lovecraft, the most influential author of horror fiction of the first half of the twentieth century, and Crowley, the most influential occultist of the last hundred years. The name of Lovecraft's monster, channeled by Crowley two decades earlier, is linked to the city sacred to the ancient plague-god and underworld gatekeeper, Nergal/Resheph/Apollo.

Again, this is speculation into a realm that we see "through a glass, darkly," but the connections between this ancient entity and our modern world don't end there.

Now we've met two prominent deities of the ancient Near East closely connected to war: Ishtar/Inanna/Astarte and Resheph/Nergal/ Apollo. Both entities were worshiped by the people around ancient Israel long before Abraham was called by God from his home in northern Mesopotamia.

Over time, the warlike aspects of Astarte and Resheph were downplayed, especially after they were absorbed into the Greek pantheon as Aphrodite and Apollo. Astarte was primarily known for the sexual rites involved with her cult. Her martial side had been split into her male aspect, the war-god Attar, who was a minor character in the Amorite pantheon at Ugarit mainly known as the god who wasn't big enough to sit on Baal's throne after the storm-god had been carried off to the underworld by the god of death, Mot.

By the time of the judges in Israel, the most violent aspects of Astarte's personality had been ascribed to another goddess, Anat, whose name probably derives from a root meaning "force" or "violence."[221] Like Inanna/Ishtar, Anat was volatile, unpredictable, and shockingly violent.

She fixed heads to her back;
she attached palms to her girdle.
Her knees she steeped in the blood of soldiers;
her thighs in the gore of warriors.[222]

For his part, Resheph is best remembered as Apollo, the Greek god *par excellence*; god of music, oracles, and poetry; the ideal of athletic, beardless youth; the god who hitches the team of heavenly horses to the solar chariot that carries the sun-god Helios across the sky each day. His role as a death-dealing warrior and god of plagues is downplayed these days, especially in popular fiction marketed to teens and preteens. It's very different from the description of the "destroyer" of Revelation 9.

13

The God of War

Another war-god mentioned in the Bible has been a key player in the long drama unfolding over the last five thousand years. He embodies the destructive, uncontrolled martial aspects of Resheph/Nergal/Apollo and Astarte/Ishtar/Inanna. He's not referenced in Scripture as often as Baal or Astarte, but his followers were a thorn in the side of Israel for a thousand years.

This god's cult existed in the region a thousand years before the Exodus, and he's still active as part of the Fallen's long game to destroy as much of God's creation (and as many of His people) as they can before the end.

I refer to the national god of Moab, Chemosh.

You may find that surprising. While Moab and Israel fought a lot in Old Testament times, Moab was never an existential threat to Israel the way Egypt, Assyria, and Babylon were. Despite being called "the abomination of Moab,"[223] you get the sense that Chemosh was on the infernal JV team. He gets little play in the Bible, mentioned in only eight verses. That's misleading.

The god of Moab was worshiped alongside Resheph and Dagan in Ebla, the ancient city in northern Syria we've mentioned before. There, Chemosh was spelled Kamish, and he was one of the most important deities in what was the most powerful kingdom in the Levant at the time. Texts from between 2400 BC and 2200 BC show that Kamish/Chemosh was one of six deities for which a month was named:

1) Feast of Dagan — First month
2) Feast of Ashtabi (War-god; Hurrian name for Attar) — Second month
3) Feast of Hada (Adad/Baal, storm-god) — Third month
4) Feast of Adamma (Goddess, consort of Resheph) — Ninth month
5) Feast of Ishtar — Eleventh month
6) Feast of Kamish (Chemosh) — Twelfth month[224]

This is an interesting pattern. The first month of the year was named for Dagan, called *bēl pagrê* ("lord of the corpse"), and the next two were named for warrior gods (the Syrian storm-god is usually depicted in a "smiting" pose). The next grouping of three months named for gods began with the feast month for Adamma, a Hurrian goddess whose name meant something like "soil" or "earth," which makes sense for the consort of the gatekeeper of the underworld. Her feast month was followed by two more months named for warrior deities.

The pattern of feasts for the gods of Ebla was: Underworld god, warrior, warrior, underworld goddess, warrior, warrior. And remember, the city's patron deity was Deber, the pestilence-god. I'll say again: Ebla must have been a really fun place to live.

We also note that the Ebla texts record dealings with the ancient city of Carchemish, which means something like "port" or "market of Kamish,"[225] about sixty miles northeast of Aleppo on the modern border between Syria and Turkey. It's mentioned several times in the Bible[226] and was the site of a key battle between Egypt and Babylon in 605 BC. More recently, it was the scene of intense fighting for the modern village of Jarabulus during the Syrian civil war in late August 2016.

Back to the point: The worship of Chemosh was around for centuries before Moab was founded by the oldest son of Abraham's nephew, Lot.[227] The cult and rituals involved with Chemosh aren't well known because there haven't been many texts recovered from ancient Moab. Most of what we know comes from two sources—the Bible and the Mesha Stele, also known as the Moabite Stone.

Mesha was the king of Moab in the time of Jehoshaphat, king of Judah, and Ahab's son Joram, king of Israel, around 850 BC. His kingdom had been conquered by David, but the Moabites recovered their independence while the Israelite tribes were occupied with the rebellion of the northern tribes after the death of Solomon. Israel's King Omri reconquered northern Moab, and it had been controlled by Israel for several decades by the time of Mesha's rebellion.

Second Kings 3 and the Mesha Stele record different aspects of this fight, but both shed light on the character of Chemosh. The records agree that while the coalition of Israel, Judah, and Edom routed Mesha and his army, forcing them to take refuge in his capital city of Kir-hareseth, they did not succeed in stripping Moab of its independence. On his commemorative stone, Mesha described instructions he was given by his patron god.

> And the men of Gad lived in the land of Ataroth from ancient times, and the king of Israel built Ataroth for himself, and I fought against the city, and I captured, and I killed all the people from the city as a sacrifice for Kemoš and for Moab.…
>
> And Kemoš said to me: "Go, take Nebo from Israel!" And I went in the night, and I fought against it from the break of dawn until noon, and I took it, and I killed its whole population, seven thousand male citizens and aliens, female citizens

and aliens, and servant girls; for I had put it to the ban of Aštar Kemoš. And from there, I took the vessels of YHWH, and I hauled them before the face of Kemoš.[228]

This account of the slaughter of Nebo, which was probably at or near the place where Moses got his only look at the Promised Land, is similar to the treatment given by Joshua and the Israelites to the Amorite cities declared *khērem* ("under the ban"), a phrase usually translated into English as "devoted to destruction" or "annihilated." The sense of the word is hard for us in the modern West to grasp because we aren't taught that things can be so sacred or set apart that we humans touch them or possess them on pain of death. For example, the first use of the word *khērem* in the Bible is in Exodus 22:

Whoever sacrifices to any god, other than the LORD alone, shall be devoted to destruction. (Exodus 22:20)

Khērem is the root behind the name of Mount Hermon, the mountain where the Watchers of Genesis 6 began their rebellion and where the pagan Amorites believed their creator-god El held court with his consort and their seventy sons.

The Mesha Stele confirms that Chemosh and his followers understood the concept of *khērem*. And that's not all. Before the slaughter of the Israelites of Nebo, this happened:

When the king of Moab saw that the battle was going against him, he took with him 700 swordsmen to break through, opposite the king of Edom, but they could not. Then he took his oldest son who was to reign in his place and offered him for a burnt offering on the wall. And there came great wrath against Israel. And they withdrew from him and returned to their own land. (2 Kings 3:26–27)

So, Chemosh accepted child sacrifice. Verse 27 can be a hard pill to swallow for Jews and Christians; why, after the prophet Elisha told the kings of Judah, Israel, and Edom that God would grant them victory over Moab, was there "great wrath against Israel"? Whose wrath was it—God's or Chemosh's?

There are a couple of possible explanations. First of all, we should make clear that this passage does not depict a victory by Chemosh over Yahweh. It's probable that God's anger was directed at the armies of Judah and Israel for losing faith in His ability to deliver on His promise.

The practice of child sacrifice was well known in the ancient Near East, even in times of battle. Classical historians record the horror of the mass sacrifice of at least two hundred children in 310 BC when the people of Carthage were surprised by an army from the city-state of Syracuse on Sicily.[229] Inscriptions from Egyptian temples commemorating military victories of the New Kingdom pharaohs (Eighteenth through Twentieth Dynasties, which covers the period from about a hundred years before the Exodus to about the time of the birth of Israel's first king, Saul) confirm that rituals of child sacrifice like this were not uncommon in exactly the situation described in the Bible.

> The pharaoh [Ramesses II, the Great] attacks the city of Ashkelon; in the city we can see four beseeching men, and three women kneeling below them. The hands of these men are directed toward the sky. The chief, with the brazier, can be clearly made out, and in front of him is depicted a man together with a young child. The hairlock of youth plus the diminutive size of the second figure removes any doubt concerning its age. The child is definitely being sacrificed as the battle rages on. Moreover, the same act is being repeated to the left. On both occasions, it is clear that the two children are not being carried up to the citadel, but thrown down; and from the depiction of the limp arms and legs of the child at the right, we can conclude that one, at least, is definitely dead.[230]

It appears that the armies of Judah, Israel, and Edom, seeing King Mesha slaughter his firstborn son on the wall of his capital, assumed the war-god Chemosh was about unleash his fury and they simply lost heart. As a result, thousands of Israelites in Ataroth and Nebo later died, and Mesha, according to his account, expanded his kingdom northward by capturing territory that had belonged to the Israelite tribes of Reuben and Gad for the better part of five hundred years.

The other point we need to emphasize from the Mesha Stele is the link between Chemosh and Ashtar, an alternate spelling of the male aspect of Astarte, Attar, the war-god. It appears that to Mesha and the Moabites, Attar and Chemosh were the same entity.

How can that be? Both Attar and Chemosh were worshiped in Ebla about fifteen hundred years earlier. Well, trying to pin down precise correlations between the gods and goddesses of the ancient world is a great way to drive yourself crazy. They change names and genders over the centuries—and besides, they lie. It's possible that the names of these deities are, at least in some cases, more like job titles than proper names. For example, in the Hebrew Old Testament, Satan is actually "*the* satan." And since *hašāṭān* means "the accuser" or "the adversary," it's what that spirit would put on the second line of its business card instead of the first. In fact, during the Second Temple period, Jews believed in multiple satans,[231] and even named some of them—Gadreel,[232] Mastema,[233] Belial, and Samael.[234]

In the same way, the etymology of some of the names of ancient deities seems to fit that pattern, like "plague," "pestilence," "thunderer," and so on. It may explain why some that we'd assume to be evil characters, like Resheph and Deber (Plague and Pestilence), are found in the Bible serving God's purposes, as in Habakkuk 3:3–5.

That begs the question: Did Chemosh take on the mantle of "the *attar*," the war-god, sometime after Israel established itself in Canaan? About the same time, the violent, male side of Astarte, the war-god Attar/Ashtar, was deemphasized, if not entirely split from her character. By the time she became Aphrodite of the Greeks and Venus of the Romans, the warlike aspect of her personality was nearly gone, maybe set aside in favor of emphasizing her identity in the Western world as the Queen of Heaven.[235]

Attar, however, continued his career as an independent male war-god elsewhere. More about that in an upcoming chapter.

Chemosh began to fade from history after Nebuchadnezzar conquered the Levant in the early sixth century BC. The last known inscription attesting to the name Chemosh is dated to the fourth century BC.[236]

What happened to him? We get a clue from coins issued during the reign of Roman emperor Septimius Severus (AD 193–211) found at Moab's capital city, featuring the emperor on one side and a war-god on the reverse. By that time, Moab's ancient capital, Diban, had been renamed Areopolis in honor of the region's patron god—who was then identified as the Greek war-god, Ares.[237]

Like Chemosh, Ares (Mars to the Romans) was not a pleasant god to have around. In his Greco-Roman form, he embodied the unrestrained, destructive aspect of war—sometimes necessary but never welcome. In other words, Ares/Mars was very much like the bloodthirsty Anat of the Canaanites and Ishtar/Inanna of Babylon and Sumer.

So, Chemosh did *not* disappear; he simply did what other deities of the ancient world have done for thousands of years—changed his identity. He's been known to the world for the last two thousand years as the god of the red planet, Mars.

And a time was coming when the unrestrained violence of Chemosh/Ares/Mars would be put to very effective and deadly use by the rebels in their long war against Yahweh.

14

Wars of the Fallen

The history of the ancient world suggests a series of conflicts not just between the fallen angels who rebelled against the Creator and declared themselves gods, but between one another. In their minds, this war is not Satan vs. God; it's a supernatural game of thrones.

The evidence is in the rise and fall of various city-states and nations that followed different gods. For a time, "the" god, known throughout history as Enlil, El, Kumarbi, Dagan, Kronos, Saturn, and Baal-Hammon, was supreme. Even after he was replaced by Marduk or the storm-god, known as Hadad/Baal, Teshub, Zeus, and Jupiter, "the" god still influenced societies from Mesopotamia to north Africa to Europe, where we find evidence of child sacrifice as late as the Christian era.

If our theory is correct, and the entity behind the myths and faces of "the" god is the leader of the Watchers who descended to the summit of Mount Hermon, then we can add one more name to his rap sheet: Shemihazah, who convinced his coconspirators to swear a mutual oath to sin against the Creator by sharing forbidden knowledge that humanity was not meant to know.

Even though the storm-god was king of the pantheon for most of the civilizations in the Mediterranean world by the time of the Exodus, the moon-god, who'd been worshiped for at least fifteen hundred years by that point, was still a leader among the gods. Some of the Israelites' earliest confrontations with the spirit realm were clearly directed at Sîn, like God's gift of manna when Israel entered the Wilderness of Sîn, the giving of the Law at Mount Sinai, and the destruction of Jericho, which carried the Amorite name of the moon-god, Yarikh.

The sun-god, whose cult goes back to the earliest days of ancient Sumer (and probably earlier), was a junior partner in the Sumerian and Amorite divine assemblies. He rose to the top of the heap in Egypt, first as Ra, and then later as the merged solar deity Amun-Ra. Throne names of the pharaohs during the Israelite sojourn in Egypt, even those of the Baal-worshiping Hyksos kings, included Ra as a theophoric element (the "god-name"). So, the Exodus, as a whole, was Yahweh's smackdown of the fallen angel who chose to be worshiped as the deified sun.

But the sun-god wasn't alone. We noted earlier that the crossing of the Red Sea was orchestrated by God to demonstrate His power over the sea, which was supposed to be the domain of Baal. The warrior-god of plagues, who held down a second job as gatekeeper of the netherworld, was also a target of God's judgment during the Exodus; the evidence identifies the hard-hearted pharaoh who contended with Moses as Amenhotep II, who believed that the plague-god Resheph, a protector of horses and chariots, was his personal guardian. So, God used a series of plagues and then destroyed Amenhotep's chariot corps of as the *coup de grâce*.

After Joshua's Long Day, Baal became the main supernatural threat to Israel. The influence of the storm-god on ancient Israel was so profound that the name of Baal's holy mountain, Zaphon, became the Hebrew word for the compass point "north." Baal is the pagan deity mentioned most often in the Bible, and with good reason. Isaiah 14 identifies the mount of assembly of the divine rebel from Eden as Mount Zaphon;

Ezekiel 38–39 names Mount Zaphon as the rally point for the army of Gog, who is the Antichrist of the Book of Revelation; and in the New Testament, Jesus twice specifically linked the storm-god to Satan.[238]

In the background, throughout the history of the ancient Near East, the worship of the goddess of sex and violence, variously called Inanna, Ishtar, Astarte, Aphrodite, and Venus, among others, was always drawing the faithful away from the Most High. From ancient Sumer to the present day, her gender-fluid cult of carnality has lured millions to destruction. She even influenced the bloodline of the Messiah (see the Genesis 38 account of Judah and Tamar; what a reversal!). Ishtar's mindless rage when challenged has been on full display here in the US recently, but in a broader sense—the "battlefield is her playground" sense—her irrational violence and sacralization of carnality has been with us for centuries.

We can only speculate, because most of us don't see into the spirit realm, but Paul's reminder that our daily struggle is against these unseen entities rather than other humans supports our theory that geopolitics is really theopolitics, the visible consequences of what happens in the spirit realm. Similarly, the prophecy of Daniel describing a future war between the princes of Greece and Persia, which foretold the coming of Alexander the Great about two hundred years later, clearly referred to spirits. The prince of Persia delayed the angelic messenger from reaching Daniel for three weeks. It was only when "Michael, one of the chief princes" arrived that the messenger was able to reach Daniel, "for I was left there with the kings of Persia."[239]

Based on how easily the angelic messengers to Abraham's nephew, Lot, dealt with the mob in Sodom, it's not possible that the prince or kings of Persia were human.

Interestingly, we often skip over the messenger's comment at the beginning of the eleventh chapter of Daniel:

And as for me, in the first year of Darius the Mede, I stood up to confirm and strengthen him. (Daniel 11:1)

The angel talking to Daniel "stood up" to support, encourage, and protect Darius the Mede. Against whom, or what? In this context, it appears that the enemies of Darius were supernatural, possibly the prince and kings of Persia mentioned a few verses earlier—beings powerful enough that the archangel Michael, the special protector of Israel,[240] had to intervene.

Who were the supernatural princes of Persia and Greece? We don't have any way to know. The chief deity of the Medes and Persians who conquered Babylon in 539 BC was Ahura Mazda. Some scholars believe that Ahura Mazda was a Persian manifestation of Marduk, the city-god of Babylon,[241] which could explain why that city was taken so easily by Cyrus. The priesthood of Marduk couldn't have been happy that the last king of Babylon, Nabonidus, wanted to replace Marduk at the top of the pantheon with Sîn, the moon-god. So, just as modern-day Shia Muslims in Iraq are willing to work with their Iranian neighbors despite their cultural and ethnic differences (Arab vs. Persian), it's possible that the priests of Marduk were willing to cut a deal with a foreign king if it meant *their* god remained number one in the official state religion. But then the pesky storm-god worshipers from Greece came along two centuries later and established a Greco-Roman foundation for Western civilization.

It seems clear. The pagan gods of the ancient world struggled with one another even as they rebelled against their Maker. That is, until it became clear that the gospel of Jesus Christ was not going away.

Earlier, we mentioned Paul's observation that if the supernatural rulers of the age had realized what God was doing, "they would not have crucified the Lord of glory."[242] But they didn't get it. As we noted earlier, if they understood that Jesus was talking about them in the Parable of the Tenants, they still couldn't resist sending him to the cross.

They were caught off guard. They didn't grasp that Jesus' death in the physical realm wasn't a tragedy, it was His *victory*. It was a terrible price, yes, but God was willing to pay it for you, me, and countless billions who have been saved by His immeasurable love—followed by His glorious Resurrection on the morning of the third day.

But the principalities and powers didn't just give up. If they had, the world today would be a far happier place.

Part III

A Waterless Place

15

The Arabian Strategem

How does this ancient history affect us today? Unless we pin that down, this is nothing but an academic exercise for history geeks like this author.

That, dear reader, is the point of this book: The pagan gods of the ancient world did not humbly submit after the Resurrection. Instead, they've continued in their rebellion. Maybe they figure they've got nothing to lose. Like Inanna in the *Epic of Gilgamesh*, who tried to destroy Uruk because she'd been rejected by the hero of the tale, they're willing to destroy everything rather than let the Messiah return to establish His throne over a world restored to its intended glory.

But they're also arrogant enough to think they can *win*. The entities conspiring against God are playing multidimensional chess. We humans are barely able to perceive this game with access to only three spatial dimensions, so I won't pretend to have all of the answers. This book will only cover one of the most significant aspects of the rebellion, a front opened by the small-*g* gods after they realized they'd been outplayed.

Their first response to the Resurrection was to inspire the Roman government and Jewish religious authorities to try to crush the growing body of believers. By the fourth century AD, when it was clear that Christianity was not going away despite the persecution from Rome, the Fallen tried a different tactic. The empire of the storm-god first legalized the faith with Constantine's Edict of Milan in AD 313. Then in 380, Christianity became the official state religion when Theodosius issued the Edict of Thessalonica. Once the Church became a path to wealth and political power, there was no shortage of men and women who chose the clergy as a career—but it wasn't because they were interested in saving sinners from the fires of hell.

Making Christianity the official religion of the Roman Empire was a brilliant move. Corruption in the Church persists to this day and it infects all denominations. But that has only weakened the body of believers, not killed it; as of this writing, the followers of Jesus Christ still outnumber all other religions on the earth.

But the Enemy employed another stratagem, one that's exploited the Church's weakness and the dilution of the gospel since the Renaissance and Enlightenment. Let's begin by tracking the activity of the pagan gods in the years after the Resurrection.

Looking at the ebb and flow of history from high above the page, as it were, we can sometimes see patterns that are hidden when we zoom in too close, sort of like trying to make out an image in an old newspaper by looking at it under a microscope. All we see are blobs of ink—the pixels, to use a more modern reference. The picture only comes into focus when you look at it from farther away.

In the same way, trying to see into the spirit realm is a good way to drive yourself crazy. We aren't designed to do that, and God has warned us not to try. But we can make out some of the shapes and patterns, the actions of the principalities and powers, if we step back and look at how history has progressed through the ages.

A rough outline of the spiritual history of the ancient Near East shows that there were at least two transfers of power in the pantheon.

First, a primordial god of heaven was overthrown by his son, who was considered "the" god between about 3000 and 2000 BC.

Around the time that the Amorites emerged as the dominant people group in the Near East, "the" god was replaced as king of the pantheon by the storm-god—except in Akkad and Sumer, where the city-god of Babylon, Marduk, occupied that place of honor.

However, the personal god of the founding dynasty of Babylon was the moon-god. As we noted earlier, some scholars now believe that the Sumerian god Amurru was actually an epithet of the lunar deity, "god of the Amurru (Amorite) land." A text only translated within the last ten years reveals that the moon-god, Sîn, was believed to preside over the Mesopotamian divine council at least some of the time.

The nations led by these various deities fought with one another throughout the period of history covered by the Bible. Beginning around 1800 BC, the time of Abraham and Isaac, Marduk and his followers ruled Babylonia and Sumer, while Baal worshipers dominated western Mesopotamia (Canaan), followers of the sun-god controlled most of Egypt, and the moon-god was the chief deity of the nomadic tribes of the steppe and deserts of Syria and Arabia.

The fall of the Neo-Babylonian Empire to the Medes and Persians in 539 BC was probably another rebuke of the moon-god by Yahweh, who revealed to the prophet Isaiah, about a hundred and fifty years earlier, His plan to use Cyrus to return the Jewish exiles to Jerusalem.[243]

Oddly, if scholars are correct about the Persian god Ahura Mazda, this replaced one empire subject to Marduk with another that worshiped the same god under a different name.

So, was Marduk/Ahura Mazda the "prince of Persia" who fought against the angelic messenger who came to the prophet Daniel? It's impossible to know, and wondering about the prince's identity leads to other questions we can't answer. For example, did the prince of Persia resist the angel because he didn't want Cyrus to free the Jews of Babylon?

These questions can only be answered with speculation. It's curious that Marduk doesn't fit the pattern of succession among the gods. Across the ancient Near East, and even as far away as Scandinavia and India, the storm-god rose to the top of the pantheon, but at Babylon, a city-god about whom we know nothing prior to that city's rise to power, claimed the throne of the gods. We can only ask, "Why?"

Is it possible that the rise of the Zoroastrian religion in Persia, which emerged just before the Medes and Persians conquered the lands of the Bible as far west as Greece, was part of a civil war among the rebel angels? Given that the moon-god, Sîn/Yarikh, was the patron deity of the founders of Babylon (and of most Amorites in the days of Abraham), then maybe Marduk was a figurehead who was head of the infernal council in name only. There isn't a single event in the Bible that appears to be specifically directed at Marduk, except maybe the reference to the size of Og's bed.

Continuing with our speculation, the rise of the Persian Empire and its devotion to Ahura Mazda, possibly another aspect of Marduk, may have been that entity's play to go solo by rebelling against the rebels. Of course, God used it for His purposes, to free His people from Babylon and humble the moon-god (Belshazzar's feast was during the fall *akitu* festival for Sîn).

But Marduk's shot at glory didn't last long; within two centuries, people of the storm-god, first the Greeks and then the Romans, pushed the Persian Empire back to Mesopotamia. And with the rise of Islam in the seventh century AD, Zoroastrianism faded into the background. Today, it's estimated that there are fewer than three million Zoroastrians in the world; in the 1990s, the *Guiness Book of World Records* began labeling Zoroastrianism as the "major religion nearest extinction."[244]

There are hints in pagan texts of other rifts between the Fallen. Two letters to the king of Mari from the ambassador of Yamkhad, a powerful kingdom based at Aleppo, mention the delivery of the clubs used by the storm-god "with which the deity boasts to have struck his enemy, the sea" to the temple of "the" god, Dagan, in the city of Terqa.[245]

Scholars don't know exactly what the letters mean, but there are two probable messages: First, they implied that Mari was subordinate to Yamkhad, just as Dagan (El, Enlil, etc.) had been replaced at the top of the pantheon by the storm-god, Adad (Baal). Second, in a backhanded way, it claims a victory for Adad/Baal that had been credited to Marduk.

> Thus says Adad.... I brought you back to the throne of your father, I brought you back. The weapons with which I fought the Sea [*Têmtum*] I gave to you. With the oil of my bitter victory I anointed you, and no one before you could stand. My one word hear![246]

Têmtum is the Akkadian word for Tiamat, the chaos dragon defeated by Marduk in the *Enuma Elish*. Now, this may be political posturing, sort of like saying, "Our gods are better than your gods, nyaah nyaah nyaah," but it may have been inspired in the spirit realm as members of the infernal council plotted and schemed against one another.

Another example of this comes from the western Amorite kingdom of Ugarit in a myth about a drunken feast at the house of the creator-god El.

> Yarikh [the moon-god] arched his back like a d[o]g;
> he gathered up crumbs beneath the tables.
> (Any) god who recognized him
> threw him meat from the joint.
> But (any god) who did not recognize him
> hit him with a stick beneath the table.
> At the call of Athtart [Astarte/Ishtar] and Anat [the Canaanite war-goddess] he approached.
> Athtart threw him a haunch,
> and Anat a shoulder of meat.
> The porter of El's house shouted:

"Look!
Why have you thrown a haunch to the dog,
(why) to the cur have you thrown a shoulder?"[247]

This is a great example of a text that drives scholars crazy. The meaning is unclear; it could refer to ritual drinking to reach an altered state of consciousness, or it could simply be a long and convoluted cure for a hangover.[248] Either way, the moon-god, bearing his Amorite name, Yarikh, is depicted as a dog, and canines were not man's best friend in the ancient Near East. This text comes from the final years of Ugarit in the thirteenth century BC. That was the time of the judges in Israel, after the conquest—in other words, after the moon-god had been humiliated at the Wilderness of Sîn, Mount Sinai, Jericho, and the Valley of Aijalon.

Does this text reflect a demotion in the infernal council? The moon-god was at or near the top of the pantheon in Mesopotamia until Joshua led the Israelites across the Jordan. After the Long Day, the moon-god faded into the background until his devotee Nabonidus took the crown of Babylon nearly a thousand years later.

Then the Medes and Persians destroyed Babylon as an independent kingdom, and a couple of centuries later, the Greeks and Romans came. Quick, now: How many myths about the Greco-Roman moon-goddess, Selene/Luna, do you know? Probably not many, if any. In the pantheon of Greece and Rome, the moon-deity was strictly supporting cast, a back-bencher.

Again, this is speculation, an attempt to discern the history of the unseen realm from evidence in the natural. We have limited ability to see into the spirit realm. It does, however, fit recorded history. Before Christ, the Fallen fought amongst themselves as well as with God. After the Resurrection, it appears that they put aside some of their mutual distrust. We'll explore that in more depth as we go along.

The conquest of Babylon by Cyrus apparently frustrated the plans of the moon-god to take over the empire of Nebuchadnezzar. But worship of the moon-god didn't disappear with the Chaldean kingdom. The land south and southeast of Edom, around the north end of the Gulf of Aqaba, ancient Midian, was still moon-god territory. Tayma, the second home of Babylon's last king, Nabonidus, was there, although it was no longer called Midian by his day.

Most of what scholars know about the pre-Islamic gods of northwestern Arabia, the area closest to the kingdom of Judah, comes from inscriptions found at Tayma and the other major oases in northern Arabia, Dumah and Dedan (Al-Ula).[249] All three were strategically located along caravan routes connected to the spice trade between southern Arabia, Mesopotamia, and the Mediterranean world.

Tayma, sometimes spelled Tema, is especially important because the last king of Babylon, Nabonidus (*Nabû-na'id*, "Nabu [god of wisdom] is praised"), established himself there for ten years, leaving his son, Belshazzar, in Babylon as his coregent. This didn't sit well with the priesthood of Marduk because certain rituals at the annual *akitu* festival required the king.

But we need to remember that fake news wasn't invented by the American media. Politicians have a long and sordid history of spinning news for their own goals. When histories are written based on fake news, they solidify into "fact" because most of us don't have time to chase down original sources to get closer to the truth.

Cyrus the Great of Persia was certainly used by God. There is no question about it. But he was a shrewd political operator who used what was at hand to win over the public. That was especially important in a time and place when transfers of power didn't happen on schedule every four years, but whenever enough people with swords and spears decided another ruler offered them a better deal.

Here's what Cyrus had going for him: When it became obvious that the Medes and Persians were about to attack, Nabonidus transferred idols of many of the Mesopotamian gods from their home cities to Babylon.

In the month of [...?] Lugal-Marada and the other gods of the town Marad, Zabada and the other gods of Kish, the goddess Ninlil and the other gods of Hursagkalama visited Babylon. Till the end of the month Ulûlu all the gods of Akkad—those from above and those from below—entered Babylon. The gods of Borsippa, Cutha, and Sippar did not enter.[250]

Why did he do this? Idols were thought to be spiritual focal points for the gods. The statues gave the deities locality from which they'd protect their cities, as long as they were properly cared for. Nabonidus, knowing this (and painfully aware of the superior army Cyrus had assembled), brought the priests needed to care for the gods to Babylon as well. Not only was this to prevent the gods of Babylonia from falling into Persian hands, but Nabonidus hoped it would strengthen Babylon's defenses by adding divine protection.

Several months before the final clash of arms at Opis on the Tigris, Nabonidus was already facing the eventuality of a Persian invasion and was making preparations accordingly. These preparations included the gathering of statues in the capital.... During the months preceding the Persian invasion, Babylon became a vast repository of cult statues attended to and cared for by hundreds, if not thousands, of members of their respective clergies.[251]

As a veteran military commander, Nabonidus had to know he was in deep trouble. By the summer of 539 BC, the Medes and Persians had already conquered everything north and east of the Fertile Crescent. Looking at a modern map, Cyrus controlled everything from Afghanistan in the east to all of Turkey in the west. To make matters worse, his patron deity, the moon-god Sîn, went into partial eclipse on June 13 of that year, which was Simānu 14 on the Babylonian calendar.[252] In a thirty-day lunar month, the moon should have been nearly full that night, and it wasn't.

The Babylonian astrological text *Enuma Anu Enlil* offers several possible interpretations for a lunar eclipse falling on Simānu 14. They vary with certain factors—weather conditions, color of the moon, etc.—but they're described by scholars as "uniformly catastrophic for the land."[253] With the army of Cyrus massing for invasion, it's not surprising that the moon-god worshiper Nabonidus reacted with something like panic.

Now, if Nabonidus had somehow won the war, Mesopotamians would naturally have credited the gods for the deliverance of Babylon. Instead, Babylon fell without a fight a few days after its army was beaten at the Battle of Opis, which was fought at a strategic site on the Tigris River about fifty miles north of modern Baghdad. This dropped a magnificent propaganda opportunity into the Persian king's lap: Cyrus scored major PR points with his new subjects by returning their gods to their home cities, no doubt to the relief of a conquered people who felt spiritually naked without their patron deities. Then Cyrus poured it on by accusing "the deposed king (Nabonidus) with having brought them to the capital against their will."[254]

In other words, Cyrus took advantage of Nabonidus' desperate effort to line up divine protection to show how he, the great and beneficent Cyrus, had freed the gods from captivity and sent them home.

Jews and Christians, here's a key point: The decree of Cyrus in 538 BC that sent the Jewish exiles home was no doubt part of this propaganda campaign. In his mind, Cyrus was *allowing* Yahweh to return to Jerusalem!

But it doesn't matter. Remember, God *knew* this would happen. And He had revealed it to Isaiah more than a century earlier.

What was the result of Nabonidus' long sojourn in the desert? The king lived at the oasis of Tayma in what is today northwestern Saudi Arabia, between about 553 BC and 543 BC. Scholars are divided on whether he was there to personally oversee Babylon's control of the profitable spice trade or just seeking prophecies from the moon-god.

If you've ever been to the land that was once called Edom, the area southeast of the Dead Sea in present-day Jordan, you can be forgiven for wondering why anyone in their right mind would willingly move there, especially the king of one of the most powerful nations on earth. Edom is well-named; it means "red," and the rocks and sand of Edom certainly are that.

Tayma, however, is a well-watered oasis that's been occupied for thousands of years. Nabonidus recognized its strategic value; Tayma sits at the north end of the spice road, an ancient caravan trail that ran along the east side of the Red Sea. In the days before reliable sea travel, caravans were the most economical way to transport the valuable spices from southern Arabia, especially after domesticated camels were introduced to the region around 1400 BC.[255] The frankincense and myrrh brought to Jesus by the magi were probably carried by camel through Tayma, which was on the route that branched northeast toward Babylon and Persia.

The wealth produced by this valuable trade route financed the powerful kingdom of the Nabataean Arabs, which emerged in the second century BC and carved the fabulous city of Petra out of the red sandstone of Edom. Nabataean sites keep archaeologists busy to this day. The Saudi government, recognizing an opportunity, recently announced it will spend billions of dollars to develop Al-Ula, the wealthy biblical kingdom of Dedan mentioned by Jeremiah and Ezekiel, into a tourist site to rival Petra in Jordan.[256]

Like all good politicians, Nabonidus recognized a big source of revenue when he saw one. So, around 551 BC, he moved to take control of the three key north Arabian oases along the caravan route: Tayma, Dedan, and Dumah.

First, the king had to break the power of Edom, which controlled the routes to the port at Gaza and had extended its authority as far south as Tayma. Scholars date the destruction of Edom's largest city, Bozrah, to the time of Nabonidus' campaign,[257] which was apparently a prelude to setting up shop at Tayma.[258]

Teman, a place-name that refers to Edom in the Bible (Amos 1:12 and Habakkuk 3:3), may be one and the same as Tayma.[259] This suggests that ancient Edom extended much farther south in the days of the prophets than is shown on most Bible atlases. It would explain why Nabonidus destroyed Bozrah before moving on to Tayma, Dedan, and Dumah.

It also adds a layer of meaning to the verse in Habakkuk. If Teman was Tayma, then it was linked to Mount Sinai by the prophet, who called Sinai by its alternate name, Paran. That means Tayma was a center of the cult of Sîn for about a thousand years before Nabonidus made it his base of operations.

While Nabonidus was in residence at the oasis, it's a good bet that the moon-god was the main deity of the local pantheon, but after the fall of Babylon in 539 BC, the chief god was Salm or Salam, the sun-god.[260] During the Persian period that followed, Salm was depicted as a bull, sometimes with a solar disc between his horns. On a stela found at the oasis in 1877, Salm was described as one of "the gods of Tayma" alongside Ashima, possibly equated with Ishtar/Astarte, and Sangila, a deity whose name may derive from Sîn, the moon-god. No surprise there; we noted earlier that the sun, moon, and Venus (Ishtar) were commonly worshiped together as an astral triad in Mesopotamia.

Getting a handle on the rest of the gods of Arabia between the fall of Babylon and the rise of Islam in the early seventh century AD is a challenge. Trying to pin down precise one-to-one correlations across times, places, and tribes is an exercise in frustration. For our purposes, the best approach is to draw some general conclusions.

It appears that several deities were most prominent throughout Arabia, although they were worshiped under different names. The other oases in northern Arabia, Dedan and Dumah worshiped a pantheon headed by Attarshamain, the "queen of heaven."[261] The name of the goddess is a composite: Attar + *shamain* ("Attar of the skies");[262] in other words, she was the Canaanite Astarte and Babylonian Ishtar by a slightly different name.

Dedan, seventy miles southwest of Tayma, was the center of a tribal confederacy that included the powerful Qedarites, a tribe named for Kedar, son of Ishmael.[263] Attarshamain, represented by the planet Venus, was part of an astral triad with Nuhā and Rudā'u, the sun-god and moon-god.[264]

In southern Arabia, modern-day Yemen and Oman, over one hundred deities have been attested but only one was worshiped throughout the region—the war-god Athtar, the male aspect of the dualistic Canaanite god/dess Astarte/Attar.[265] Other important south Arabian gods included the moon-god Syn or Sayin (a variant of Sîn); Wadd, another name for the moon-god; the sun-goddess Shams (variant of Shapash, the Ugaritic version of Shamash, the sun-god); 'Amm ("paternal uncle"), a god whose name suggests ancestor worship; and a trio of goddesses named al-Lāt ("the goddess"), al-'Uzzā ("the most powerful"), and Manāt.[266] Scholars are divided on the origins of those three, other than to note that they appear to have been brought to Arabia in the second century BC.[267]

We're painting with a broad brush here. To draw a general conclusion: As we look at the religions of Arabia in the eleven hundred years or so between the fall of Babylon in 539 BC and the rise of Islam in the AD 620s, the deities who survived were the old Mesopotamian astral triad—sun, moon, and Venus—and the male aspect of Astarte, the war-god Athtar. Remember, we noted in a previous chapter that Astarte/Athtar may have been seen as separate entities as early as the ninth century BC, with the war-god identity linked to Moab's national deity, the ancient war-god Chemosh.

But we can draw one more conclusion that seems solidly grounded in history: While the worship of Jesus Christ spread widely in the centuries after the Resurrection, reaching as far east as China and as far west as Britain, there is one land frequently mentioned in the Bible where Christianity never gained a firm foothold—Arabia.

Extrapolating from that bit of history, we offer this theory: The gods of the ancient world, stunned and alarmed by the Resurrection, withdrew, like the unclean spirit of Matthew 12:43–45, to a waterless place—Arabia.

And there they planned their counterstrike.

16

The Lord of Shara

And so, we turn our attention to a city that is the center of a religion that erupted onto the world stage in the early seventh century AD—Mecca.

The history of Mecca before the rise of Islam is obscure. With all due respect to Muslims, their historians have tended to retcon—that's shorthand for "retroactive continuity," a Hollywood term for changing the backstory of a television series or movie franchise—the history of lands Islam has occupied. It is an inconvenient truth for Islam that there are no clear references to Mecca in any text known to scholars written before the eighth century AD.[268]

You'll probably be surprised to learn that the Quran only mentions Mecca once.[269] Given the significance of Mecca today, how is that possible? Imagine the Bible with only one reference to Jerusalem! There is more to the story of how Mecca became the holy site of Islam than we are told.

A second reference in the Quran, Becca,[270] is assumed by most people to mean Mecca, but it's not necessarily a synonym for the city. Muslim scholars distinguish between the two: Becca is the holy site surrounding the Ka'ba, while Mecca is the city in which Becca is located.[271]

Additionally, Quranic descriptions of the city just don't fit the actual geography of Mecca. For example, the Quran and hadiths describe it as a city in a valley[272] with a "rain water passage" between two mountains,[273] where grass[274] and trees[275] once grew—none of which is supported by archaeology. Mecca is in a barren valley unsuited for raising crops or herds.

Taken together, the evidence strongly suggests that the Ka'ba was not in Mecca during the lifetime of Muhammad.

Further, tales of Mecca as a thriving center of trade in Muhammad's day, which are taken at face value by most, aren't supported by documented history. By the sixth century AD, the ancient world's demand for incense had evaporated with the spread of Christianity. Unlike the pagan gods, Jesus never asked His followers to honor Him with offerings of frankincense and myrrh. As the faith spread, demand for spices and incense dried up. The few camel caravans that still carried such goods from southern Arabia traveled a road that bypassed Mecca altogether.[276]

Muslim histories trace the origin of Mecca to the descendants of Ishmael. But the Romans, who took over western Arabia in the second century AD, seem to have been completely unaware of a center of trade and/or religious pilgrimage called Mecca.[277] It wasn't until AD 741 that Mecca is even mentioned in a foreign text, and that author located it in Mesopotamia, halfway between Ur and Harran in what is now Iraq.[278]

For context, by AD 741, a little more than a hundred years after Muhammad's death, the armies of Islam had conquered Persia, Mesopotamia, Egypt, north Africa, most of Anatolia (modern Turkey), and the Visigothic kingdom in Spain. Between 674 and 678, an Islamic army laid siege to Constantinople, the capital city of the Eastern Roman Empire.

Yet, Mecca, the holiest city in Islam, was so unimportant that the Western world *didn't even know where it was!*

How is that possible?

Here's another bit of data to chew on: It's well known that Muslims are expected to pray in the direction of Mecca five times a day. This is called the Qibla (Arabic for "direction"). Most mosques have a niche built into a wall that indicates the direction of the Ka'ba in Mecca.

Note the word "most." Not all—most.

It's known from the Quran that the Qibla was changed during the lifetime of Muhammad.[279] If Mecca wasn't the original target of Muslim prayers, what was?

Jerusalem.

> According to Yunus b. 'Abd al-A'la—Ibn Wahb—Ibn Zayd: The Prophet turned towards Jerusalem for sixteen months, and then it reached his ears that the Jews were saying, "By God, Muhammad and his companions did not know where their Qiblah was until we directed them." This displeased the Prophet and he raised his face toward Heaven, and God said, "We have seen the turning of your face to Heaven."[280]

So, around AD 624, the Qibla shifted from Jerusalem to Mecca. It was not just for sixteen months, but for more than thirteen years—the time Muhammad preached in Mecca plus sixteen months in Medina—that Muhammad taught his followers to pray towards Jerusalem.[281]

Canadian historian and author Dan Gibson decided to test that belief several years ago by measuring the orientation of the Qibla in the oldest mosques still standing. Using modern satellite photography, GPS, and other architectural tools, he found, to his surprise, that mosques built during the first hundred years of Islam were not oriented toward Mecca.

But they don't face Jerusalem, either.

Of the twelve surviving mosques for which Gibson could obtain reliable data, all are oriented toward Petra, the fabulous Nabataean city carved into the red sandstone cliffs of southern Jordan. The largest error in alignment, the Qaṣr Humeima mosque in Jordan, is off by only 7.3 degrees from Petra, and the average error for the twelve mosques is only 2.5 degrees, one of which is in China![282] The oldest of the mosques was built in Medina in AD 626, six years before Muhammad's death and four years before he and his followers captured Mecca.

The first known mosque to orient its Qibla in the direction of Mecca was built in AD 727,[283] more than a century after Muslim scholars acknowledge the Qibla changing from Jerusalem.

If correct, this is stunning. It would mean two things: Muhammad didn't teach his followers to pray toward Mecca, because the "Mecca" of Muhammad was not the one in modern Saudi Arabia; and the change in the Qibla directed Muslims to revert to the veneration of a pagan object—a Ka'ba ("cube") in the city of Petra.

Gibson believes the first Ka'ba may have been in front of the temple of Dushara, the chief god of the Nabataeans.[284] After the death of the Umayyad caliph Mu'awiya in AD 680, one of the last of Muhammad's surviving companions, Abdullah ibn al-Zubayr, refused to swear allegiance to the new *amir*, Yazid. By 683, out of patience with the rebel, Yazid dispatched a force to Medina that defeated and slaughtered the followers of Ibn al-Zubayr—but their leader had left town before the amir's army arrived. Ibn al-Zubayr had decided to hole up in the *bayt allah*, "House of God," apparently daring the new caliph to desecrate it by launching an assault against the faithful barricaded inside.

To this day, Muslims assume the "House of God" was the Ka'ba in Mecca, but no contemporary writings say so.[285] In fact, the clues point farther north.

The weight of evidence would suggest a location to the north of the Hijaz, midway between Kufa and Alexandria. Since this is precisely the region with which Muhammad himself appears to have been most familiar, and since Ibn al-Zubayr was consciously aiming to defend the Prophet's legacy, the likelihood must surely be that the House of God in which he barricaded himself stood not in Mecca but between Medina and Palestine: in that "blessed place" named by the Prophet himself as Bakka.[286]

Petra is north of the Hijaz between Medina and Palestine. Unlike Mecca, it fits the geographic descriptions of Islam's holy city. Petra is a settlement in a valley with a "rainwater passage" between two mountains where grass and trees once grew.

There's another link between Petra and Mecca. The fourth-century Christian bishop Epiphanius, from Salamis on the island of Cyprus, is best-known for his book *Panarion*, written between AD 374 and 377. The book is a refutation of eighty heresies, a sort of guidebook to Christian apologetics. Among the pagan beliefs he railed against was the religion of the Nabataeans.

First, at Alexandria, in the Coreum, as they call it; it is a very large temple, the shrine of Core. They stay up all night singing hymns to the idol with a flute accompaniment. And when they have concluded their nightlong vigil torchbearers descend into an underground shrine after cockcrow and bring up a wooden image which is seated naked < on > a litter.... And they carry the image itself seven times round the innermost shrine with flutes, tambourines and hymns, hold a feast, and take it back down to its place underground. And when you ask them what this mystery means they reply that today at this hour Core—that is, the virgin—gave birth to Aeon.

This is also done in the same way in the city of Petra, in the temple of the idol there. (Petra is the capital city of Arabia, the scriptural Edom.) They praise the virgin with hymns in the Arab language calling her, in Arabic, Chaamu—that is, Core, or virgin. And the child who is born of her they call Dusares, that is, "the Lord's only-begotten."[287]

There are two important takeaways from this text. First, the ritual at Alexandria involved circumambulating a shrine seven times. Take note; we'll refer back to that later.

Second, the ritual at Petra involved the chief deity of the Nabataeans, Dushara, and the tribes of northern Arabia worshiped the god with a ritual circumambulation.

But while Epiphanius meant well, he lost something important in translation.

It appears that Epiphanius confused the Arabic word *ka'ba*, which means "stone, cube, betyl," with words such as *ka'iba* or *ku'ba*, which mean "young females" or "female breasts." Because of this confusion, Epiphanius concluded that Dushara was born from a virgin, misinterpreting Dushara's actual worship in the form of a stone.[288]

A betyl (pronounced "beetle") is a sacred stone believed by pagans to be endowed with life. So, the chief god of Petra wasn't born of a virgin; the hymns of praise were for Dushara because he was the stone cube—the *ka'ba*.

According to Epiphanius, the faithful worshiped him by circumambulating the stone cube. Does that sound familiar?

17

Lord of the Cube

If historian Dan Gibson's theory is correct, then Petra, a center of religion and trade just one hundred miles from Jerusalem, was a perfect location for the Fallen to launch their new religion. It could also explain how Muhammad traveled to Jerusalem and back on his famous Night Journey. A good endurance horse can cover a hundred miles in a day. The Tevis Cup is an annual one-hundred-mile endurance ride through the Sierra Nevada mountains in California, and winners usually complete the rugged course in fourteen to seventeen hours.[289] With two good horses and some strong coffee, it would have been possible for a rider to leave Petra one day and return the next.

Setting aside whether Muhammad's horse Buraq ("Lightning") really had wings and legs that supernaturally lengthened according to the terrain (rear legs longer uphill, front legs longer downhill),[290] Mecca is 940 miles from Jerusalem. Barring divine intervention, Muhammad did not cover that distance in a single night.

It's possible the supernatural horse was invented by later Islamic writers to explain the journey after Petra was retconned out of the official history. It's also possible Muhammad really did experience something supernatural that night. Still, it's worth noting that locating the original holy place of Islam at Petra may shed light on more questions than we think.

Anyone who visits Petra can't help but notice the large sandstone "djinn blocks" along the path to the Bab as-Siq, the narrow gorge that leads into the city itself. These stone cubes, which measure roughly fifteen to twenty feet square and stand up to twenty-six feet high, are actually tombs.[291] Their shape, however, may be inspired by the cube that represented the chief god of the Nabataeans, Dushara, the way so many Christian funerary monuments feature a cross.

Walking through the Siq into Petra, visitors pass by a number of niches for betyls carved into the walls along the grand caravan entry to Petra, but there are niches with betyls all over the city. These betyls are symbolic forms representing their gods, a practice called "aniconism."

The Israelites practiced a strict aniconism, allowing no graven images of Yahweh. Nabataean aniconism was more relaxed. They allowed anthropomorphic representations of their gods, although aniconic symbols, such as the betyls, are far more common. An archaeological expedition in the late 1990s identified a total of nearly 530 betyls at Petra![292]

The word "betyl" (sometimes spelled "baetyl") comes from the Greek *baitylia*. Philo of Byblos, who claimed he translated an earlier work by Sanchuniaton of Phoenicia (now lost), wrote in the early second century AD that the sky-god Ouranos created betyls ("animated stones") to somehow help him when his children, led by the Titan Kronos, rebelled.[293] It was believed these stones fell from the heavens, possessing magical powers.[294] Other Greek and Roman writers describe "round or spherical, red or black meteorites that were especially venerated as sacred stones in the Roman East."[295] Roman coins with images of betyls were minted from the late third century BC through the fourth century AD.[296]

Here's the connection between Petra and the Bible: The Greek word *baitylia* derives from the Hebrew *byt'l*—"beth-el," or "house/temple of El/God."[297]

Well, now. Remember the story of Jacob's "ladder"?

Jacob left Beersheba and went toward Haran. And he came to a certain place and stayed there that night, because the sun had set. Taking one of the stones of the place, he put it under his head and lay down in that place to sleep. And he dreamed, and behold, there was a ladder set up on the earth, and the top of it reached to heaven. And behold, the angels of God were ascending and descending on it! And behold, the LORD stood above it and said, "I am the LORD, the God of Abraham your father and the God of Isaac. The land on which you lie I will give to you and to your offspring. Your offspring shall be like the dust of the earth, and you shall spread abroad to the west and to the east and to the north and to the south, and in you and your offspring shall all the families of the earth be blessed. Behold, I am with you and will keep you wherever you go, and will bring you back to this land. For I will not leave you until I have done what I have promised you." Then Jacob awoke from his sleep and said, "Surely the LORD is in this place, and I did not know it." And he was afraid and said, "How awesome is this place! This is none other than the house of God, and this is the gate of heaven."

So early in the morning Jacob took the stone that he had put under his head and set it up for a pillar and poured oil on the top of it. He called the name of that place Bethel. (Genesis 28:10–19)

Archaeologist Robert Wenning connects the dots:

It was but a small step to connect "beth-el" with the sense of the "dwelling of the god" as the presence of the god in the stone. That is precisely what a betyl represents.[298]

Jacob's divine revelation apparently inspired the pagans around ancient Israel to worship the *stone* on which he experienced his dream vision instead of the God who *created* the stone.

Who was this god of Petra, Dushara? His name is a contraction of Dhu-Shara, "The One (or Lord) of Shara."[299] That's a reference to the Shara mountains that run along the east side of the Aravah rift near Petra, south of the Dead Sea. Shara is the biblical Seir,[300] a fascinating link to the mountain from which Yahweh began the conquest of Canaan.

The LORD came from Sinai
and dawned from Seir upon us;
he shone forth from Mount Paran;
he came from the ten thousands of holy ones,
with flaming fire at his right hand. (Deuteronomy 33:2)

Wait—what? Is Mount Sinai in Seir—Edom? Mount Paran is another name for Sinai,[301] which suggests that all three places named in that verse point to the same location. The only one we can locate with some degree of certainty of is Seir, which is Edom, the land south of the Dead Sea and mainly north of modern Saudi Arabia.

That's an intriguing question. Friends of ours have devoted entire books to it. Hold on to that idea for now because it would rabbit-trail us off point.

"Dhu-Shara" is a title, similar to the various *baalim* of the Bible, like Baal-Peor ("lord of Peor"), Baal-Berith, Baal-Hermon, and so on. Scholars have tried to identify the god behind the title for decades. Guesses have included the Semitic storm-god, Hadad (Baal), the moon and sun gods, and the Greek deities Zeus, Ares, and Dionysus, the god of wine and madness.

It's likely that Dushara was a local god adopted by the Nabataeans when they moved into the region after the Babylonian army crushed Edom in the middle of the sixth century BC. Logically, this makes the most sense. Sources outside the Bible confirm that a god named Qôs was the national deity of Edom. Egyptian texts place Qôs in the Transjordan as early as the thirteenth century BC,[302] and he was worshipped as late as the third century AD, long after the Nabataeans had taken the place of the Edomites in the land.[303] Even though he isn't mentioned in the Bible, with his fifteen-hundred-year track record, "'The One of the Sharâ-Mountains' can hardly refer to any deity other than Qôs."[304]

If the original Ka'ba was indeed at Petra, then the national god of Edom, Qôs, was probably the one who occupied the place of honor at the shrine of the black stone.

Ah, but wait! Not so fast. Later Islamic sources tell us that a god named Hubal was "Lord of the Ka'ba" right up until the time that Muhammad received his revelation.

So, who was Hubal?

Evidence points to Hubal originating in the north, maybe in Syria but possibly with the Nabataeans themselves, sometime in the third century AD.[305] Histories of Islam describe Hubal as the most prominent of 360 idols in the Ka'ba, which may have represented the days of the year.[306] Muslim tradition recalls that Muhammad's grandfather, Abd al-Mutallib, received an oracle in the Ka'ba by praying to Allah while standing next to the idol of Hubal,[307] which sat near a well owned by Muhammad's tribe, the Quraysh.[308]

Muslim apologists argue that this doesn't mean al-Mutallib was praying to Hubal; he was just standing next to an idol that was later smashed by Muhammad. Frankly, this sounds like another example of retconning. This event took place long before Muhammad had his "epiphany," so it seems unlikely that al-Mutallib would have been praying to a god he did not yet know.

If Muhammad's grandfather did, in fact, pray to Allah, then another inconvenient fact rears its ugly head: Islamic sources call Hubal "the greatest" of the images in the Ka'ba.[309] And if Hubal was in the house, then Allah was not—unless Hubal *was* Allah.

> Naturally Quraysh were polytheist, but the deities of polytheist Arabia preferred to be housed separately. No pre-Islamic sanctuary, be it stone or building, is known to have accommodated more than one male god, as opposed to one male god and female consort.... If Allah was a pagan god like any other, Quraysh would not have allowed Hubal to share the sanctuary with him—not because they were proto-monotheists, but precisely because they were pagans.[310]

There is no evidence in existence today to prove that 360 idols were present or worshiped inside the Ka'ba at Mecca. We remind you that Mecca is not mentioned in any extant text written before the mid-eighth century AD, more than a hundred years after the death of Muhammad, even though the religion he founded had conquered most of the world from Afghanistan to Spain.

Petra, however, was filled with more than enough idols, in the form of betyls, to last for more than eighteen months if one paid homage to only one god per day.

So, Hubal, a god who emerged in Syria or northern Arabia sometime in the third century AD, became the main deity at Petra, a religious center important to the Nabataean Arabs. Thus, Hubal was probably one and the same as Edom's patron god Qôs, called Dushara, the Lord of Shara (Seir), who was worshiped at Petra in the form of a *ka'ba*, a stone cube.

Nearly two thousand years before Hubal arrived at Petra, Jacob's divine revelation inspired him to set up the stone he used as a pillow to commemorate his dream vision at *byt'l*, Bethel, the "house/temple of El/God." His act of anointing a stone with oil was twisted over time into the veneration of sacred stones called *baitylia* (betyls). These were often the remnants of meteorites, which were believed to house the presence of a god.

By the Islamic era, the veneration of a cube-like betyl, a *ka'ba*, was a centuries-old practice at Petra, a city that fits the descriptions of Islam's holiest site far better than Mecca. Petra even appears to be the place to which early Muslims directed their prayers, based on the Qibla of the oldest mosques.

And the description of the Ka'ba as the "House of God," the *bayt allah*, connects the sacred stone of Mecca back to its likely inspiration, *byt'l*—the stone on which Jacob dreamt of a stairway to heaven. Is it a coincidence that many Nabataean tombs, especially those at Petra, feature crowsteps—an ascending and descending stairstep pattern that became "one of the most significant features" of Nabataean architecture?[311]

Maybe. But I'm not a coincidence theorist. Now let me add one more bit of speculation for you to consider.

Christians have tried to identify Islam in prophecy ever since the first Muslim raiders rode out of the Arabian desert. Bible teachers have pointed to the four horsemen of Revelation 6, the Antichrist, and the False Prophet. Recently, Joel Richardson made a case for Islam as the fourth kingdom of Nebuchadnezzar's dream in Daniel 2, the one with the toes of iron mixed with soft clay.

Let me suggest another verse that has gone unnoticed until now, to the best of my knowledge:

The oracle of the word of the LORD to Israel by Malachi.
"I have loved you," says the Lord. But you say, "How have you loved us?" "Is not Esau Jacob's brother?" declares the Lord. "Yet I have loved Jacob but Esau I have hated. I have laid waste

his hill country and left his heritage to jackals of the desert." If Edom says, "We are shattered but we will rebuild the ruins," the Lord of hosts says, "They may build, but I will tear down, and they will be called 'the wicked country,' and 'the people with whom the Lord is angry forever.'" (Malachi 1:1–4)

The word translated "jackals" is the Hebrew *tannôt*, based on a root it shares with the Hebrew word for "dragon," *tannin*. (The King James Bible translators chose "dragons" over "jackals" for this verse.)

Petra was in the heart of Edom. It was the site of a bloody battle between the Judean king Amaziah and the Edomites sometime in the 790s BC.[312] The city was called Sela in the Old Testament, which—like Petra in Greek—simply means "rock."

If Petra is the true birthplace of Islam, as the evidence suggests, is it possible that the prophet Malachi was shown a vision of "dragons of the desert"—dark angels who commandeered Esau's heritage to launch a religion that aspires to conquer the Holy Mountain of God?

18

Allah, Inc.

It would be easy to categorize Islam as worship of the moon-god. The flags of many Muslim nations feature a crescent moon and star, and the clock tower at the Abraj Al-Bait ("Towers of the House [of God—i.e., the Ka'ba]") in Mecca is topped by a golden crescent moon. So are the nine minarets that surround the Grand Mosque.

It's hard to argue the point. The crescent moon atop the Makkah Royal Clock Tower makes the hotel beneath it the third-tallest building in the world, and the Abraj Al-Bait, a government-owned hotel complex, is yards away from the Great Mosque of Mecca, the world's largest mosque and Islam's holiest site. Since the complex was only completed in 2012 (by the Saudi Bin Laden Group),[313] the lunar symbol is not a remnant of Islam's early days. And it's highly unlikely it was included in the design without the approval of the religious authorities of the Saudi kingdom.

Muslims reject the idea that their religion is based on older pagan religions that worshiped the moon. One prominent American convert to Islam, referring specifically to the claim that Allah was originally a moon-god, wrote that the idea "is not only an insult to Muslims but also an insult to Arab Christians who use the name 'Allah' for God."[314]

This may surprise you, but I agree—Allah was *not* a moon-god. But it begs the question: If he's not, then why *is* that big crescent moon on top of the clock tower? Why are the star and crescent on so many Muslim flags, an ancient symbol that looks a lot like the Sîn and Ishtar (Moon and Venus) portion of the old Mesopotamian astral triad?

The truth is the star and crescent weren't part of the iconography of early Islam. It's an ancient symbol; something very like it is featured at the top of the Ur-Nammu Stela, found in the 1920s at the site of Ur in southeastern Iraq. The stela, a limestone slab that shows the moon-god Nanna (his name in ancient Sumer) receiving a drink offering from Ur-Nammu, the king of Ur around 2100 BC.[315] As we've noted, the moon and Venus (Nanna/Sîn and Inanna/Ishtar) are frequently featured with the sun-god as a triad in Mesopotamian art.

Use of the star and crescent appears to have spread westward over the centuries as the religion of Mesopotamia influenced the people of Anatolia and Greece. The kings of Pontus, a country in what is northern Turkey today, adopted the symbol in the early third century BC and introduced it to the Bosporus.[316] That's the strait that connects the Black Sea to the Sea of Marmara, and, more importantly, is the location of what was then called Byzantium.

The star-and-crescent symbol was still in use more than five hundred years later when the Roman emperor Constantine renamed the city Constantinople after himself—it's good to be the king—and made it the capital of the eastern empire in AD 330. It appears that the Byzantines especially venerated the Titan Hecate, an ancient goddess linked to the moon, because they believed she'd protected them from the invading army of Alexander the Great in the fourth century BC.[317]

It would be logical to assume that the star and crescent were simply adopted as a symbol of conquest by Mehmed the Conqueror when his Ottoman armies captured Constantinople in 1452. However, there is little evidence that the mainly Christian city used the symbol during the eleven hundred years between the name changes from Byzantium to Constantinople to Istanbul,[318] and the symbol wasn't adopted by the Ottoman Empire until 1844.

After the breakup of the empire in the early 1920s, some of its successor states (Tunisia, Libya, and Algeria) incorporated the symbol into their new flags, and a dozen national flags adopted in the twentieth century likewise feature the star and crescent, all representing countries that are predominantly Muslim.

To be fair, it should be noted that many Muslim scholars are aware that "the faith of Islam historically had no symbol, and many refuse to accept [the crescent moon]."[319] That's why the Islamic State flies a variant of the Black Standard under which Muhammad went forth to conquer.

That just brings us back to the question: If Islam has no symbol, why did the royal house of Saud, presumably with the approval of Islamic religious authorities in Mecca, put a golden crescent moon 1,972 feet in the air right next to the Ka'ba?

That's kind of a rhetorical question. We could just as well ask why the Roman Catholic Church installed an obelisk representing the missing piece of Osiris, the Egyptian god of the dead, right in front of the Vatican in Saint Peter's Square, or why so many government buildings here in the United States are topped by statues of pagan deities. The answer: The infernal council constantly whispers in our ears. All too often, we listen.

So, with all of the crescent moons hanging over Islam's holy of holies, why do I claim that Allah was never a moon-god? Simple. Islam is too big to be the work of just *one* small-*g* god. It's the supernatural equivalent of a corporate merger—a new religion created by the rebel gods as a desperate response to the Resurrection.

In other words, Allah is an artificial entity, a figurehead who represents a supernatural board of directors forced to put aside their mutual distrust and jealousy when they realized how badly they'd been outplayed at Calvary. It's similar to creating a corporation that's treated like a person under the law. Islam is essentially "Allah, Inc.," a partnership of ancient deities who banded together because they shared a single goal: To destroy the growing faith in Jesus Christ.

Well, that and staying out of the Lake of Fire.

When the new sect of Christianity began to spread from Jerusalem around the middle of the first century AD, the ruling authorities in Rome and Israel tried to exterminate it by killing as many believers as they could catch. Obviously, that didn't work. By the beginning of the fourth century, when Constantine legalized Christianity, it had reached Britain in the west and may have spread as far as China in the east.[320]

By the early seventh century, Christianity was the majority religion in most of the Roman and formerly Roman world, as Germanic and Celtic peoples in western Europe and Britain converted to the faith from their polytheistic paganism. The eastern empire had been Christian for centuries, with the oldest centers of Christianity in the lands of the Bible—places like Antioch, Alexandria, Damascus, and Jerusalem. Missionaries had spread the gospel throughout most of northern Africa, Egypt, and the land on the west side of the Red Sea, the kingdom of Aksum in what is now Eritrea and northern Ethiopia.

Only in Arabia did Christianity fail to take root. Other than a short run during the sixth century in what is now Yemen, the tribes of Arabia remained faithful to the pagan gods of their ancestors.

It was from there that the counterattack came.

There had been hints at this developing coalition for centuries. We mentioned earlier the stela commemorating the Assyrian king Ashurnasirpal II that featured the symbols of his patron deities: Ashur, Assyria's version of "the" god; Sîn, the moon-god; Shamash, the sun-god; Ishtar, goddess of sex and war; and the storm-god, Adad, better known to you and me as Baal. Add the war-god Chemosh/Ares/Mars and the plague-god Resheph/Apollo, and there, thirteen hundred years before Muhammad, you've got the infernal council of Islam—Allah, Inc.

You may be wondering how "the" god, confined to the abyss until the Judgment, can still wield influence on earth. While even pagans believed the old god was confined to the netherworld, he's still persuaded or intimidated humans for millennia to trade the lives of children for the promise of divine favor in everything from success in business to victory in war. Despite his imprisonment, statistics argue that his power is still felt in the natural realm. The number-one cause of death around the world in 2018 was abortion; nearly forty-two million unborn children were terminated, roughly one out of every four pregnancies worldwide.[321] There were more deaths by abortion than from malaria, HIV/AIDS, smoking, alcohol, and traffic accidents combined.[322]

But while this god still pulls the strings of human agents on the earth, he's not alone in his rebellion. And he's lent his title to the figure-head of the cause.

To recap from earlier: The god's name, *en-lil*, comes from *i-lu-lu*, based on the Semitic root *'l* ("god"), repeated to emphasize that the title referred to "*the* god" (*'l'l* = *il-ilu* = *en-lil*), or "god of (all) the gods."[323]

It's not a coincidence that the proto-Semitic word for "god," *'l* ("*il*"), became the generic Hebrew word for a god, *el*—hence, *elohim* and the less common *eloah*. This is consistent with evidence that connects this old god, under the names Enlil, El, Dagan, Kumarbi, Baal-Hammon, Kronos, and Saturn, with northwestern Mesopotamia. Although the oldest known writing on earth comes from Sumer, it appears that the god who emerged as the head of the Sumerian pantheon in the third millennium BC may have been known even earlier to the people of what is now Syria, Lebanon, and southern Turkey as El—"the" god.

Over time, beliefs change and so does language. The title "the god" was applied to various deities over the years. The divine name *el* of Northwestern Semitic spread throughout Mesopotamia and persisted through the centuries. It's changed, but it's still in use to this day. By the time of Muhammad, the word for "god" among the tribes of northern Arabia had been transformed from *ilu* to *el* (or *eloah*) to *ilah*.[324]

That brings us to Allah. It is a title, not a proper name; it's a contraction of the Arabic *al-ilah*, "the god,"[325] the same title claimed by the rebellious entity who dared to lead the Watchers' rebellion on Mount Hermon.

The pagan Arabs of the pre-Islamic world knew *Al-Ilah*. Muhammad's father was named Abdallah, which is a contraction of "Abdul Allah" ("servant of Allah"). Muhammad apparently believed he was reforming the faith by convincing his followers to renounce other deities in favor of "the" god, thereby demoting the moon-god, sun-god, war-god, and the rest of the pagan pantheon to an "exalted assembly"[326] similar to the divine council described in the Bible.[327]

But Muhammad was deceived. The dark angel who called himself Jibril convinced the would-be prophet that Jews and Christians had twisted the true faith of "the" god, and the false revelations he delivered to Muhammad formed the basis of a new religion based on total submission to the will of Allah.

But Allah, "the" god, is actually a Wizard of Oz-like simulacrum operated by coalition that hides behind a spiritual curtain, an infernal council of angelic rebels who have partnered in a desperate attempt to destroy as much of God's creation as they can before their time is up.

Part IV

Desert Storm

19

Covenant with Death

Although Islamic historians have rewritten and whitewashed many parts of their history, many descriptions of Islam from its formative years have survived. From those texts, and from the long record of Islam's dealings with the West, characteristics of the old gods shine through in the teachings of Muhammad.

By the time of his "revelation" in AD 610, most of the known world—at least, the world known to us Westerners—had abandoned polytheism for a monotheistic faith.[328] Yahweh was worshiped from Mesopotamia to Britain, while the Zoroastrians of Persia followed Ahura Mazda.

Obviously, this analysis doesn't consider the religions of the far corners of Asia, Africa, Australia, and the Americas. But since the supernatural war of rebellion is for control of the *har môʿēd*, the "mount of assembly," the lands closest to Israel are most relevant. That's why the Fallen used them to launch their counterattack.

The Arabian tribes continued to worship the old Mesopotamian gods long into the Christian era. Names changed and their roles sometimes shifted—for example, the split of the dual-gendered god/dess of sex and war Astarte/Attar into male, the war-god Ashtar, and female—either al-Lat ("the goddess"), al-'Uzza, or both. Worship of the moon-god and sun-god continued under various names, and regional gods never lost their importance to the tribes that lived on their home ground—for example, Qôs, the national god of Edom, who was adopted by the Nabataean Arabs as their national god, Dushara, when they settled in the Edomites' former territory.[329]

Alone among the peoples who lived in and around Israel in the centuries after the Resurrection, most of the tribes of Arabia, with the notable exceptions of the Ghassanids and Lakhmids in the north, retained their polytheistic paganism. They also practiced rituals that were absorbed into later Islamic doctrine, such as the annual pilgrimage to a place called the Al-Masjid al-Haram, or the "forbidden gathering place." But the real question is this: How did this new coalition of pagan gods guide Muhammad and his followers when they brought this new religion to the world?

We've discussed the connections between death and "the" god earlier in this book. In brief, the evidence suggests that this is the entity who led the rebellious Watchers to the summit of Mount Hermon, called Shemihaza in the Book of 1 Enoch. For their sin, the Watchers, the angels of Genesis 6 "which kept not their first estate,"[330] were sentenced to spend all of time until the judgment chained in darkness. Peter's description of the imprisonment of these angels in Tartarus, based on the Greek word *tartaroō*, identifies these rebels with the Titans of Greek myth. They were led by Kronos, the god who ate his children to forestall their rebellion.

Other names for this dark god over the ages include El, Enlil, Dagan, Kumarbi, Saturn, and Baal-Hammon, all of whom had some link to the realm of the dead. And the religion founded by Muhammad, which serves a corporate deity called "the god," Allah, is likewise inextricably linked to death.

It's well established that Muhammad began his ministry around

AD 610. His first ten years of preaching met with little success. It was only after his fellow Qurayshi tribesmen, tired of Muhammad preaching against their polytheistic ways, drove him and his followers away from the *masjid al-haram* to take refuge in the oasis of Yathrib (later renamed Medina) that Muhammad had an epiphany that changed everything. Even sympathetic mainstream historians acknowledge his change in tactics, although they tend to try to justify it:

> Muhammad and the emigrants from Mecca had no means of earning a living in Medina; there was not enough land for them to farm, and, in any case, they were merchants and businessmen not agriculturalists. The Medinese, who were known as the *ansar* (the helpers), could not afford to keep them gratis, so the emigrants resorted to the *ghazu*, the "raid," which was a sort of national sport in Arabia, as well as being a rough-and-ready means of redistributing resources in a land where there was simply not enough to go round.[331]

You can spot the holes in that story from thirty thousand feet. Muhammad's band was made up of merchants and businessmen, so they couldn't farm to support themselves. But somehow, almost instantly, they became a military force that conquered the Arabian Peninsula within ten years? And the practice of—let's be honest—looting property that belonged to others, called "piracy" on the high seas, was nothing more than the redistribution of resources?

It's a good bet that the people on the wrong end of the swords had a different word for it.

The "national sport" Muhammad played wasn't to keep himself and his ragged band of followers alive. The principalities and powers behind the prophet had a longer game in mind, and his first efforts hadn't yielded results quickly enough.

That Muhammad had only won over some one hundred followers after a decade of peaceful preaching in Mecca—but nearly the whole of Arabia after a decade of successful raiding, "an average of no fewer than nine campaigns annually"—speaks for itself.[332]

In a nutshell, losers in the caravan raids had two choices: death or submission—which is, after all, what "Islam" means. Submission required the recitation of the *shahada*, the first pillar of Islam: "There is no god but Allah and Muhammad is the messenger of Allah." Those who refused to submit were killed or enslaved.

However, Muhammad's instructions to his followers forbid them from taking the lives or possessions of those who chose to submit.[333] Obviously, that was a powerful tool for evangelizing. As an added incentive for new converts, Muhammad preached that the carnal rewards of a raider—wealth, slaves, and women—were even better in the afterlife for those who died during *jihad*.

"I guarantee him either admission to Paradise," said Muhammad, "or return to whence he set out with a reward or booty." As for "the martyr"—the *shahid*—he "is special to Allah," said the prophet. "He is forgiven from the first drop of blood [he sheds]. He sees his throne in paradise.... Fixed atop his head will be a crown of honor, a ruby that is greater than the world and all it contains. And he will copulate with seventy-two *Houris*."

The houris are supernatural, celestial women—"wide-eyed" and "big-bosomed," says the Koran—created by Allah for the express purpose of gratifying his favorites in perpetuity.[334]

For hot-blooded young men, this was a win-win.

Note that the rewards promised by Muhammad are all carnal, things that appeal to the flesh—food, drink, gold, and physical pleasures, a sharp contrast that with the promises of Jesus. The rewards for Muhammad's potential recruits were in terms they could easily understand. Join the army of Allah! Win the fight and take home all the loot and women you can carry! If you die, you get even *more*!

No wonder Islam overwhelmed Arabia within a decade. After a few key victories early on, it wasn't hard for any man who could wield a sword to figure out which way the wind was blowing.

For the dark, child-eating god chained up in the abyss, there must have been some satisfaction in knowing that an engine of death had been loosed on the world—one that would swiftly capture Zion and march right to the very gates of the most powerful city in Christendom.

If there is only one thing we can learn from the last fourteen hundred years of Muslim history, it's that Islam has relied on the sword for expansion since the very beginning. Remember, the faith went only as far as Muhammad's closest relatives until he revealed that Allah was not only okay with caravan raiding, but had decreed it a holy calling.

Christendom has had its share of war over the centuries, without question. But war as a tool for converting unbelievers, much less for profit, was never sanctioned in the Bible.[335] Rather than spreading the gospel by force, Jesus told His disciples to just shake the dust from their feet of a town that refused to hear their words.[336] Islam, as we noted earlier, only began its explosive growth when Muhammad began pandering to the basest instincts of men who could fight well enough to take what they wanted.

Here is where we detect the influence of the god, or gods, of war. This is an area in which several of the deities worshiped in ancient Mesopotamia had some expertise. The storm-god, Baal/Zeus, and the plague-god, Resheph/Nergal/Apollo, were warriors in their own right. They were usually depicted in a smiting pose, with one arm raised, holding a club or mace. But it's the mindless, unrestrained violence and bloodshed of the goddess Ishtar/Inanna and the war-god Chemosh/Ares/Mars behind the wars of Islamic expansion and modern Islamist suicide bombers. Those spirits have convinced millions over the centuries that shedding blood in the cause of Allah, Inc., is a holy act.

Whether the war-god was always independent or emerged as a distinct entity in his own right after Moab became an established kingdom during the Israelite sojourn in Egypt is unknown. Evidence is fragmented; the violent goddess Inanna/Ishtar was the original transgender, and by the time of the patriarchs she was worshiped in Canaan as the female sex-goddess Astarte and the war-god Attar. As we noted earlier, Moab's King Mesha called his god "Ashtar Chemosh" on the Moabite Stone, suggesting that the two were one by the ninth century BC, despite evidence for the worship of Chemosh more than fifteen hundred years earlier in northern Syria.[337] We can only speculate. Our window into the spirit realm is cloudy at best.

While Christian missionaries traveled peacefully as far as Ireland and China within a few hundred years of the Resurrection, Islam took a quicker path to grow its numbers—conversion or death. That tactic yielded many new converts, but it also spilled a lot of blood. We assume that either outcome was acceptable to the infernal council.

Within half a century of Muhammad's death in AD 632, the armies of Islam had ended the four-century rule of the Sassanid dynasty in Persia (AD 651) and besieged the capital of the Eastern Roman Empire, Constantinople (AD 674–678). A century after Muhammad's passing, a Muslim army fought the Franks led by Charles Martel at Tours, deep inside what is modern France. If the Romans or Franks had lost either one of those battles, European history—and thus American history—might be very different from the one we know.

Still, the effectiveness of the war-god's approach to spreading the message of Muhammad has been aided by the tendency of Europeans to forget who we are. We're like the man described by James, our Lord's half-brother, who walks away from a mirror and immediately can't remember his own face. Even with fourteen centuries of history as a guide, Western liberals tell us that Muslims in the Middle East hate us because of our support for Israel while conservatives believe they hate us because of our freedom.

What absolute nonsense.

In 1786, when the government of the United States still operated under the Articles of Confederation, Jefferson and Adams met with the ambassador to England from Tripoli. They sent a report of that meeting to Secretary of Foreign Affairs John Jay.

> We took the liberty to make some inquiries concerning the Grounds of their pretentions to make war upon Nations who had done them no Injury, and observed that we considered all mankind as our friends who had done us no wrong, nor had given us any provocation.
>
> The Ambassador answered us that it was founded on the Laws of their Prophet, that it was written in their Koran, that all nations who should not have acknowledged their authority were sinners, that it was their right and duty to make war upon them wherever they could be found, and to make slaves of all they could take as Prisoners, and that every Musselman who should be slain in battle was sure to go to Paradise.[338]

It's a bit surprising that educated men like Jefferson and Adams were caught off guard by the reasons for Muslim attacks on American ships and sailors. But they were products of the Enlightenment, which, in a spiritual sense, was a clever tactic by the Enemy that served in part to blind the West to the threat of Islam. Two of the most intelligent men in American history struggled to understand how anyone could take an invisible god so seriously as to use the words of his prophet as pretext for war. Centuries later, our brightest minds still ask the same question:

The first reaction to the Brussels massacres [note the bombings of March 22, 2016, that killed thirty-two and wounded three hundred] among postmodern European intellectuals was predictable: What did we, Europeans, do to them, our Muslims?[339]

It's the same answer today. All nations who have not acknowledged Allah's authority are sinners, and it's their right and duty to make war upon us wherever we can be found.

If that sounds harsh and closed-minded of me, well—too bad. Allah, Inc., is a bloodthirsty bunch of small-*g* gods who inspire their most devout followers to say things like:

> It is neither hunger nor poverty that has driven us from our land [Arabia]. We, the Arabs, are drinkers of blood and we know there is no blood more tasty than that of the Greeks. That is why we have come, to spill and to drink your blood. Khalid bin al-Walid, the "Sword of Allah"[340] (AD 636)

See if you can spot the similarity in the following statement from ISIS, issued 1,380 years later:

> Fox News reports that jihadi web sites are rejoicing over today's terrorist attacks in Paris. The line we have heard more than once from ISIS-related sites is, "The American blood is best, and we will taste it soon."[341] (AD 2015)

Khalid bin al-Walid was a companion of Muhammad and one of early Islam's most effective military leaders. He led the campaign that captured Damascus in AD 634. and the army that defeated the Roman forces at the Battle of Yarmouk in 636, which led to the fall of Jerusalem in 637. His words are echoed by violent jihadis today, fourteen centuries later. Yet "virtually no one in the West understands that they are quoting the verbatim words—and placing themselves within the footsteps—of their jihadi forbears."[342]

Even the term, "the West," has its roots in the bloody history of Islam, as it refers to the remnant of Christendom after the armies of Allah, Inc. conquered three-quarters of it.

> The West is actually the westernmost remnant of what was a much more extensive civilizational block that Islam permanently severed.... It further implies that all those "eastern" lands conquered by Islam were never part of "Western civilization," when in fact they were the original inheritors of its Greco-Roman and Christian heritage.[343]

Constantine the Great moved the capital of the Roman Empire to Byzantium, later Constantinople (and now Istanbul), in the fourth century because it was closer to most of the wealth and civilization of the Roman world. Even though Rome and the western half of the empire collapsed in the fifth century, the Eastern Roman Empire—which never called itself "Byzantine" or "Eastern," just Roman—survived for another thousand years. For most of that time, it was the most powerful economic and military force in Europe, an odd and unfamiliar fact to most of us educated in "the West."

Again, if Constantinople had fallen in AD 674—or anytime before 1453, for that matter—the history of the West would be very different. Instead, the city held out long enough against Muslim pressure for European civilization and technology to develop to the point that it was no longer possible for the Islamic world to destroy what was left of Christendom.

Oddly enough, in a scenario that's been repeated again and again over the years, disunity among the Christian defenders of Europe made it more vulnerable to attack. I won't go so far as to suggest the Reformation touched off by Martin Luther in the early sixteenth century was a bad thing, but it came at a bad time for Europe.

By portraying the Catholic pope as more of an "Antichrist" than the Ottoman sultan—an office held by Muslim leaders responsible for the slaughter and enslavement of hundreds of thousands of Christians—Luther and other Reformation leaders ushered in a sort of relativism that prevails to this day, one that cites (often distorted) episodes from Catholic history to minimize ongoing Muslim atrocities.

The Catholic Church responded with its own invective "and frequently tried to discredit Protestant doctrine by likening it to Islam—Muhammad was an early Protestant and the Protestants were latter day Saracens." It finally got to the point that both Catholics and Protestants began "heaping praise upon the infidel" in an effort to portray each other as unparalleled evil.[344]

In 1683, more than one hundred sixty years after Spain established a colony in the Americas, and more than sixty years after the Pilgrims landed at Plymouth Rock, the army of the Ottoman Empire assaulted the walls of Vienna, Austria. The Ottoman forces were led by Kara Mustafa Pasha, an Albanian Muslim who served as Grand Vizier to Sultan Mehmed IV. Mustafa was described as "fanatically anti-Christian," which seems appropriate; after capturing a Polish town in 1674, he had the citizens flayed alive and sent their stuffed hides to Mehmed.[345] The ambitious Mustafa was driven to accomplish what the famed sultan Suleiman the Magnificent had failed to do by capturing the capital of the hated Habsburg Empire.

Only the last-minute arrival of a relief army led by heroic Polish king Jan III Sobieski kept the Ottomans from taking the city and controlling key trade routes from the Mediterranean and Black seas to western Europe. Vienna was essentially the gateway to Europe; "from it, Italy (and Rome) to the south and the disunited German kingdoms to the north could easily be invaded."[346] If not for Sobieski, Saint Peter's Basilica in Rome might have been turned into a mosque decades before the American colonies declared independence.

But even after the Ottomans' defeat at Vienna, Muslim pirates made life on and around the Mediterranean dangerous. Robert C. Davis, a professor at the Ohio State University, estimated in his 2003 book *Christian Slaves, Muslim Masters* that more than one million Europeans may have been enslaved by Muslim pirates between 1530 and 1780.[347] Between 1627 and 1633, the island of Lundy, off the west coast of Britain, was occupied by the pirates as a base to launch raids on England.[348]

Yet, two of America's learned founding fathers were stunned to learn that Muslims felt entitled to confiscate the new nation's cargo ships and enslave its sailors. Thus, America's first war as a nation began even before George Washington was elected its first president. The fighting against the Muslim pirates of North Africa dragged on for more than thirty years, provoked Congress to create the United States Navy in 1794, and finally ended in 1815. One of the battles inspired the line "to the shores of Tripoli" in the "The Marines' Hymn."

Western academics often rationalize these encounters by referring to the Crusades, as though the Vatican is responsible for the violence done in the name of Allah since the twelfth century. President Barack Obama famously scolded Americans at the National Prayer Breakfast in 2015, drawing a moral equivalence between the Islamic State and the Crusades of nine hundred years ago.

"Humanity has been grappling with these questions throughout human history," he told the group, speaking of the tension between the compassionate and murderous acts religion can inspire. "And lest we get on our high horse and think this is unique to some other place, remember that during the Crusades and the Inquisition, people committed terrible deeds in the name of Christ. In our home country, slavery and Jim Crow all too often was justified in the name of Christ."[349]

The former president's view is shared by many academics, who have an inexcusable blind spot when it comes to the Crusades. When the history of post-Roman Europe is reviewed, the terms Arabic, Turk, Tatar, Moorish, or Ottoman are used easily enough, but the words "Muslim" or "Islamic" rarely appear—as though the shared religion of the forces that nearly conquered all of Christendom is coincidental. The truth is the Crusades were a response to centuries of Muslim war against the West. Yes, atrocities were committed by the Crusaders; and no, "they did it first" is not justification for those atrocities.

The difference is that only one of the two religions under discussion here has made bloodshed for profit a sacrament, and it's not the one under the banner of the cross. As Saudi journalist Abdelrahman al-Rashid wrote in 2004: "It is a certain fact that not all Muslims are terrorists, but it is equally certain, and exceptionally painful, that almost all terrorists are Muslims."[350]

The bottom line is this: War, and the booty to be gained from it, was one of the driving forces of Islamic expansion from its earliest days. The prospect of wealth from successful raiding or an eternity of carnal pleasure for dying in the attempt has enticed millions of young men over the centuries to take up the banner of *jihad*.

The blood spilled for Allah, Inc., over the last fourteen hundred years has only whetted the appetites of the old gods for revenge against the Most High. They are determined to press on until Armageddon— the final battle for the mount of assembly, Jerusalem.

20

Perversion

Taking a secondary role in the formation of Allah, Inc., must have been difficult for Ishtar. Her name isn't on the label, and besides, women generally don't get much respect in Islam.

On the other hand, Ishtar and her other incarnations—mainly Inanna (Sumer), Astarte (Canaan), and Atargatis (Syria)—didn't conform to gender roles or stereotypes, so maybe this is a better fit than it appears at first look. She was, after all, the goddess of carnal sex and bloody violence, and Islam, to be blunt, has inspired plenty of both.

We've already discussed the long history of war since Muhammad led his first caravan raid, so we won't cover that again. No doubt the spirit behind Ishtar was all in with that business model. It's her other aspect, and the perverse sexuality that she's inspired among the followers of Muhammad, that we will discuss here as delicately as we can.

One of the most disturbing episodes of America's seemingly never-ending war in Afghanistan was revealed by the *New York Times* in 2015.

In his last phone call home, Lance Cpl. Gregory Buckley Jr. told his father what was troubling him: From his bunk in southern Afghanistan, he could hear Afghan police officers sexually abusing boys they had brought to the base.

"At night we can hear them screaming, but we're not allowed to do anything about it," the Marine's father, Gregory Buckley Sr., recalled his son telling him before he was shot to death at the base in 2012. He urged his son to tell his superiors. "My son said that his officers told him to look the other way because it's their culture."[351]

The *Times* went on to reveal that a former Special Forces captain had been relieved of his command for beating up a US-backed militia commander "for keeping a boy chained to his bed as a sex slave."[352] The soldier had left the military by the time of the article's publication. Worse, the Army tried to forcibly retire a second soldier, a decorated Green Beret sergeant, who assisted his captain in that thrashing,[353] presumably to make sure the message was received: *Rape the boy again and things will not go well for you.*

Maybe the war in Afghanistan is still simmering after more than seventeen years as of this writing because our so-called allies treat the locals worse than the Taliban did.

It's not like this has been a secret. Less than five months after the United States invaded Afghanistan, the *Times* reported that it was this homosexual abuse of young boys that actually helped the Taliban come to power.

Back in the 19th century, ethnic Pashtuns fighting in Britain's colonial army sang odes talking of their longing for young boys.

Homosexuality, cloaked in the tradition of strong masculine bonds that are a hallmark of Islamic culture and are even more pronounced in southern Afghanistan's strict, sexually segregated society, has long been a clandestine feature of life here. But pedophilia has been its curse.

Though the puritanical Taliban tried hard to erase pedophilia from male-dominated Pashtun culture, now that the Ministry for the Promotion of Virtue and Prevention of Vice is gone, some people here are indulging in it once again....

An interest in relationships with young boys among warlords and their militia commanders played a part in the Taliban's rise in Afghanistan. In 1994, the Taliban, then a small army of idealistic students of the Koran, were called to rescue a boy over whom two commanders had fought. They freed the boy and the people responded with gratitude and support.[354]

In January 2018, the Special Inspector General for Afghanistan Reconstruction (SIGAR) published the results of an investigation into allegations of child sexual abuse in Afghanistan launched after the 2015 article in the *New York Times*. The report was released internally in June 2017, but it had been considered so toxic that it was originally classified SECRET/NOFORN ("No Foreign"), with a recommendation that it not be declassified until 2042.[355] While the report released to the public is heavily redacted, it does reveal that SIGAR found "no evidence that U.S. forces were told to ignore human rights abuses or child sexual assault."[356] Further, SIGAR reported:

On 5,753 occasions from 2010 to 2016, the United States military asked to review Afghan military units to see if there were any instances of "gross human rights abuses." If there were, American law required military aid to be cut off to the offending unit.

Not once did that happen.[357]

What a relief. We'd hate to think the seventy-one billion dollars we've given to Afghan security forces forces[358] was being misused.

Or maybe the Inspector General decided there weren't any "gross human rights abuses" because "it's their culture." The practice is so widespread that a powerful CIA-backed warlord ran for president in Afghanistan's 2014 election even though many believe he's a pedophile.[359]

The practice is called *bacha bazi*. Roughly translated, it means "boy play." It is exactly what your imagination tells you it is—the enslavement and rape of young boys.[360]

It's difficult to say with absolute authority, but a culture that prevents men from ever seeing anything but the feet of wives or close female relatives might have something to do with it. How did this culture come about?

Well, there are well-known verses in the Quran hint at "boy play" as one of the rewards for the faithful in paradise.

There will circulate among them [servant] boys [especially] for them, as if they were pearls well-protected. (Surah At Tur 52:24, Sahih International)

There will circulate among them young boys made eternal. When you see them, you would think them [as beautiful as] scattered pearls. (Surah Al-Insan 76:19, Sahih International)

While those verses don't specifically *say* what the young boys are for, they're ambiguous enough to keep good lawyers employed for years.

To be fair, the Bedouin culture that produced Muhammad and his companions was very similar to the Amorite milieu that surrounded Abraham, Isaac, and Jacob,[361] or the people of Midian with whom Moses sought refuge when he had to get out of Egypt.[362] While Bedouins protect the honor of young ladies, the old custom of allowing wealthy and powerful older men to take multiple wives and concubines makes it more difficult for single young men to find available female partners. You can see how this might encourage the practice of homosexuality in early Muslim society.[363] Scholars of literature have noted "an unusually rich and varied body of homosexual love poetry" from the early years of Islam.[364]

This culture endures to the present day. It's not unique to Afghanistan. Several news organizations have reported that sexual abuse of boys is common in Pakistan, especially among professional truck drivers. Boys employed as truck cleaners in Pakistan told researchers that sexual abuse by truckers is "part of the job."[365] A 2014 British documentary, *Pakistan's Hidden Shame*, revealed the shocking extent of the practice; it's estimated that 90 percent of the street children in Pakistan, most of them boys (parents, not surprisingly, tend to keep little girls at home), have been victims of sexual abuse. A survey of eighteen hundred Pakistani men found that one-third believe that raping young boys isn't even immoral.[366]

No less an authority than the would-be Mahdi of the Islamic State, Abu Bakr al-Baghdadi, advised his followers via a *fatwa* posted to Twitter that "it is permissible for the mujahid [jihadi] to enjoy young boys in the absence of women."[367]

Nice. And the abuse isn't limited to young boys.

The influx of Pakistanis into England in recent years recently forced the British government to confront an unpleasant reality: About fourteen hundred girls in the northern town of Rochdale, some as young as 13 and most of whom were white,[368] were groomed, abused, and trafficked by what the media usually described as "Asian" men. That editorial choice concealed, for a while, the fact that most of the men in the grooming ring were, in fact, Pakistanis—and Muslims.

Nine men were eventually convicted and jailed, and three ringleaders, convicted of conspiracy to engage in sexual activity with children under the age of 16 and trafficking for sexual exploitation, were stripped of their UK citizenship in 2018.[369] It would be nice to report that these men were outliers, evil exceptions to the Muslim rule. But they're not.

Even liberal media in the US couldn't ignore some of the Islamic

State's most outrageous behavior, like auctions of women and girls as young as eight captured from Christian and Yazidi communities in Iraq and Syria.[370] But this wasn't out of character for historic Islam. On the contrary, it was a *return* to historic Islam.

> Starting in the mid-600s and for nearly three centuries thereafter, "Viking raids were elicited by the Muslim demand for white-skinned European slaves." Indeed, it is "impossible to disconnect Islam from the Viking slave-trade," argues M. A. Khan, a former Muslim from India, "because the supply was absolutely meant for meeting [the] Islamic world's unceasing demand for the prized white slaves" and for "white sex-slaves." Emmet Scott goes so far as to argue that "it was the caliphate's demand for European slaves that called forth the Viking phenomenon in the first place."[371]

Get your head around that. The Vikings who terrorized Europe for centuries were motivated by the Muslim demand for European slaves, especially sex-slaves.

The Hudson Institute reported in 2015 that girls age nine and under drew the highest prices at ISIS auctions.[372] Should this be a surprise? It's well known from Muslim sources that Muhammad's third wife Aisha, his favorite, was six years old when they married and nine when the marriage was consummated.[373] Muslim apologists have tried to whitewash this over the last century or so, but this information comes from the *hadith*, sayings attributed to Muhammad or his companions, and Aisha herself is the one who remembered being married off as a nine-year-old.

ISIS didn't hijack Islam. They're trying to return it to its roots. Rather than admit that Muhammad had serious issues with sexuality, some Islamic scholars tie themselves into moral knots justifying deviant behavior—including necrophilia.[374]

If we're brutally honest, the biggest change from the earliest days of Islam is that instead of buying sex slaves from Europe, Muslim men, thanks to the EU's open-minded immigration policies, are now being imported by Europeans to pick out their own victims. On New Year's Eve of 2015, Germany was shocked when some twelve hundred women were assaulted by about two thousand men in Cologne, Hamburg, and Frankfurt,[375] including twenty-four alleged rapes in Cologne.[376]

> Even more remarkable has been the response. First, the German authorities misleadingly reported merely a small handful of attacks by German-speaking men with no evidence of immigrant involvement. Then social media, and the Breitbart news website, started to report the victims' graphic testimony and a very different picture emerged. In Cologne women were sexually assaulted and both men and women robbed by a throng of migrants a thousand strong. The victims identified virtually all these attackers as of north African, Arab or "dark" appearance.[377]

We could belabor the point, but you get it. The roles of men, women, and children in Islam are fundamentally different than those described in the Bible.[378]

There is no question that Christian societies have never been free from the evil of sexual perversion, including abuse of children and violence toward women, but it's also clear that the Bible instructs men to protect and cherish women and children. While women are instructed to respect their husbands, men are commanded to love their wives the way Christ loved the church.[379] That means being prepared and willing to give up everything—including our lives.

Since Jesus defined adultery as simply lusting after a woman who is not a man's spouse, the type of abuse suffered by women and children at the hands of men—Muslim, Christian, or other—cannot be reconciled with the teachings of Jesus.

And that's the point. Through the perversion of sexuality, Allah, Inc., has been deconstructing the divine order God decreed at Mount Sinai—the foundation of human society, and the smallest battle formation in the spiritual war, the family.

21

The Yoke of Sharia

One of the most striking things about Islam is that sincere conversion doesn't matter to Allah, Inc. Muhammad himself taught that a captive only needed to speak the words of the *shahada* to avoid enslavement or death. Faith didn't enter into it. Making submission (Islam) to Muhammad was your ticket into the club.[380]

This is 180 degrees removed from the teachings of Jesus. He taught His disciples that it wasn't the rules they followed that saved them, but His grace offered to those who believed that He died for their sins, rose again on the third day, and accepted Him as Lord and Savior.[381]

Killing or enslaving people who wouldn't convert wasn't part of the Great Commission, either.

In its approach to the faith, Islam reflects the legalistic spirit that was attributed to the ancient sun-god, called Utu in Sumer, Shamash in Babylon, and Shemesh in Hebrew. As we noted previously, although the neighboring Canaanites called the solar deity Shapash, he was a she in Canaan for reasons we just don't know.

The great Amorite king Hammurabi of Babylon recorded his famous law code on a stela that features an inscription of Shamash handing the law to Hammurabi. Now, society need laws; besides making it possible for citizens to lead peaceful lives, a legal authority that enforces contracts is critical to economic growth and prosperity. Investors don't like to risk money where they can't bank on returns.

But building a bridge between this world and the next is different. Alone among the world's religions, the followers of Christ have been taught that there is nothing we can do to cross the divide that separates us from an eternal reward. Salvation is by faith alone, because "none is righteous; no, not one."[382] In a revolutionary departure from the Jewish origins of the faith, first-century Christians, most of them Jews, were taught that even the Law given to Moses was powerless to save them.

> Now if perfection had been attainable through the Levitical priesthood (for under it the people received the law), what further need would there have been for another priest to arise after the order of Melchizedek [i.e., Jesus], rather than one named after the order of Aaron? For when there is a change in the priesthood, there is necessarily a change in the law as well.…
>
> For on the one hand, a former commandment is set aside because of its weakness and uselessness (for the law made nothing perfect); but on the other hand, a better hope is introduced, through which we draw near to God. (Hebrews 7:11–13, 18–19)

The 613 *mitzvot*, or commandments, derived from what Christians call the Old Testament by learned rabbis like Maimonides, a twelfth-century Torah scholar, were summed up by Jesus of Nazareth in just two.

> And he said to him, "You shall love the Lord your God with all your heart and with all your soul and with all your mind.

This is the great and first commandment. And a second is like it: You shall love your neighbor as yourself. On these two commandments depend all the Law and the Prophets." (Matthew 22:36–40)

Paul emphasized the point:

For the whole law is fulfilled in one word: "You shall love your neighbor as yourself." (Galatians 5:14)

Keeping the Law has no power to save us from our sins, but keeping the commands of Allah and belief in his "oneness," a practice called *tawhid*, is the only hope of salvation for Muslims. Even then, they can't be sure of their eternal destination.[383]

Sadly, since legalism is the bedrock of Islam, Muhammad and Islamic legal experts over the centuries have gone to disturbing lengths to justify bad behavior like theft, killing, and slavery, which, after all, was the whole point of caravan raids and the wars of conquest after Muhammad's death.

The Quran does forbid unlawful sexual intercourse, but men are allowed four wives and married women captured in war.[384] Then there is the odd solution that scholars in the Twelver Shiia sect devised that allows men to satisfy their lusts outside of marriage—the *nikah mut'ah*, or "pleasure marriage." It's a short-term contract to have sex for pay without committing fornication, justified by a single verse in the Quran.

And [also prohibited to you are all] married women except those your right hands possess. [This is] the decree of Allah upon you. And lawful to you are [all others] beyond these, [provided] that you seek them [in marriage] with [gifts from] your property, desiring chastity, not unlawful sexual intercourse. So for whatever you enjoy [of marriage] from them, give them their due compensation as an obligation. And there is no blame upon you for what you mutually agree to beyond the obligation. Indeed, Allah is ever Knowing and Wise. (Surah 4:24, Sahih International)

Sunnis dispute with Twelver Shia over this verse—not whether it allows pleasure marriages, but whether Muhammad later rescinded his permission for "pleasure wives." Sunnis say yes, Twelvers say no.[385] (One Sunni imam from Manhattan told a reporter that *mut'ah* marriages are "prostitution with a religious stamp.")[386] But either way, why was it allowed in the first place?

The answer seems obvious: to give a "holy" rationale for the pursuit of carnal pleasure. Hey, that's what made Islam popular in the first place.

Another disturbing aspect of the legalistic spirit who sits on the board of Allah, Inc., is that it persuaded Muhammad to teach that deception, trickery, and outright lying is a holy calling as long as it's in the service of Islam. The practice is called *taqiyyah*.

Koran 3:28 is one of the primary verses that sanction *taqiyya*: "Let believers [Muslims] not take infidels [non-Muslims] for friends and allies instead of believers. Whoever does this shall have no relationship left with Allah—except when taking precaution against them in prudence." Al-Tabari (d. 923), author of a mainstream Koran commentary, offers the following exegesis of 3:28: "If you [Muslims] are under their [non-Muslims'] authority, fearing for yourselves, behave loyally to them with your tongue while harboring inner animosity for them...[know that] Allah has forbidden believers from being friendly or on intimate terms with the infidels rather than other believers— except when infidels are above them [in authority]. Should that be the case, let them act friendly towards them while preserving their religion."[387]

So, according to their holy book, it's perfectly okay for Muslims to lie, as long as it's to non-Muslims—although, because of the long, bitter rivalry between Sunni and Shia, the minority Shia have often relied on *taqiyya* to hide their faith in Sunni communities to avoid persecution.[388]

Remind me again—why is Muslim immigration into Europe and the Americas a good idea? I don't mean to spread fear or distrust without cause, but seriously, when this is a mainstream interpretation of verses in their holy book, how can any promise of loyalty or goodwill be believed?

Look, all of us rationalize to some degree. Every day, we do things we know we shouldn't or could have done better, or we fail to do things we should. We constantly rewrite the script of the movie playing inside our heads to make ourselves worthy of the starring role. It's easier to get through the day when we can picture ourselves as heroes.

In the same way, patriotic Americans want to see our nation as a force for good in the world, even though a lot of places would be better off if we'd left them alone.

Likewise, Islam has established a legal system that allows its adherents to claim that it's a religion of peace and ethics, built on law. A close examination of its moral code says different. Whereas the Bible forbids adultery, lying, stealing, and coveting your neighbor's stuff, Muhammad and the Islamic scholars who interpreted his revelations have crafted a legal framework that allows all of these actions and attitudes while maintaining a pretense of holiness.

According to Jesus, even harboring thoughts of lust or hatred breaks the commandments against adultery and murder—an impossible standard, which is why His atoning sacrifice on the cross was necessary. Muslims, on the other hand, are free to fantasize all they want. By not acting on their dreams fueled by lust, hatred, or jealousy, they're actually doing *good* and earning the favor of Allah.

There is no way around this conclusion: By following the teachings of Islam, Muslims are freely and openly sinning in the eyes of God.

It can be disheartening to realize how radically different Islam is from the gospel of Jesus Christ. Think of the billions of Muslims who have been led to destruction by Allah, Inc., over the last fourteen hundred years. Jesus died and rose from the dead for them, too—although, sadly, Muhammad rejected both the death and Resurrection of Christ.[389]

The principalities and powers behind Allah, Inc., have been playing a long game of *taqiyya* on the Islamic world. Sadly, "I was misinformed," will not be an acceptable excuse in front of the Great White Throne.

22

The Baal

By AD 630, only eight years after Muhammad implemented his radical new approach to evangelizing, the armies of Islam had conquered the city that chased them out into the desert. The sacred city—probably Petra rather than Mecca—belonged to Islam.

This accomplished two things for Muhammad. First, it gave him control of a major pilgrimage site. The merchants of Arabia had been forced to refocus their trade on leather goods and serving as middle men for Indian spice dealers when the demand for incense disappeared in the Christian era. Dealing leather and spices was not a business that produced the kind of wealth enjoyed by the Nabataeans of five hundred years earlier.[390]

Second, capturing the holy city put Muhammad in position to preach to pagan pilgrims from all over Arabia and the Levant. The *hajj* was an old custom even in Muhammad's day,[391] and if Epiphanius' description of the rituals of the Nabataean god Dushara is correct, pilgrims had been coming to Petra and its *ka'ba* for at least two hundred and fifty years by the time of Muhammad's victory.

When his forces entered the city, one of Muhammad's first acts was to destroy the idols in the Ka'ba. Johann Burckhardt, the Swiss adventurer who rediscovered Petra for the Western world in 1812, wrote after his visit to Mecca that three hundred and sixty idols had adorned the Ka'ba, presumably one for each day of the year.[392] As noted earlier, this tracks with the recent tally of more than five hundred betyls in Petra.

Islamic records agree that one of the three hundred sixty was considered supreme. Their histories record that an early leader of the Khuza'a tribe named Amr ibn Luhayy obtained an idol of Hubal in Hit, a city northwest of Baghdad in what is now Iraq's Anbar province, and installed it in the Ka'ba,[393] probably in the third century AD.[394] It appears the Khuza'a became guardians of the Ka'ba when the power of the Nabataeans waned, and they retained that power until the Quraysh, Muhammad's tribe, took over as protectors (and beneficiaries) of the shrine in the fifth century.[395]

Until now, historians have generally agreed that during the three or four centuries between ibn Luhayy and Muhammad, worship at the Ka'ba had turned from Hubal to Allah.

> Officially, the shrine was dedicated to Hubal, a Nabatean deity, and there were 360 idols arranged around the Kabah, probably representing the days of the year. But by Muhammad's day, it seems that the Kabah was venerated as the shrine of Allah, the High God.[396]

That's mainly taken as a given by readers of Islamic history. However, it's not clear why a god who was worshiped in what is now Syria and Iraq should become the most prominent god in Mecca, which is a long way away, or why Allah later overtook Hubal as chief of the Meccan pantheon by the time of Muhammad.

We already addressed the latter question in a previous chapter; the polytheist Arabs did not house more than one male idol per shrine.

Muhammad's grandfather prayed to Allah while standing next to the idol of Hubal; thus, Allah *was* Hubal. And if the original Ka'ba was in Petra, much closer to Damascus than to the heart of the Arabian Peninsula, then the worship of a god known mainly in Syria makes a lot more sense.

It also identifies Hubal/Allah as Dushara. But we still don't know much about Hubal. Etymology to the rescue.

> The name for this god was "Hubal," without the *ayin*. This would seem to indicate that his origin was from among a dialect group which used the *bl*-form, and which also used the *ha/hn*-article. Dialects like these found representation in the northern Hijaz and Syrian areas.[397]

In other words, the form of the name "Hubal" points to his origin far to the north of Mecca, which is at the southern end of the Hejaz. That's seven hundred miles or more from the northern Hejaz and Syrian areas, which is where Petra is located.

If we take an *ayin*, the Hebrew character that looks like a reverse apostrophe, and add it to "Hubal" we arrive at *Huba'al*—and suddenly things make sense.

> The name Hubal, then, begins to be comprehensible to us, seeing as there is no sound argument against understanding Hubal to be a *ba'al*. Hubal appears late on the scene, relatively speaking. We do not see any real evidence for his existence until the time of the Nabataeans, and from there he goes wherever the Arabs go—to Palmyra, the Hijaz, and so forth. The name, itself, seems to suggest that it originally was a title or epithet of a high god. Hubal means "THE lord," seeming almost as if to differentiate him from others who might conceivably be given that title.[398]

So, Hubal was "the *ba'al*." Well, now. Things just became a whole lot clearer. Remember, we connected Hubal to the national god of Edom, Qôs. It seems odd that Qôs is never mentioned in the Bible, while the prophets had some choice words for the national gods of Ammon and Moab. But maybe he *is* there and we just haven't recognized him.

The root word behind Qôs is the Arabic *qaus*, meaning "bow."[399] This appears to be a reference to the powers of the storm-god since the same root word appears in God's covenant with Noah.

I have set my **bow** in the cloud, and it shall be a sign of the covenant between me and the earth. (Genesis 9:13, emphasis added)

While the Hebrew *qešet* does mean the bow of a warrior, in this context it suggests that we're on the right track: Qôs may have been the Edomite name for the West Semitic storm-god, Hadad—Baal. *The* Baal, or Hubal.

Here's another connection: Hubal was the god of oracles or divination. Worshipers seeking guidance, like Muhammad's grandfather, would ask questions of the god at the Ka'ba by consulting a group of seven arrows marked with words—sort of a low-tech Magic 8 Ball.

This practice connects Hubal and the Ka'ba to several partners in Allah, Inc.—the storm-god, one of the gods of divination in ancient Mesopotamia (although with animal guts instead of arrows), and the arrows link Hubal both to Qôs and to Resheph/Apollo, the archer, who was the god of oracles in the Greek world.

Worship of this god appears to have begun in what is now southern Jordan, the heartland of the biblical Edom.[400] A mountain named Jabal al-Qaus sits about fifty-five miles south-southeast of Petra, near the modern border with Saudi Arabia. The point is this: If Qôs, the god of ancient Edom who became Dushara to the Nabataeans, was the god behind Hubal in the Ka'ba, it supports the theory that Islam began not in Mecca, hundreds of miles to the south in Arabia, but at Petra, a (black) stone's throw from Jerusalem.

But wait—there's more!

We've suggested already that Qôs might be identified with the storm-god, Baal, because of the link between *qaus* ("bow") and the rainbow. Baal, who was originally called Hadad ("Thunderer"), was king of the West Semitic gods.

At Ugarit, religious texts name three daughters of Baal: Pidray, Tallay, and Arsay.[401] This is another link in the chain that binds Baal, Hubal, and Allah: The "Satanic verses," Surah 53:19–20, name al-Lat, al-Uzza, and Manat as daughters of Allah.[402]

Early in his career, trying to reconcile with the leaders of his Quraysh tribe, Muhammad softened his monotheistic doctrine and rebranded the three major pre-Islamic Arabic goddesses as angels[403] whose "intercession is accepted with approval."[404] While the Quraysh were delighted,[405] Jibril later revealed to Muhammad that Satan had tempted the would-be prophet to insert those verses into the revelation of God.

Oops.

A temple to al-ʿUzzā, the Temple of the Winged Lions, sits right across the Colonnaded Street in Petra from the Temple of Dushara (Hubal/Baal/Allah). Muslim history remembers her as one of the most important deities to the Quraysh,[406] another piece of evidence supporting the theory that Islam originated at Petra rather than Mecca.

If we're correct, then the storm-god was part of the supernatural coalition that banded together in the deserts southeast of Jerusalem and the Dead Sea. But he was more than just a weather deity; the Bible IDs him as one of the most dangerous rebels of the infernal council.

It was well known in the ancient world that Baal's palace was located on Mount Zaphon. Today, it's called Jebel al-Aqra, an imposing mountain on Turkey's Mediterranean coast just north of the border with Syria. Its peak is more than fifty-two hundred feet above sea level, and it was sacred to nearly every version of the storm-god in the ancient Near

East—Baal, Teshub, Tarhunz, and Zeus. Even though the Greek storm-god ruled from Olympus, Zaphon is where he defeated the chaos-god, Typhon, whose desperate efforts to dodge the thunderbolts of Zeus, the story goes, dug the channel of the Orontes River.

We tell you all of that so you'll understand the significance of this famous passage from Isaiah.

> How art thou fallen from heaven, O Lucifer, son of the morning!
> How art thou cut down to the ground, which didst weaken the nations!
> For thou hast said in thine heart, I will ascend into heaven,
> I will exalt my throne above the stars of God:
> I will sit also upon the mount of the congregation, in the sides of the north:
> I will ascend above the heights of the clouds; I will be like the most High. (Isaiah 14:12–14, KJV)

I usually read the English Standard Version, but I want to emphasize that the prophet was referring to the divine rebel here. In verse 13, the Hebrew phrase rendered "sides of the north," *yarkete tsaphon*, is only used three places in the Bible: Here, in Isaiah 14, to describe Lucifer's "mount of the congregation"; in Psalm 48, where the psalmist compares Zion with Zaphon, to demonstrate that God's "mount of the congregation" is superior; and in the apocalyptic prophecy of the war led by Gog of Magog—the Antichrist—in Ezekiel 38 and 39.

Some English-language Bible translators recognized the significance of Mount Zaphon:

> You said to yourself,
> "I will climb up to the sky.
> Above the stars of El
> I will set up my throne.

**I will rule on the mountain of assembly
on the remote slopes of Zaphon."** (Isaiah 14:13, NET, emphasis
added)

You said in your heart,
"I will ascend to the heavens;
I will raise my throne
above the stars of God;
I will sit enthroned on the mount of assembly,
on the utmost heights of Mount Zaphon." (Isaiah 14:13, NIV,
emphasis added)

This long war, from Eden until today, has been fought for control
of the mount of assembly, or mount of the congregation. In Hebrew,
the phrase is *har mô'ēd*, which underlies the Greek word rendered into
English as "Armageddon" in Revelation 16:16. The fight is for the *har
mô'ēd*, and the prize is Zion—Jerusalem.

In a nutshell, Isaiah, Ezekiel, and the psalmist weren't writing about
someplace in the *physical* north (although Mount Zaphon is north of
Israel). Zaphon was the home base of the greatest supernatural enemy of
the people of God in the Bible. How do we know? Because Jesus specifically linked the storm-god to Satan.

But when the Pharisees heard it, they said, "It is only by Beelzebul,
the prince of demons, that this man casts out demons." Knowing
their thoughts, he said to them, "Every kingdom divided against
itself is laid waste, and no city or house divided against itself will
stand. And if Satan casts out Satan, he is divided against himself.
How then will his kingdom stand?" (Matthew 12:24–26)

"Beelzebul" means "Baal the prince (of demons)." Later, in Revelation 2:13, Jesus calls the city of Pergamum in western Turkey the place

"where Satan's throne is" and "where Satan dwells." This was probably a reference to the Altar of Zeus in the acropolis of Pergamum. Zeus was the storm-god, like Baal, and thus he is also Satan/Lucifer.

We've hit you with a lot of names in this chapter. To summarize, the evidence points to Zeus, Baal (Hadad), Qôs, Dushara, and Hubal being the same entity—the storm-god, who Jesus identified as Satan, the divine rebel who was ejected from Eden, "the holy mountain of God."[407]

And since Hubal was "lord of the Ka'ba," then Satan himself is part of Allah, Inc.

That begs the question: Why would Satan partner with anyone? It's inconsistent with what we've been taught about the devil. He's the one whose unrestrained pride in his beauty and splendor led him to imagine that he could exalt himself above the stars (i.e., the angels) of God.

True. But he's also not stupid. Cooperating with other rebels, at least for now, is his last, best chance to make himself "like the Most High."

23

From Hermon to Mecca

This finally brings us back to the moon-god. After documenting the powerful influence of the other gods in the ancient pantheon on the religion of Muhammad, what can possibly be left that we can lay at the feet of Sîn?

Ritual. Remember from an earlier chapter we described the *akiti* festival at ancient Ur, a festival that involved ritual circumambulation of the fields. This practice dates to at least 2500 BC. We speculated that it may have originated even earlier than that, based on the spiral wall around the summit of Mount Hermon, apparently for ritual purposes, that Sir Charles Warren described in his 1869 report for the Palestine Exploration Fund.

Warren, a brilliant man, speculated on the connection between Hermon and the holy city of Islam.

> Hermon, no doubt, as being pre-eminent among the high places of Syria and Palestine, must have been the scene of the ancient worship: its stone oval may have been for the same purpose as that of the Kaaba at Mecca.[408]

Warren then cites the report of Johann Burckhardt, the Swiss explorer who brought Petra to the attention of the West in 1812.

> The devotee then begins the *Towaf* or walk round the Kaaba, keeping that building on his left hand. This ceremony is to be repeated seven times...[409]
>
> Prior to the age of Mohammed, when idolatry prevailed in Arabia, the Kaaba was regarded as a sacred object, and visited with religious veneration by persons who performed the *Towaf* nearly in the same manner as their descendants do at present.... The Mohammedan Hadj or pilgrimage, and the visit to the Kaaba, are, therefore, nothing more than a continuation and confirmation of the ancient custom.[410]

In an earlier chapter, we learned that the fourth-century bishop Eplphanius connected pagan rituals at Alexandria and Petra. The former involved worshipers circling an idol of a virgin goddess (a *ka'iba*) seven times; the latter required the faithful to circle the idol of Dushara, a stone cube—a *ka'ba*.

Warren then added an intriguing note in his report, suggesting another connection between the Ka'ba and Mount Hermon.

> It appears possible that Hermon may be one of the holy mountains spoken of in the Mohammedan mythology. Burckhardt tells us (vol. i. p. 297), with reference to Adam building the Kaaba, that "he collected the stones for the building from the five holy mountains—Lebanon, Tor Syna (Mount Sinai), El Djoudy [Ararat], Hirra, or Djibel Nour, and Tor Zeyt." The sheikh of the mosque at Jerusalem tells me that Tor Zeyt is the Mount of Olives, considered holy by them because Isa [Jesus] ascended from it; if this is the case, then this myth would be of later origin than the Christian era. Perhaps by Lebanon, Mount

Hermon is intended, and the stone oval may have some connection with the *towaf* of the Kaaba.

Of the five holy mountains, we have those on which the ark rested, the law was given and from which Isa ascended: this disposed of three; the fourth, Hura, or Gibl Nour, at Mecca, the scene of some local tradition; and the fifth, Lebanon. How comes the latter to be classed among the five, unless it is on account of its connection with some pagan tradition?[411]

It would be interesting, to say the least, if the black stone in the Ka'ba came from Mount Hermon, but the relevant point is the pagan ritual that connects Mount Hermon to the Ka'ba—counterclockwise circumambulation of a sacred site.

We can't know for sure, of course, but at the very least it appears that Muhammad incorporated into his new religion old pagan traditions that had been practiced in Arabia, and specifically Petra, for centuries at least, and in Mesopotamia for millennia. Petra, at the south end of the Jordan Rift Valley, was well within traveling distance of the high place on the summit of Mount Hermon.

To be fair, Christians also have a long history of adopting pagan practices. There is nothing in the Bible about praying to saints (that's from the Greek hero cults, which in turn came from Canaanite worship of the Rephaim),[412] exchanging wedding bands (that's from ancient Egypt), or contemplative prayer (Eastern mysticism). But circumstantial evidence points to an archaic ritual that Muhammad may not have recognized as coming from the pagan gods he thought he was rejecting, a rite with a very long pedigree—one that's documented three thousand years before the birth of Islam at the city of the moon-god, Ur in ancient Sumer.

And it may go all the way back to the Watchers on Mount Hermon.

I have no doubt that Muslims and open-minded people of other faiths will find this chapter particularly hard to accept, and maybe even to take seriously. That's fine. If I had read what I just wrote twenty-five years ago, I would have either laughed at the conspiracy nutball author or I'd have been disturbed that such closed-minded people drew breath on this earth. If someone had told me twenty-five years ago that *I* would be writing this stuff, I would have demanded an apology.

Well, we live and learn.

Jesus really meant it when He said that He was the only path to heaven. He backed it up by predicting His own Resurrection, and then fulfilling the prophecy. Without the testimony of the eyewitnesses to the risen Jesus, this book could be filed alongside the "ancient alien" stuff in the paranormal section of the bookstore.

But He did come back. This isn't a book of apologetics, and there are scholars far more qualified than me to give you the proofs, but the bottom line is the Resurrection is one of the best-attested historical events of the classical era. No serious scholar doubts the historicity of Jesus, although they may deny His divinity. Fair enough; the evidence convinced me. What you do with it is up to you.

So, everything Jesus confirmed, like the Old Testament, is likewise true, and teachings about the nature of the spirit realm from the apostles in the New Testament have to be taken seriously as well. When Paul used words like "principalities," "powers," "thrones," "dominions," and "rulers," he wasn't talking about Roman or Jewish politicians. When the Hebrew prophets railed against Baal, Asherah, El, and the Rephaim, they weren't condemning figments of pagan imagination. And when Peter and Jude referred to the angels who sinned, they were writing about ancient entities who are bound in chains right now, as you read this, in pitch darkness.

It took some years for me to get from a squishy "all roads lead to heaven" theology to grasping the implications of the historical fact of the Resurrection. If Jesus is the *only* way, then all the other ways must be... wrong. That makes life easier and a lot more difficult at the same time; it's easier to know the path to follow, but it's also easier not to not offend people when you play the post-modern "No Absolute Truth" card—you know, "This is *my* truth, but it may not be true for you."

What drivel. To paraphrase Ravi Zacharias, when you cross the street, it's either you or the bus. Not both.

Here is truth: It's either Jesus or nothing.

So, when we consider how the religions of the ancient world were transformed after the Resurrection, it seems self-evident that they must have been shaped in response to Jesus' shocking victory over death. The principalities and powers were shocked. If they'd known what was coming on the morning of the third day, "they would not have crucified the Lord of glory."[413]

Quoting Isaiah, Paul wrote:

What no eye has seen, nor ear heard, nor the heart of man imagined, what God has prepared for those who love him. (1 Corinthians 2:9)

With our human senses, we cannot imagine what God has prepared for us. Clearly, the rebel gods, the coalition that's gathered a following more than a billion and a half strong under the sign of the crescent moon, weren't expecting what happened, either.

Though they can study His Word with supernatural intellects far older and more powerful than we can imagine, they still cannot perceive the "secret and hidden wisdom of God," which has been decreed and will inevitably come to pass according to His will.

What's coming is beyond awesome, and I mean that in the original sense of the word—overwhelming, beyond the human capacity to grasp, and unprecedented in history.

What lies ahead is the end of history—the death of the gods.

Part Five

The Oracle Concerning Arabia

24

How This All Ends

U p to this point in the book, we've dealt with history. Some of it is documented, and some is necessarily speculative. We can only guess as to what's happened in the spirit realm. But while history can help us understand how we got to where we are, it's perfectly natural if you're asking right about now, "So what? How does this affect me?"

That's what we'll try to figure out from here on, using Bible prophecy as a road map—even though it's one we're reading in a mirror with insufficient light.

Here are a few assumptions about the end times that are behind the analysis you'll read in the forthcoming pages:

- Apocalyptic prophecy in the Bible has yet to be fulfilled. I do not subscribe to a preterist view of prophecy; Nero was not the Antichrist of the end times.
- The seventy weeks of Daniel 9:24–27 refers to seventy seven-year periods. That clock began ticking when Artaxerxes I, king of Persia, issued a decree to rebuild Jerusalem in 445 BC.[414]

- We are currently in a period between the sixty-ninth week, when "an anointed one shall be cut off" (the crucifixion of Jesus),[415] and the seventieth, when all hell breaks loose.

The Hebrew for "anointed one" is *mashiach* (Messiah), so Daniel 9:25 is a clear prophecy of the coming of Jesus.

Sixty-nine "sevens" equals 483 years. From 445 BC, that would put the crucifixion at AD 37. (483–445, minus one more because there is no Year Zero), a bit too late for the best estimate of the date of Jesus birth, September 11, 3 BC.[416]

However, the Babylonian calendar year was 360 days. Sixty-nine "sevens" times 360 equals 173,880 days. Dividing that number by a 365-day year and adjusting for leap years, Daniel prophesied the death of the Messiah in AD 30,[417] when Jesus was about thirty-three.[418]

We are still waiting for the final events of the age, which will begin with "the prince who is to come," the Antichrist, making "a strong covenant with many for one week." That week is the final seven-year period before the Day of the Lord.

There are other assumptions about the interpretation of the images and symbols used by the prophets, but we'll deal with those as we get to them. Daniel's seventy weeks is the big one, the foundation of most systems for understanding the timeline of end-times prophecy.

One last thing: As I noted earlier, we must always remember we're looking "through a glass, darkly."[419] That's by design. God is not called Lord of Hosts—Yahweh of Armies—for nothing. Much of prophecy will remain hidden from our understanding until the events are right on top of us.

Why? Because the rebel spirits would love to have that information too, to spin a really convincing lie. As it is, the signs and wonders performed by false christs and false prophets will be so amazing that, if it were possible, even the elect will be deceived.[420]

So, bearing in mind that I reserve the right to change my mind with new information or acquired wisdom, here's how Islam fits into end-times prophecy.

Before we propose a scenario for how the end times will play out, it's helpful to look at what Muslims and Jews believe about the last days, since the three Abrahamic religions ostensibly received divine revelation from the same source.[421] Because there are some serious disagreements between the eschatological doctrines of the three faiths, however, somebody is wrong.

Since I'm not an expert on the teachings of Jews and Muslims, the next two sections of the book will be very broad overviews. To make things even more complicated for us nonexperts, Islam and Judaism are divided into sects with differing and often contradictory beliefs—a lot like us Christians, in fact. Not every Muslim will hold all, or even any, of the beliefs I'm about to describe.

My goal is to demonstrate that the Enemy—specifically, Allah, Inc., in this case—has put in motion a brilliant end game that will draw in many otherwise good people to their doom, people who may well believe they're doing God's work as they volunteer to serve the Antichrist.

It is my view—and I write this with no joy—that Muslims will play the most tragic role of all.

25

Islam and Armageddon

Muslim eschatology is dominated by two prophesied figures. The Mahdi, or "rightly-guided one," is similar to the Jewish under-standing of the *mashiach*, a mortal man who plays a central role in defeat-ing the enemies of Allah. The Dajjal is the Islamic Antichrist figure.

Western pundits, politicians, and preachers fail to understand the depth of Muslim belief that we are in the end times right now. Unlike American Christians, some 80 percent of whom do not anticipate the literal return of Jesus anytime soon, most Muslims in the Middle East and South Asia, upwards of three-quarters in some places, expect to see the Mahdi before they die.

> Looking at specific countries, the highest percentage of the pop-ulation expecting the Mahdi's near-term appearance is found in Afghanistan (83 percent), followed by Iraq (72 percent), Turkey (68 percent) and Tunisia (67 percent). Sixty percent of Pakistanis, 51 percent of Moroccans, 46 percent of Palestinians and 40 percent of Egyptians are looking for the Mahdi in their

lifetimes. The conventional wisdom in recent decades among many journalists, and not a few area "experts," has been that Mahdism is an eccentric outlier belief held mainly by (Twelver) Shi`is and the uneducated on the fringes of the Sunni world. This Pew data, among other things, shows the intellectual vacuity of such biases. The average for the 23 countries Pew surveyed on this issue of Mahdism comes out to 42 percent, and extrapolating from that to the entire Muslim world means there are over 670 million Muslims who believe the Mahdi will return here in the first half of the twenty-first century.

What does this Pew information on Mahdism mean? First and foremost, Mahdism must be taken seriously as an intellectual, sociological and even political strain within the entire Islamic world—not dismissed as archaic, mystical nonsense.[422]

It's hard to overstate the importance of that data. What it means is this: The Islamic State and other Sunni "Mahdist" movements, of which there have been many over the years, haven't hijacked Islam; they practice a *purer form* of Islam—one that believes it can jump-start the Apocalypse and bring the Mahdi to earth sooner rather than later.

While most Muslims do not support the methods and/or aims of ISIS, "Islamic history is rife with violent jihads led by self-styled Muslim messiahs and waged by their followers."[423] ISIS caliph Abu Bakr al-Baghdadi and the Islamic State is only the most recent iteration such a movement. If only 1 percent of the world's Muslims who believe the Mahdi is due to return rally to a would-be Mahdi's cause, he'll have nearly seven million jihadists at his disposal.[424]

Oddly enough, two of the starring characters of the Islamic endtimes scenario aren't even mentioned in the Quran.

In the seventh century AD, as the armies of Islam swarmed out of Arabia and overwhelmed the armies of the two greatest powers in the Near East, Persia and the Eastern Roman Empire, a pseudepigraphal text called the *Apocalypse of Pseudo-Methodius* emerged, attributed to the fourth-century bishop Methodius of Olympus. The text was an effort by stunned Christians to make sense of the new world order, as Muslim conquerors captured nearly all the major centers of Christendom—Damascus, Antioch, Jerusalem, and Alexandria—by 642, just ten years of Muhammad's death. In 674, the armies of the Umayyad caliph began a four-year siege of the Eastern Roman capital, Constantinople.

For traumatized Christians in the Middle East reeling before the Islamic onslaught, it must have felt like the end of the world. Without the military strength to fight back, Christians turned to the pen. *Pseudo-Methodius* depicted Roman emperors as agents of God's will and prophesied that a final emperor would arise in the last days to deliver Christendom from the "sons of Ishmael."

But it provoked an equal and opposite reaction from Islamic teachers—creation of the Mahdi. Yes, it appears the messianic savior of Islam was invented out of whole cloth after Muhammad's death in response to the Final Roman Emperor, who was created in response to the Islamic invasion by an unnamed Christian cleric in northern Syria. In other words, the Mahdi is the product of an "anything you can do, we can do better" game of one-upmanship.

Isn't it bizarre that seventh-century fiction has such an impact on the world today?

Unlike the Quran, which was compiled under the authority of early Islamic authorities in Medina, the *hadith* weren't collected until the eighth and ninth centuries. The sayings attributed to Muhammad, based on stories passed down from people who'd known him, were never evaluated by a central authority. Islamic scholars in the centuries since have divided the *hadith* into *sahih* (authentic), *hasan* (strong), and *da'if* (weak). Here's the thing: There is no universal agreement on which *hadith* are which. Sunni and Shia Muslims have different collections of *hadith*, and there is a small group of Quranists who reject the *hadith* altogether.

Since everything Muslims know about their two main players in the end times, the Mahdi and the Dajjal, come from the *hadith*, it's nearly impossible to summarize an authoritative list of "What Muslims Believe about the End Times." Sunnis and Shias have disagreed over Islamic doctrine for more than thirteen hundred years, often violently, and those differences naturally carry over into eschatology.

For example: Sunnis believe the Mahdi has yet to appear on earth while Shias believe he's hidden now but will return. Those views are as different as Christian and Jewish views of the Messiah.

Two other figures play key roles in Islamic eschatology. Isa, the Muslim conception of Jesus, appears in the Last Hour to kill the Dajjal (or help the Mahdi do so), and the Sufyani, a Muslim tyrant or national hero depending on the sect, emerges in Damascus just before the Mahdi's arrival.

What's odd about Isa's return is that it's prophesied in the Quran. However, Muslims believe Isa/Jesus did not die on the cross but was taken up into heaven before death like Enoch and Elijah. Despite his miraculous birth (Muslims do believe Mary was a virgin) and rescue from the cross, Isa will die like any other mortal man some years after his return.

The Sufyani, like the Mahdi and the Dajjal, is an apocryphal figure mentioned only in the *hadith*. The differences in how he's perceived in the Muslim world illustrates the depth of the hostility between Sunnis and Shias. His name stems from his ancestor, one Abu Sufyan, the leader of Muhammad's tribe who persecuted the self-proclaimed prophet and his followers at first. Although he and his family eventually converted to the faith, Abu Sufyan's son, Yazid, fought Muhammad's son-in-law, Ali, for control of the new Islamic empire and eventually became the caliph.

Ali's supporters, the Shi`at Ali ("partisans of Ali," and later just "Shi`a"), formed their own sect that persists to this day. After the death of Ali's son, Husayn, in AD 680, the Umayyads had firm control of Islam. Shia imams, perhaps drawing inspiration from *Pseudo-Methodius*, began teaching that the Mahdi would return someday to defeat the champion of the Sunnis, the Sufyani. Many Shias today believe the Sufyani's emergence is imminent—a bad thing for them because he's the enemy of the Mahdi.

Conversely, some Sunnis see the Sufyani as a sort of national hero, especially in Syria, the historic homeland of the Sufyani's ancestors. (More evidence that the tribe of Muhammad and the original Ka'ba were not from Arabia.) And unlike Shia prophecies that portray Syria in a bad light because it will be the birthplace of the Sufyani, it holds a place of honor for Sunnis as the site of the prophesied future victory over the forces of Rome.

Think about that. Some 670 million Muslims, including an overwhelming majority in the Middle East and western Asia, expect to see the Mahdi in their lifetimes—sometime during the first half of the twenty-first century. But Sunnis and Shias, like Jews and (most) Christians, are looking for different men to fulfill their prophecies.

Now, the typical Muslim is probably no better informed about his or her faith than the typical Christian. So, while large majorities in nations like Syria, Iraq, and Afghanistan expect the Mahdi's return in the near future, their expectations, which are already built on sometimes contradictory *hadith* of questionable authority, may be shaped to fit current events by charismatic and persuasive imams or political leaders.

So, in broad strokes, here is what Muslims generally believe about the end times:

1. The "Last Hour" will be preceded by corruption, widespread unbelief, oppression of Muslims, declining standards of living, wars and anarchy, sexual immorality, the emergence of false prophets, and an increase in technology.
2. The armies of Rome will land at al-A'maq, a valley near Antakya (Antioch) in southern Turkey, or Dabiq, a rural village in Syria between Aleppo and the border with Turkey. Muslims triumph

over the "Romans" and go on to conquer Constantinople (Istanbul). This belief is at the center of the apocalyptic theology of the Islamic State, and it's why the official news agency of ISIS is called Amaq and its now-defunct official magazine was titled *Dabiq*. (Not surprisingly, when Syrian rebels, Turkish troops, and US Special Forces overran Dabiq in October 2016 with virtually no resistance, the Islamic State just told the faithful that the relevant *hadith* refers to a *future* battle at Dabiq, not the one they'd just lost.)

3. The Dajjal emerges from the east, possibly from Khorasan, the traditional name of a region in eastern Iran and western Afghanistan, and remains on earth deceiving and oppressing people for forty days, forty months, or forty years.
4. Isa (Jesus) descends from heaven at Damascus and either helps the Mahdi kill the Dajjal or kills the Dajjal himself.
5. The Sufyani fields an army to fight the Mahdi, but the earth swallows the Sufyani and his followers before they reach him.
6. When the fighting is over, Isa and the Mahdi will lead prayers at Jerusalem. Al-Mahdi will try to defer to Isa, but Isa will insist on remaining subordinate to the Mahdi. The two will rule over the earth for forty years before dying of old age.

Obviously, there is far more than the above to Islamic eschatology, but since a lot of it isn't believed by most Muslims or deals with supernatural events after the defeat of al-Dajjal, it doesn't concern us here.

Then there are multiple variations on the main theme that are unique to either Sunnis or Shias. Some Sunnis believe the Dajjal will come from Iran; some Shias believe the civil war in Syria is a sign that the end times are upon us.

This is a key point: Both Sunnis and Shias firmly believe the *other* sect will mistake the Dajjal for the Mahdi. Young Muslim men willing to travel from Iran, Chechnya, Dagestan, the United Kingdom, and

America for the privilege of fighting each other in the Syrian civil war convey the sense that Sunnis and Shias are enthusiastically slaughtering each other for the privilege of going toe to toe with the Dajjal.

Sunnis, nearly 90 percent of Muslims worldwide, have traditionally derived religious authority from the caliphate. The first caliph was appointed by the companions of Muhammad at his death because the prophet didn't leave a male heir. Shias, however, follow the bloodline of Muhammad, believing that his true heir descends from the prophet's cousin and son by marriage, Ali. To Shias, and more specifically Twelver Shias, the Mahdi is the Twelfth Imam, Muhammad al-Mahdi, who went into hiding in AD 873 at the age of four.

Or so it's claimed. His father, Hasan al-Askari, lived his life under house arrest. He was apparently poisoned at the age of twenty-eight, probably by the Abbasid caliph, and died without a male heir. That might have been the end of Shia Islam right there. But one Abu Sahl al-Nawbakhti of Baghdad saved the day by claiming that al-Askari did, in fact, have a son who had gone into *ghaybah*—"occultation," or "hiding." Like King Arthur, who returns at the hour of Britain's greatest need, the Twelfth Imam will emerge from occultation at the end of the age to usher in an era of peace and justice—and, of course, establish Islam as the global religion.

In short, the Mahdi's appearance will either be the arrival of a "rightly guided" Sunni Muslim leader, a mortal man who will rule for a time and then die, or the return of a Shi`i Imam who's been supernaturally preserved for more than eleven hundred years.

This is a key distinction: For Shias, the Mahdi must reappear as one specific person. In Sunni theology, "the mantle of the Mahdi can be appropriated, in the right context, by a charismatic leader megalomaniacal enough to believe Allah is directing him to wage divinely-guided jihad."[425] Unlike Sunnis, Shias don't believe that human action can affect the timing of the arrival of the Last Hour. The Mahdi will appear when Allah wills it and not one heartbeat sooner. In fact, Shias believe they're not even supposed to fight for victorious global jihad *until* the Twelfth Imam returns.

Furthermore, there are reasons to believe that Shias, especially in Iran, may not be all that eager for the Mahdi's return. The ayatollahs rule about 40 percent of the world's Shia Muslims. The return of al-Mahdi would undercut their authority, sort of like the Sanhedrin's reaction to Jesus. When Mahdi returns, they're suddenly unemployed. There go the nice cars, pretty wives, and big houses.

One Israeli scholar puts it bluntly:

> Shi`ism in general, and post-revolutionary Iranian Shi`ism in particular, is *not* only *not* messianic or apocalyptic in character, but is in fact the fiercest enemy of messianism to be found anywhere in the Muslim world or Islamic history.[426]

That may be a surprise to Americans who've heard conservative media pundits claim for years that Twelver Shias want nothing more than to trigger the Apocalypse by destroying Israel. I was guilty of that myself; during my run as a secular radio talk show host in 2006–07, I regularly referred to the president of Iran as "Mahmoud I'm-in-a-jihad."

But since Shias believe the Mahdi and Isa are prophesied to lead Muslims in prayer at Jerusalem, the ayatollahs have a good reason *not* to turn the Temple Mount into a radioactive crater. The Mahdi wouldn't like it.

That's not to say Iran isn't a threat to Israel and the West. Iran is a state sponsor of terror. Americans should never forget the 241 soldiers killed at the Marine barracks in Beirut in 1983.

Regardless of how the end times unfold, it's a safe bet that the Temple Mount will be the site of violence in the future. Zion is at the center of the spiritual war, and its significance is recognized by Muslims, Jews, and Christians. And Sunni Muslims, whose long history of radical Mahdist movements lives on in movements like the Islamic State, generally believe the Last Hour can be triggered, which explains the bloody trail of destruction across Syria and Iraq.

Scholar Dr. Timothy Furnish summarizes the geopolitical threat posed by Sunni Mahdism:

> First, a civilization laden with eschatological expectations AND a historical track record of militant movements motivated by messianic leaders, infused with intolerance toward its own schematics, convinced of ongoing problems with demonic entities and witches and in thrall to a literalist reading of a violent religious text might not be amenable to rational actor theory in international relations.
>
> Second, political consolidation and/or jihadist movements led by self-styled Mahdis should be considered as real possibilities in the twenty-first century, especially as we approach key dates such as the hundred year mark from the dissolution of the Ottoman caliphate (2024) or the year 1500 of the Muslim calendar (2076)–since Mahdism, historically, clusters around such important dates which spark attempts to create rival caliphates, often violently. The vast geographic breadth, and surprising depth, of Mahdist belief in the Islamic ummah evidenced in this Pew data makes Mahdi-inspired movements, including jihads, quite plausible in the near future.[427]

Most analyses of end-times Bible prophecy don't consider the influence of the apocalyptic worldview of Sunni Muslims on how those prophecies might be fulfilled. Those that do often take a flat view of Islam, lumping Sunnis, Shias, and their various sects and subsects together, ignoring the fact that many Muslims, especially in the West, don't take the Quran and the *hadith* literally.

That's too simplistic. And with all due respect to prophecy teachers who believe Islam is the soil from which the Man of Sin will spring, a

Muslim Antichrist is far too obvious. That's not a deception that would "lead astray, if possible, even the elect."[428] A more plausible end-times scenario will be much subtler, one that draws in Jews and Christians (if the Church is still here when the Antichrist steps onto the world stage).

In broad terms, the beliefs of Jews and Christians about the end times are closer to those of Shia Muslims than those of Sunnis, at least about the influence humans can have on the timeline of the Apocalypse. Since Christians and Jews share the prophecies of the Hebrew prophets, it follows that there are some similarities in their beliefs. But it's in the differences, and the failure of most Christians to understand the basics of Bible prophecy, that danger lies.

At this point, we need to address a question that's probably occurred to you: If our theory is correct, that Islam is an unholy alliance between fallen angels worshiped as gods in ancient Mesopotamia, then why did these spirits allow sectarian disputes to divide their new religion? Wouldn't a united front against the growing Christian faith have been more effective?

Considering how quickly Islam overran most of the Eastern Roman Empire, a more effective approach is frightening to think about. A united front certainly seems to have been the goal of Allah, Inc.; by defining Islam as a sort of "super-tribe,"[429] with fellow Muslims in it, regardless of race, ethnicity, or language, and the rest of the world outside it, the principalities and powers behind Muhammad created a fighting force that Christendom struggled for centuries to counter.

Of course, it also meant that when political Christendom put on the blinders of modern secular philosophy after the Enlightenment, Islam remained frozen in the tribal worldview of seventh century Arabia, which in turn was pretty much unchanged since the time of Abraham. What seems barbaric to the twenty-first century Western mind was not all that unusual in seventh-century Arabia, or in the days of the Old Testament prophets and patriarchs. For example, 1 Kings 11:15 tells us that David and Joab "struck down every male in Edom," and about two centuries later, King Amaziah of Judah ordered his troops to throw ten thousand Edomite prisoners off a cliff.[430]

There are a few possible explanations for the divisions that emerged in Islam less than twenty-five years after Muhammad's death. The Sunni-Shia conflict may reflect competition between the members of Allah, Inc. Or it could be that the internal conflict was encouraged by spirits faithful to God in the same way that the Enemy has spread dissent among the faithful from the beginning. (Except that, unlike the Muslim sectarian dispute, Protestants and Roman Catholics haven't been killing each another in large numbers—at least not for the last three hundred years.)[431]

Another possibility is that the Fallen instigated the civil wars to keep control of the growing Islamic empire in the hands of men motivated by wealth and power rather than true seekers trying to find spiritual truth. Men and women on that path might stumble onto *genuine* divine revelation, the way many Muslims today are finding Christ through dreams and visions.[432]

Of course, by making the acquisition of wealth and power a sign of Allah's favor almost from the start, the spirits behind Muhammad guaranteed that the new faith attracted the right kind of followers—men enticed by the prospect of plunder—and the whole world outside the *umma* (the "supertribe") was fair game. So, while the ruling elites of Shia Islam appear indifferent to the Mahdi's return, Sunnis expect the imminent fulfillment of the riches and pleasures Muhammad promised his followers fourteen hundred years ago.

But the key issue is understanding what the spiritual directors of Allah, Inc., hoped to achieve through the twisted prophecies they revealed through the *hadith*.

The supernatural war is for control of Zion. Consider: While Mecca and Medina are the holiest sites in Islam, they play virtually no role in Muslim prophecies of the end times. Damascus and Jerusalem are far more important in Islamic eschatology. That's not a coincidence.

Damascus is where the apostle to the Gentiles, Paul, was brought into the faith and began his mission.

And Jerusalem, of course, is the site of Yahweh's mount of assembly. That's been the goal of the Fallen since the beginning.

26

The Temple Mount and Two Messiahs

Arab Muslims have controlled the Temple Mount since the conquest of Jerusalem in AD 638, with brief exceptions during the eleventh and twelfth centuries when European crusaders occupied the city. The Al-Aqsa Mosque, the third-holiest site in Islam, and the Dome of the Rock, which sits on the spot from which Muslims believe Muhammad ascended to heaven, were constructed in the late seventh century, despite the claim by the Grand Mufti of Jerusalem, Sheikh Muhammad Ahmad Hussein, that Al-Aqsa was either built by Adam or by angels "during his time."[433]

When Israel captured the Temple Mount during the Six-Day War in 1967, the geopolitical fallout of taking full control of the site was considered so dangerous that the first action of Israel's Defense Minister Moshe Dayan was to take down the Israeli flag that his paratroopers had raised over the mount.

The Temple Mount today is administered by the Waqf, an Islamic religious trust that has overseen the area since 1187. The government of Jordan acts as custodian, although security is provided by Israeli police. This arrangement makes no one happy. It's a constant source of irritation and provocation to Jews and Muslims alike.

Christians, as spiritual descendants of Judaism, also attach special significance to the Temple Mount. In addition to the Old Testament history linked to the site, some of the major events of Jesus' life took place on the Temple Mount. Still, its importance to Christians, especially in the mostly secular West, pales in comparison to the significance of the Temple Mount to Jews. American Christians can only guess at the level of frustration religious Jews must feel at being forbidden to pray on the mount.

Moshe Dayan and Israel's secular leadership in 1967 apparently believed that the mount was a holy site only for Muslims and nothing more than "a historical site of commemoration of the past" for Jews.[434] By granting Jews access to the Temple Mount, Dayan thought demands for worship and sovereignty there would be satisfied; by allowing Muslims to keep religious control of it, he hoped to remove the site as an inspiration for Palestinian nationalism. It was the ultimate no-win situation.

The Roman Catholic Church recently waded back into these shark-infested waters; on June 26, 2015, the Vatican signed a treaty with the "state of Palestine," essentially acknowledging the independence of a sovereign Palestine.[435] The Israeli government wasn't happy about that; if the Palestinian Authority can achieve independence through outside pressure on Israel, why negotiate?

News of this agreement stirred up old suspicions among some Jews that the Vatican is conspiring with Palestinian leaders, and possibly with Israeli elites as well, to take control of the Old City and/or the Temple Mount. Stories have circulated for years that the Vatican is working with Jewish elites on a secret deal to turn over administration of the Old City to the Roman Catholic Church.[436]

This isn't entirely conspiracy theory. The 1947 United Nations Partition Plan for Palestine included a proposal to designate Jerusalem *corpus separatum* (Latin for "separated body"), a zone under international control because of the city's shared religious importance. The proposal was included in the plan largely because of a powerful diplomatic effort by the Vatican, which had been concerned about the status of Christian holy sites in the Holy Land since the nineteenth century.

The partition plan failed. War broke out almost immediately after Israel declared its independence, and it's hard to talk when bullets are flying. Months of intense fighting left Israeli forces in control of western Jerusalem, and Israel kept that territory when an armistice was signed to end the 1948–49 war.

Today, at least one Middle East think tank, the Jerusalem Old City Initiative, formed by Canadian diplomats after the failure of the Camp David talks in 2000, "concluded that an effective and empowered third party presence was imperative in the Old City."[437] A similar proposal was reportedly made by the Obama administration in late 2013. US Secretary of State John Kerry, in Israel trying to broker a deal for a Palestinian state, is said to have offered a "third party solution" for administering eastern Jerusalem. Under the proposal, the Vatican would have controlled holy sites in partnership with a coalition of Muslim countries such as Turkey and Saudi Arabia. Israeli leaders were unreceptive, especially to Turkey's participation.[438]

A suggestion that Jordan might replace Turkey in the international coalition got a lukewarm response in Amman. King Abdullah wasn't eager to get involved in a delicate, potentially explosive situation in Jerusalem with the Syrian civil war raging just across Jordan's northern border.

The relationship between Israel and Turkey used to be friendly, but it's soured in recent years, probably due to the regional ambitions of Turkey's President Recep Tayyip Erdogan. Turkey supported the so-called Gaza Freedom Flotilla, a 2010 mission to deliver construction materials and humanitarian aid to the Gaza Strip coordinated by the Free Gaza Movement and the Turkish Foundation for Human Rights and Freedoms and

Humanitarian Relief. However, since Gaza has been blockaded by Israel and Egypt since 2007, aid is normally delivered to Israel and then transferred to Palestinian authorities. The flotilla tried to make a political and public relations point by running the blockade.

When Israeli forces intercepted the flotilla on May 31, 2010, nine people were killed on board the Turkish ship MV *Mavi Marmara*. Although Erdogan said in 2013 that relations with Israel could be normalized if certain conditions were met, he has since called for Sunnis and Shias to set aside their differences and "protect" the Temple Mount.[439]

In the current political climate, Israel will probably grow increasingly resistant to pressure to give up the Temple Mount. The Netanyahu administration, which has governed Israel since 2009, has been quietly investing in efforts to prepare for the construction of the Third Temple.[440] This includes educating young Israelis about the importance of the Temple, and preparation of the architectural plans, utensils, and even sacrificial animals needed to make the Temple a reality.

In September 2018, a perfect one-week-old red heifer was certified by a board of rabbis as meeting all of the biblical requirements for the ritual purification needed to build the Third Temple.[441] Meanwhile, close allies of Prime Minister Benjamin Netanyahu—specifically a deputy defense minister and a key US fundraiser—have been making large financial contributions to advance the cause of the Temple's construction.[442]

This could be the tinder waiting for a spark that touches off a confrontation of literally biblical proportions. While modern Israel is mainly secular, in recent years respected Orthodox and Haredi rabbis have issued regular proclamations of the Messiah's imminent arrival. Rabbi Chaim Kanievsky, a leading authority in mainstream Haredi (ultra-Orthodox) Judaism not previously given to messianic predictions, has been advising Jews since 2014 to make *aliyah* (relocate to Israel) as soon as possible to prepare for Messiah's arrival.

It should be noted that Rav Kanievsky predicted the Messiah's arrival in the first year after the Shemitah, which would have been by September of 2016.[443] The point isn't whether he was right, it's that this is what religious Jews are being taught *right now* and what many believe. One's actions are determined by one's beliefs, so making sense of the end times, which culminate in an earth-shaking battle at Jerusalem, requires understanding at least a little of what Jews believe about the last days.

As with Christian interpretations of end-times prophecy, Jews believe Israel will face an existential threat from a coalition of enemies invading from the north. That's the prophecy of the war of Gog and Magog recorded in Ezekiel chapters 38 and 39. Typically, Christians understand that this war will end when God intervenes and supernaturally destroys the invading army with "pestilence and bloodshed… torrential rains and hailstones, fire and sulfur."[444]

Jews believe the *mashiach* takes an active part in this battle. In fact, *two* are expected in Jewish prophecy—Mashiach ben Yosef and Mashiach ben David. Unlike the Christian understanding of the Messiah, Jews believe Mashiach ben Yosef and Mashiach ben David are human men, observant Jews, rather than supernatural saviors.

The origin and character of the Messiah of the tribe of Joseph are rather obscure. It seems that the assumed superhuman character of the Messiah was thought to be in conflict with prophecies of his death. Jews never really accepted the idea of the Messiah as a suffering servant. Obviously, they wouldn't see "him whom they have pierced"[445] as Jesus. Therefore, the haggadists created a second Messiah who would come from the tribe of Joseph (or Ephraim) instead of Judah who willingly suffers for his nation and falls in the Gog-Magog war.

In a nutshell, Mashiach ben Yosef is killed during the Magog invasion. He's then replaced and later resurrected by Mashiach ben David (or, some believe, Elijah), who goes on to purify Jerusalem, gather the Jews to Israel, build the Third Temple, reinstitute the Sanhedrin, and restore the system of sacrifices.

Then comes the Final Judgment: Mashiach ben David judges the nations and their guardian angels, presumably the seventy placed over the nations by Yahweh after the Tower of Babel incident, and then throws all of them—nations and angels—into Gehenna.

Not all Jews believe in the literal return of the *mashiach*. Generally speaking, Orthodox and Hasidic Jews are most likely to await his arrival, while Conservative, Reform, and Deconstructionist Jews tend to view the *mashiach* as just a symbol for the redemption of mankind from the evils of the world.

You've noticed, no doubt, a key similarity between the Jewish *mashiach* and the Sunni Mahdi: Both will be devout men, obedient to their God, who lead their people to ultimate victory over the forces of darkness. Shias and Christians, on the other hand, are waiting for the return of a supernatural deliverer.

This sets up a bizarre scenario for the last days: Sunnis and Shias both expect the other's Mahdi to be the Dajjal, comparable to the Christian Antichrist and the evil figure called Armilus in medieval Jewish eschatology. Both Muslim camps will probably see a Jewish *mashiach* figure as the Dajjal, and it's unlikely Muslims or Jews will recognize the true Messiah for who he is.

In other words, the Fallen have woven a confusing tangle of deception that will lead a lot of people discovering, too late, that they followed the wrong man.

No kidding. That's partly why prophecy scholars still can't agree on how things play out even after two thousand years of study, prayer, and arguing. One tip for Christians: If someone claims to be the Christ and his feet are on the ground, it's not Him. Remember, Jesus said to look for a cloud, power, and great glory at His return.[446]

Of course, the main reason we haven't figured it all out is because God is the greatest military mind of all time and He hadn't told us everything He knows. Loose lips sink ships, and too many of us talk to the Enemy.

Still, read on. We're going to take a shot at a plausible end-times scenario that lays out Allah, Inc.'s, plan for Muslims and shows you the doom that's already been decreed for the hellish coalition behind Islam.

27

The Wars of Antichrist

Contrary to the way he's portrayed by Hollywood, Satan appears as an angel of light.[447] His minion, the Antichrist, will do the same. He won't be easy to spot; most of us will see the greatest politician and/or military leader the world has known in generations.

That's part of the deception; from the Enemy's perspective, there's nothing to gain by literally scaring the Hell out of people. Jesus warned that in the last days "false christs and false prophets will arise and perform great signs and wonders, so as to lead astray, if possible, even the elect."[448] So, Christians have no excuse—we've been warned, and we should be *especially* wary of anyone who claims to be the Messiah. Getting it wrong means literally siding with the devil.

It won't be easy. The Fallen are far older and more intelligent than you and me. Sending out an Antichrist who's easy to identify would be stupid, and they aren't stupid. When this character appears, it will take industrial-strength discernment to see him for what he is.

Consider the following possible scenario: War erupts between Israel and its nearby Muslim neighbors. Given recent history in the Middle East, this wouldn't be a surprise. Daniel was told about this twenty-five hundred years ago:

> And the king shall do as he wills. He shall exalt himself and magnify himself above every god, and shall speak astonishing things against the God of gods. He shall prosper till the indignation is accomplished; for what is decreed shall be done. He shall pay no attention to the gods of his fathers, or to the one beloved by women. He shall not pay attention to any other god, for he shall magnify himself above all. He shall honor the god of fortresses instead of these. A god whom his fathers did not know he shall honor with gold and silver, with precious stones and costly gifts. He shall deal with the strongest fortresses with the help of a foreign god. Those who acknowledge him he shall load with honor. He shall make them rulers over many and shall divide the land for a price. (Daniel 11:36–39)

It's generally accepted that this section of Daniel is a prophecy of the character Christians call the Antichrist. Verse 36 in this chapter begins a new section of prophecies yet to be fulfilled, as verse 35 marks a break from fulfilled prophecies of the Seleucid king Antiochus IV Ephiphanes (reigned 175 BC–164 BC), who set up the infamous "abomination that causes desolation" in the Temple.

Much has been written about Daniel 11:36–39, but after twenty-five hundred years of trying to figure it out, we have to be honest—we can only guess at which gods the angelic messenger meant.

Although this end-times figure wasn't called "Antichrist" by the prophets (the title only appears in four verses in 1 John and 2 John), he's described in several places in the Old Testament. Besides Daniel 11, there are clear references in Daniel 9:26–27 ("the prince who is to come"), Daniel 7 (the little horn of the fourth beast), and, most obviously, Ezekiel's Gog of Magog, Israel's enemy at the end of the age.

Jewish religious scholars believe the Gog-Magog war is the final conflict before Messiah's arrival. They are correct. The war reaches its climax "on that day," the Day of the Lord, which is when God Himself arrives on the battlefield to put an end to the rebellion. Besides being a commonly used reference by Hebrew prophets for Judgment Day, God told Ezekiel that everyone on earth "shall quake at My presence,"[449] and that "the nations shall know that I am the Lord, the Holy One in Israel."[450]

Did you catch that? God said, *in* Israel, not *of* Israel. This is the only place in the Bible where that phrase is used. God will be on the battlefield for this showdown, which is better known to us Christians as Armageddon.

How do we connect Ezekiel to Revelation? In Ezekiel 39:17–19, God tells the prophet to invite the birds and beasts to a gruesome sacrificial feast on the mountains of Israel—the flesh of the mighty, and the blood of the princes of the earth.[451] This same feast is described by John in Revelation 19:17–21. The imagery in Ezekiel and Revelation is so similar that commentators have noticed the parallel for hundreds of years.[452] The two prophets described the same event, when the followers of those foul spirits who have for millennia demanded sacrifice from humans, including human sacrifice, will themselves become a sacrifice for all of creation.

The war of Gog and Magog ends with Armageddon. It's not a precursor to Armageddon, and the Antichrist doesn't appear after Gog is defeated. Gog *is* the Antichrist, and his war *includes* Armageddon.

One of the points we often overlook when trying to identify the human actors in this end-times drama is that the prophets described a superhuman enemy. We can get caught up in debating whether Gog is

Putin, Erdogan, or Assad, and forget that the real enemy is behind the scenes. Because the home base of Gog's army, *yarkete tsaphon*, is usually translated into English as "far north," "distant north," or "uttermost parts of the north," we draw a line on a map northward from Jerusalem, passing through Turkey, Ukraine, and Russia on the way, and assume it's somewhere on that line. And ever since Cyrus I. Scofield published his study Bible a hundred years ago, prophecy students have identified Russia as the land of Magog.

It makes sense, right? There's nothing on the map more "uttermost north" than Russia. Scofield's theory was popular after the Bolshevik uprising in 1917, and it only became more popular during the Cold War. Since the 1970s, the idea that Russia is Magog has become so ingrained in our study of end-times prophecy that it's taken as a given.

With all due respect to generations of learned prophecy teachers, this assumption misses Ezekiel's point.

I don't want to drift too far from Daniel into Ezekiel, so I'll summarize: First, all of the nations from the north in Gog's coalition—Magog, Meshech, Tubal, Gomer, and Beth-Togarmah—were south of the Black Sea, in Anatolia (modern Turkey), in Ezekiel's day.[453] Second, the "Rosh" cited by some as a reference to Russia is simply the Hebrew word for "chief" or "head," as in Rosh Hashanah—literally, "head (of) the year," the Jewish New Year. There isn't a single valid reason to connect *rosh* with Russia.[454]

Third, the other members of the Magog coalition shouldn't be read literally. While Persia (Iran) is a safe bet as an end-times enemy of Israel, it's unlikely that Ethiopia (Cush) or Libya (Put) will ever pose an existential threat to the Holy Land. Why, then, did Ezekiel include them as last-days enemies of Israel? The answer is as simple as looking at a map. For most Jews in Ezekiel's day, Persia, Cush, and Put were the farthest nations they'd heard of to the east, south, and west. When you add the northern nations to the mix, you realize that Ezekiel was saying that the army of Gog would come from the four corners of the earth—the entire world will be against Israel in that final battle.

Not only is this consistent with John's description of Armageddon, it tracks with the apocalyptic prophecies of Joel 3 and Zechariah 14, which describe a conflict that brings "all the nations" to fight against God at Jerusalem.

Finally, and most important, *yarkete tsaphon* refers to a specific mountain, Mount Zaphon, famous in the ancient world for being sacred to the storm-god, Baal. As we noted earlier, Jesus specifically identified the storm-god as Satan.[455] Isaiah 14 names Zaphon as the mount of assembly of the rebel from Eden, which pins that rebellion on Satan and connects him to the war of Gog and Magog.

So, Gog/Antichrist is Satan's military commander, a cheap copy of the role filled by Jesus Christ in the Trinity, and Mount Zaphon, the mountain in southern Turkey now called Jebel al-Aqra, is where his army will assemble.

Since Jebel al-Aqra rises out of the Mediterranean Sea on the Turkish coast, I believe that's precisely where the Beast (the Antichrist) will emerge.

That ancient serpent, who is called the devil and Satan, the deceiver of the whole world—he was thrown down to the earth, and his angels were thrown down with him…

Then the dragon became furious with the woman and went off to make war on the rest of her offspring, on those who keep the commandments of God and hold to the testimony of Jesus. And he stood on the sand of the sea.

And I saw a beast rising out of the sea, with ten horns and seven heads, with ten diadems on its horns and blasphemous names on its heads. And the beast that I saw was like a leopard; its feet were like a bear's, and its mouth was like a lion's mouth.

And to it the dragon gave his power and his throne and great authority. (Revelation 12:9, 17; 13:1–2)

The Beast of Revelation 13 is the ten-horned beast of Daniel 7. Since we have a scriptural basis for identifying Satan as Baal, and we know that the mountain considered sacred to Baal is on the Mediterranean coast in southern Turkey, it's reasonable to assume that the scene described by John in Revelation 13 takes place at Jebel al-Aqra. Again, this is where Gog, the Antichrist, assembles his army[456] for the final assault on Zion, the Battle of Armageddon.

Interestingly, the mountain is very close to Antakya, ancient Antioch, where "the disciples were first called Christians,"[457] and the al-A'maq Valley, one of the places where Muhammad reportedly prophesied the final confrontation between the armies of Islam and Christendom.[458]

Let's dig a little deeper into Revelation 13:1. Several years ago, my wife, Sharon K. Gilbert, contacted Bible scholar Dr. Michael S. Heiser about the choice of pronoun. In other words, who, exactly, saw the beast rising out of the sea?

As I mentioned in my talk earlier this year in Orlando, I believe this verse should actually be included at the end of chapter twelve and translated this way, "And 'HE' stood upon the sand of the sea."

The "he" pronoun is vital, because it must grammatically reflect back to the DRAGON described in Chapter 12.

I'm not alone in thinking the pronoun should be "he." I've found it as a footnote in nearly every translation. To learn more, I conferred with Michael S. Heiser, Cris Putnam, [and] Tom Horn regarding the correct construction and reference for this verse and for the pronoun, and all three believe that John is most likely referring to the DRAGON as standing on the sands of the sea.

Dr. Heiser had this to say:

> The difference in the reading is one Greek letter—which, when present, yields a first singular verb form ("I") and when absent yields a third masculine singular verb form ("he"). The third masculine form ("he") is supported by several major manuscripts among the oldest we have: P(apyrus)47, Sinaiticus, Alexandrinus. All of those date between the third and fifth centuries AD. I'd go with the third person reading ("he").[459]

So, we should read Revelation 13:1 this way: "And *he* saw a beast rising out of the sea." John saw the dragon, Satan, welcoming the Beast, the Antichrist, to his mount of assembly, Mount Zaphon, the modern Jebel al-Aqra. We English speakers miss this because our Bible translations obscure the spiritual significance of *yarkete tsaphon*, rendering it as a map direction—the "uttermost parts of the north." It actually points to the home of the great end times enemy of God and Israel—*cosmic* north.

But before he gets to Armageddon, the Antichrist fights a series of wars described at the end of Daniel 11.

> At the time of the end, the king of the south shall attack him, but the king of the north shall rush upon him like a whirlwind, with chariots and horsemen, and with many ships. And he shall come into countries and shall overflow and pass through. He shall come into the glorious land. And tens of thousands shall fall, but these shall be delivered out of his hand: Edom and Moab and the main part of the Ammonites. He shall stretch out his hand against the countries, and the land of Egypt shall not escape. He shall become ruler of the treasures of gold and

of silver, and all the precious things of Egypt, and the Libyans and the Cushites shall follow in his train. But news from the east and the north shall alarm him, and he shall go out with great fury to destroy and devote many to destruction. (Daniel 11:40–44)

This account almost reads like a summary of any one of Israel's wars since 1948. The two questions we must answer here are these: Who are the kings of the north and the south, and do these verses describe two characters or three?

Many well-respected teachers of prophecy will disagree with my take on Daniel 11. That's fine; if this prophecy was crystal clear, after 2,600 years there would be no disagreement over what they mean. In my view, the unnamed "he" introduced in verse 36, the king who exalts himself above all gods, is the same "he" and "him" in verses 40 through 44, a third king separate and distinct from the kings of the north and south. This is the Antichrist.

To be honest, these verses are confusing. The text doesn't make it clear who's being referred to. Translators struggle with this section, with some English translations using "and" instead of "but" in verse 40.

At the time of the end, the king of the south shall attack him, [and] the king of the north shall rush upon him like a whirlwind, with chariots and horsemen, and with many ships. And he shall come into countries and shall overflow and pass through. (Daniel 11:40, modified)

That changes the sense of the sentence. Reading it this way, it's clearer that we're reading about three characters—the king of the south, the king of the north, and Antichrist, who's attacked by the kings of the south and north. That is my view.

The king of the south could be Egypt, or it could be a powerful ter-rorist organization in the Sinai Peninsula. This has been an unpleasant reality lately for the Egyptian government. More than a dozen violent Islamist groups in the Sinai, including ISIS, have waged low-grade war against Cairo since 2011.

Although Egypt, which is mostly Sunni, appears to want Israel as an ally against Iran, the Shia power in the region, it holds a special place in Jewish minds as the nation that enslaved their ancestors. Until recently, Egypt was still one of Israel's most dangerous enemies, fighting Israel alongside Muslim allies in the Six-Day War of 1967 and the Yom Kip-pur War of 1973. When the Muslim Brotherhood ousted former presi-dent Hosni Mubarak in 2011, with the approval and behind-the-scenes assistance of the Obama administration, it was a reminder that Egypt is only a regime change away from becoming an enemy again.

The king of the north probably represents a Muslim coalition against Israel. And here's where we begin to see the interlocking pieces of Muslim, Jewish, and biblical prophecy. Other than Egypt and occasional raiders from the southern desert like the Edomites, Midianites, and Amalekites, invaders have usually attacked Israel from the north. Syria, Assyria, Baby-lon, Persia, Greece, and Rome all came into the Holy Land from the north because marching an army across the desert east of Israel is suicide.

It's not hard to imagine Sunni nations to Israel's north, or violent factions within those nations, forming an alliance as they did in 1948, 1967, and 1973—some combination of Syria, Lebanon, Iraq (or parts thereof), Saudi Arabia, Egypt, and Jordan, with the Palestinian enclaves in Gaza and the West Bank already positioned to launch terror attacks inside Israel. With the rise of Islamist sentiment in the land of Baal's holy mountain, we can add Turkey to that list. Given the apocalyptic expectations of Sunnis in the Middle East, it's conceivable that these nations could unite behind a charismatic leader whose followers declare him the Mahdi.

In a two-king scenario, where the king of the north is the Antichrist, our picture has to be modified a bit. The king of the south—say, a powerful Saudi ruler—leads a Muslim coalition, perhaps using his status as protector of Medina and Mecca to lead the world's Muslims into war. Based on the recent Syrian civil war, one can see volunteers from all over the planet signing on to fight against the Dajjal.

Bear in mind that the king of the north doesn't have to be "northern" in the physical sense, say, from Turkey or Russia. The Antichrist will be "northern," no matter where his human form is from, because his boss, Satan, is based at "cosmic north," Mount Zaphon (*har tsaphon*, literally "Mount North").

So, however we get there, we're going to get there—a Middle East war triggered by an attack on Israel followed by a swift, devastating counterattack. Psalm 83 is the most likely precursor of the Daniel 11 "wars of Antichrist" scenario.

> O God, do not keep silence;
> do not hold your peace or be still, O God!
> For behold, your enemies make an uproar;
> those who hate you have raised their heads.
> They lay crafty plans against your people;
> they consult together against your treasured ones.
> They say, "Come, let us wipe them out as a nation;
> let the name of Israel be remembered no more!"
> For they conspire with one accord;
> against you they make a covenant—
> the tents of Edom and the Ishmaelites,
> Moab and the Hagrites,
> Gebal and Ammon and Amalek,
> Philistia with the inhabitants of Tyre;
> Asshur also has joined them;
> they are the strong arm of the children of Lot. (Psalm 83:1–8)

According to author Bill Salus, who first suggested its possible prophetic significance,[460] Psalm 83 appears to name all of Israel's immediate neighbors, all of which are majority Muslim nations.

Psalm 83 Nation	Modern Nation
Edom	Jordan
Ishmaelites	Saudi Arabia
Moab	Jordan, Palestinians of West Bank
Hagrites (after Hagar, Abraham's servant)	Egypt
Gebal (city in ancient Phoenicia)	Hezbollah (Lebanon)
Ammon	Jordan
Amalek	Bedouins, Arabs in Sinai
Philistia	Hamas, Palestinians of Gaza
Tyre	Hezbollah
Asshur (Assyria)	Syria and northern Iraq

These verses name all of the Muslim nations in the immediate vicinity of Israel. If Psalm 83 does foretell a future event, it's probably a precursor to Daniel 11:40–45, a wider regional war that ultimately goes global. To lay out the sequence, let's bullet-point a potential series of events triggered by a Psalm 83/Daniel 11 war:

- Muslim nations launch a surprise attack against Israel (Psalm 83:1–8; Daniel 11:40).
- A dynamic military and/or political figure leads Israel to an overwhelming victory (Daniel 11:40–43).

- This leader "comes into the glorious land" as a victor (Daniel 11:41).
- "News from the east and the north" provokes next phase of Antichrist's war, possibly strikes against Muslim nations farther away such as Turkey, Iran, or even Pakistan (Daniel 11:44).
- Jordan is spared (Daniel 11:41), but Israel's territory may be expanded (Obadiah 1:9).

You'll see in a moment why the role envisioned for Muslims in the last days by Allah, Inc., is tragic. They're being set up as sacrificial victims of the most insidious double-cross in history.

28

Mystery Babylon

First, we're going to take a look at one of the enduring mysteries of Bible prophecy—the identity of Mystery Babylon.

If you've read the Book of Revelation, you've noticed a three-chapter gap between the armies assembling for the battle of Armageddon (Revelation 16:16) and a gruesome sacrificial feast (Revelation 19:17–21) that we'll connect to the war of Gog of Magog in an upcoming chapter. This is significant; Ezekiel and John had the same supernatural enemies in mind—the old gods of the Amorites.

> Then one of the seven angels who had the seven bowls came and said to me, "Come, I will show you the judgment of the great prostitute who is seated on many waters, with whom the kings of the earth have committed sexual immorality, and with the wine of whose sexual immorality the dwellers on earth have become drunk." And he carried me away in the Spirit into a wilderness, and I saw a woman sitting on a scarlet beast that was full of blasphemous names, and it had seven heads and ten horns.

The woman was arrayed in purple and scarlet, and adorned with gold and jewels and pearls, holding in her hand a golden cup full of abominations and the impurities of her sexual immorality. And on her forehead was written a name of mystery: "Babylon the great, mother of prostitutes and of earth's abominations." (Revelation 17:1–5)

The Antichrist's church of the last days is called "Babylon the great," but "Mystery Babylon" is the name that's stuck. After two thousand years, scholars still can't agree on what it represents. Here's what we know: The Babylon of John's vision is a religion and a city. Ezekiel gave us important clues that modern prophecy scholars have missed because they haven't considered the history and religion of the people who lived in the ancient Near East.

Chapter 27 of Ezekiel is a lament over the city of Tyre. The great trading city was founded by the Phoenician descendants of Amorites who settled along the eastern shore of the Mediterranean. This lament has a clear parallel in Revelation. It not only cements the connection between the visions of Ezekiel and John, it shows that the iniquity of the Amorites is still with us.

The word of the LORD came to me: "Now you, son of man, raise a lamentation over Tyre, and say to Tyre, who dwells at the entrances to the sea, merchant of the peoples to many coastlands, thus says the Lord GOD:
'O Tyre, you have said,
"I am perfect in beauty."
Your borders are in the heart of the seas;
your builders made perfect your beauty.
**They made all your planks
of fir trees from Senir;
they took a cedar from Lebanon**

**to make a mast for you.
Of oaks of Bashan
they made your oars;**
they made your deck of pines
from the coasts of Cyprus,
inlaid with ivory.'" (Ezekiel 27:1–6, emphasis added)

Tyre was the most powerful commercial empire in the Mediterranean for centuries. Even after the city's influence began to fade, its colony in north Africa, Carthage, grew so powerful that its most famous general, Hannibal, nearly destroyed Rome. At the peak of Tyre's power, in Ezekiel's day, the prophet linked the strength of Tyre, its ships, to Mount Hermon and Bashan.

Senir was the Amorite name for Hermon, the mount of assembly ruled by "the" god of the western Amorites, El. But the Amorites were history by Ezekiel's day, at least under the name "Amorite." Their lands were ruled by their descendants, the Arameans, Phoenicians, and Arabs, by the time of King David, about four hundred years before Ezekiel. So, why did the prophet use the archaic name for the mountain?

Ezekiel deliberately linked Tyre to the region's spiritual wickedness in the minds of his readers. Not only was Senir/Hermon the abode of El, where the Rephaim spirits came to feast, it towered over Bashan, the entrance to the netherworld. By calling the mountain Senir instead of Hermon, Ezekiel specifically connected Tyre to the Amorites, whose evil was legendary among Jews.[461]

As we noted early in the book, Babylon was founded by Amorites. Descendants of Amorites, the Phoenicians, made Tyre the foremost commercial empire of the ancient world. The link between Tyre and Mystery Babylon is the lament over its destruction:

At the sound of the cry of your pilots
the countryside shakes,

and down from their ships
come all who handle the oar.
The mariners and all the pilots of the sea
stand on the land
and shout aloud over you
and cry out bitterly.
They cast dust on their heads
and wallow in ashes;
they make themselves bald for you
and put sackcloth on their waist,
and they weep over you in bitterness of soul,
with bitter mourning.
In their wailing they raise a lamentation for you
and lament over you:
"Who is like Tyre,
like one destroyed in the midst of the sea?
When your wares came from the seas,
you satisfied many peoples;
with your abundant wealth and merchandise
you enriched the kings of the earth.
Now you are wrecked by the seas,
in the depths of the waters;
your merchandise and all your crew in your midst
have sunk with you.
All the inhabitants of the coastlands
are appalled at you,
and the hair of their kings bristles with horror;
their faces are convulsed.
The merchants among the peoples hiss at you;
you have come to a dreadful end
and shall be no more forever."
(Ezekiel 27:28–36, emphasis added)

Now, compare that section of Ezekiel's lament over Tyre to John's prophecy of the destruction of Babylon the Great in Revelation 18.

> After this I saw another angel coming down from heaven,
> having great authority, and the earth was made bright with his
> glory. And he called out with a mighty voice,
>> "Fallen, fallen is Babylon the great!
>> She has become a dwelling place for demons,
>> a haunt for every unclean spirit,
>> a haunt for every unclean bird,
>> a haunt for every unclean and detestable beast....
>
> **And the kings of the earth, who committed sexual
> immorality and lived in luxury with her**, will weep and wail
> over her when they see the smoke of her burning. They will
> stand far off, in fear of her torment, and say,
>> 'Alas! Alas! You great city,
>> you mighty city, Babylon!
>> For in a single hour your judgment has come.'...
>
> **The merchants of these wares, who gained wealth from
> her, will stand far off, in fear of her torment, weeping and
> mourning aloud,**
>> "Alas, alas, for the great city
>> that was clothed in fine linen,
>> in purple and scarlet,
>> adorned with gold,
>> with jewels, and with pearls!
>> For in a single hour all this wealth has been laid waste.'
>
> **And all shipmasters and seafaring men, sailors and all
> whose trade is on the sea, stood far off and cried out as they
> saw the smoke of her burning,**
>> 'What city was like the great city?'

And they threw dust on their heads as they wept and mourned, crying out,

'Alas, alas, for the great city
where all who had ships at sea
grew rich by her wealth!
For in a single hour she has been laid waste.'" (Revelation 18:1–2, 9, 15–19, emphasis added)

Let's compare some key phrases from these chapters.

Tyre (Ezekiel 27)	Babylon (Revelation 18)
"enriched the kings of the earth" (Ezekiel 27:33)	"kings of the earth...lived in luxury with her" (Revelation 18:9)
Lamented by mariners, pilots of the sea, merchants, and kings (Ezekiel 27:28–36)	Lamented by kings, merchants, shipmasters, and seafaring men (Revelation 18:9–19)
"'Who is like Tyre, like one destroyed in the midst of the sea? ...with your abundant wealth and merchandise you enriched the kings of the earth.'" (Ezekiel 27:32–33)	"'What city was like the great city... where all who had ships at sea grew rich by her wealth!'" (Revelation 18:18–19)

The parallels here have been noted by Bible scholars for generations. What I propose is that this connection points to the spiritual source of this global end-times religion—the gods of the Amorites, who joined forces as the directors of Allah, Inc.

By extension, then, it also points to the city that this religion calls home—Mecca.

When God made His covenant with Abraham in Genesis 15, He

told the patriarch that his descendants would spend about four hundred years in a land that wasn't theirs, "for the iniquity of the Amorites is not yet complete." Ezekiel gave us the clues. He pointed to Mount Hermon, Bashan, and the neighbors of ancient Israel who worshiped the gods who called that region home.

Who, what, or where is Babylon the Great of Revelation 17 and 18? The connection between Mystery Babylon and the Amorites is key. Spiritual wickedness, symbolized by the Amorite kingdom of Babylon, connected to an unparalleled maritime trading empire are the two main features of Mystery Babylon.

> Then one of the seven angels who had the seven bowls came and said to me, "Come, I will show you the judgment of the great prostitute who is seated on many waters, with whom the kings of the earth have committed sexual immorality, and with the wine of whose sexual immorality the dwellers on earth have become drunk." And he carried me away in the Spirit into a wilderness, and I saw a woman sitting on a scarlet beast that was full of blasphemous names, and it had seven heads and ten horns. The woman was arrayed in purple and scarlet, and adorned with gold and jewels and pearls, holding in her hand a golden cup full of abominations and the impurities of her sexual immorality. And on her forehead was written a name of mystery: "Babylon the great, mother of prostitutes and of earth's abominations." And I saw the woman, drunk with the blood of the saints, the blood of the martyrs of Jesus....
>
> This calls for a mind with wisdom: the seven heads are seven mountains on which the woman is seated; they are also seven kings, five of whom have fallen, one is, the other has not yet come, and when he does come he must remain only a little while. (Revelation 17:1–6, 9–10)

As you see, there are other characteristics. "Sexual immorality" is a euphemism for spiritual rebellion, like Israel's "whorings" with the gods of the pagan nations against which the prophets of the Old Testament thundered.

Geography is another, but a location on seven mountains or hills is one of the easiest for potential candidates to meet. While Rome is the first name most people think of, it appears to be a status symbol for a city to claim that it, too, was built on seven hills. Other cities ostensibly sitting on seven hills include Mecca, Jerusalem, Brussels, Tehran, Istanbul, Moscow, and dozens of others.

Joel Richardson made a strong case for Mecca in his 2017 book, *Mystery Babylon*. He argues that no other city on the earth has influenced world leaders over the last century like Mecca, home of Islam's holiest site. The vast wealth accumulated by the House of Saud over the last century has enabled it to bend bankers, academics, and politicians to their will, using petrodollars to draw the West into Mecca's orbit. Until very recently, OPEC nations, led by Saudi Arabia, dominated world oil markets, with about forty percent of that black gold delivered to end users by ocean-going tankers.[462]

Some argue that OPEC's declining influence with the recent surge in American oil production means the Mecca-as-Mystery Babylon theory is flawed. On the contrary, it suggests that even as Islam grows, the Saudis themselves are not indispensable to the global economy. And since the Antichrist and his minions turn on Mystery Babylon, we know that the spirits behind Allah, Inc., consider the "great prostitute" expendable. While the scarlet woman of Revelation 17 has "dominion over the kings of the earth,"[463] she's resented by the ten principal kings represented by the ten horns on the beast. They and the beast "hate" her, and so they "devour her flesh and burn her up with fire."[464]

The faithful followers of Muhammad won't know what hit them.

It's tragic irony. The ultimate end of Mystery Babylon is to be slaughtered and served up as a sacrifice for the Beast from the Abyss—just like the thousands upon thousands of children who were passed through the fire and buried in the tophets of the ancient world.

Mystery Babylon—Mecca—will be destroyed in the war that brings the Antichrist to power; a war that sacrifices an entire religion in a diabolical double-cross to lure Jews (and Christians, if the church is still on the earth) into worshiping the Man of Sin.

29

The Double-Cross

'm about to propose a concept that won't be popular with Jews or Christians—but that's precisely why it will be effective. We can forget about a standard-issue villain from Central Casting as the Antichrist. The principalities and powers are much too devious for that. He'll be charming, intelligent, handsome, and a very effective leader. And the deception that's most likely to fool Jews and Christians, assuming the Church is still on earth, is for the Fallen to put forward an Israeli Antichrist who presents himself to the world as a Jew.

Please understand that I'm not suggesting the Antichrist will *be* Jewish, only that he will *claim* to be. This interpretation won't win many fans among conservative Christians (or Jews, obviously), but it's the scenario that makes the most sense.

First, it points to the most logical national origin of a political figure who will build the Third Temple and reinstitute the sacrifices and offerings. While Christian doctrine doesn't require a temple, Daniel 9:27 prophesies that the Antichrist will "put an end to sacrifice and offering," so the Third Temple will be built.

It's highly unlikely that an Islamic Antichrist allows this to happen. Yes, the Third Temple could be built before the Antichrist arrives on the scene, but if he's a Muslim, what are the odds he "makes a strong covenant with many for one week"[465] (seven years) and then waits three and a half years to stop the daily offerings? Possible, but far less likely than the Israeli Antichrist scenario.

Second, it's difficult to imagine that an Antichrist from anywhere except Israel would conduct the prophesied war of Daniel 11:40–45. Think about this for a moment: Imagine a dynamic Israeli political and/or military leader. He's faced with a crisis, a sudden attack by a coalition of enemies. But against all odds, he not only wins a smashing victory but expands Israel's borders, maybe even taking enough territory that it appears God has finally fulfilled his land promise to Abraham.[466]

Why would the Antichrist do this? *Deception.* Muslims ready to fight for the Mahdi will undoubtedly see this Israeli leader as the Dajjal, and they would throw themselves into the fight with the same shocking ferocity that overwhelmed the Persian and Roman empires in the seventh century.

And they will lose. Badly.

How will Jews waiting for the *mashiach* react to this stunning and overwhelming victory? They'll celebrate the arrival of Mashiach ben David, hero of the Gog-Magog war. If there is no fire from heaven or burying of the dead for seven months, it won't matter; the fact that prominent rabbis are already calling the Syrian civil war the coming of Gog shows how far they're ready to bend their interpretations of Ezekiel to fit events on the ground.

When the Psalm 83/Daniel 11 wars take place, the victorious Antichrist will be welcomed in "the beautiful land" with open arms.

An Antichrist from Israel isn't a new idea. It's actually a very old interpretation. Some early church fathers, including Hippolytus of Rome (AD 170–235) and Irenaeus (c. AD 130–202), believed the Antichrist would be a Jew.

Jeremiah does not merely point out his sudden coming, but he even indicates the tribe from which he shall come, where he says, "We shall hear the voice of his swift horses from Dan; the whole earth shall be moved by the voice of the neighing of his galloping horses: he shall also come and devour the earth, and the fulness thereof, the city also, and they that dwell therein." This, too, is the reason that this tribe is not reckoned in the Apocalypse along with those which are saved. [467]

Dan, of course, was one of Israel's twelve tribes, and Irenaeus noted the strange omission of Dan from the 144,000 Jews who are sealed in Revelation 7. After failing to push the Canaanites out of its allotted territory on the coast, the tribe of Dan migrated north and captured the city of Laish (see Judges 18) to become the northernmost tribe of Israel. The city of Dan is on the southwestern foothills of Mount Hermon, and it became the site of one of Jeroboam's golden calves, an idol to the creator-god of the Canaanites, El,[468] whose mount of assembly was Hermon.[469] This is consistent with the "threat from the north" theme that's woven through Israel's history and central to the prophecy of Ezekiel 38 and 39.

Interestingly, Hippolytus was a disciple of Irenaeus, who was a disciple of Polycarp, who was a disciple of the apostle John. So, the belief in a Jewish Antichrist held by Hippolytus and Irenaeus may have come from the man who received the Revelation from Jesus Christ Himself.

You may question how someone with the attitude described by Daniel—haughty, arrogant, serving a foreign "god of fortresses"—could possibly win over Orthodox and Haredi rabbis and be declared the *mashiach*. Good question. Here's another: How often do politicians tell people what they really think instead of what they want people to hear?

You may also wonder why the Antichrist would lead a war to destroy what you'd assume would be his most loyal and enthusiastic followers—Muslims ready to fight for the Mahdi. The answer is simple: Muslims, in the eyes of the Enemy, are already lost. Those who embrace the false teachings of Muhammad are destined for destruction. The goal of the Fallen is to destroy the followers of Jesus Christ and the people Yahweh chose for Himself, the Jews. The best use the Enemy has for Muslims is to throw them into a losing battle as cannon fodder, a bloody sacrifice to lure Jews and Christians into worshiping the Antichrist as the Messiah.

The Fallen have no use for humanity. Those of us who serve them willingly are just useful idiots.

After a decisive victory by the Antichrist over the forces of Islam, the Psalm 83/Daniel 11 war, Muslim eschatology becomes irrelevant. We don't need to worry about identifying the Mahdi because there will never *be* a Mahdi. In my view, Allah, Inc., created Islam for one purpose only: To build an army for a war that validates the Antichrist's claim to be the prophesied savior of Israel.

That army will be sacrificed by its creators; its faithful jihadis willingly slaughtered by their hellish masters to put the Antichrist on the Temple Mount as Israel's false *mashiach*.

If the Church is still here when this happens, how will American Christians receive such a man? Evangelicals typically view strong Israeli leaders in a very positive light. If we're still on earth, conservative American Christians might even help elevate a man perceived as the savior of Israel to the status of a world leader—which is his ultimate destiny, of course, if only for a little while.

But the Dominionist strain of Christianity, which ignores the Antichrist in its faulty interpretation of end-times prophecy, is working toward a Christianized version of global jihad. Based on an incorrect reading of Psalm 110:1, some Dominionist teachers believe Christ is stuck in heaven until Christians make His enemies His footstool. They believe this can only be accomplished by literally taking over the world.[470]

The apostolic-prophetic movement, dubbed the New Apostolic Reformation, might just welcome a victorious Israeli military leader as Christ incarnate, a fulfillment of their expected Manifest Sons of God. Since the self-proclaimed apostles and prophets leading this movement claim the authority of their biblical forebears, which includes the men who wrote the New Testament, they believe they are free to mold Scripture as needed to make their doctrine fit current events.[471]

Now, consider the world's reaction to the next event in the chronicle of the wars of Antichrist:

And he shall pitch his palatial tents between the sea and the glorious holy mountain. Yet he shall come to his end, with none to help him. (Daniel 11:45)

After smashing the Muslim coalition and establishing his *bona fides* as the *mashiach* of Israel, the Antichrist sets up his government somewhere between the Mediterranean coast and Jerusalem. But he meets an unexpected end, perhaps by assassination. So, how could this guy be the Antichrist if he's killed before he commits the "abomination that causes desolation" by desecrating the Temple and declaring himself a god? We return to the Revelation of John:

And I saw a beast rising out of the sea, with ten horns and seven heads, with ten diadems on its horns and blasphemous names on its heads. And the beast that I saw was like a leopard; its feet were like a bear's, and its mouth was like a lion's mouth. And to it the dragon gave his power and his throne and great authority. **One of its heads seemed to have a mortal wound, but its mortal wound was healed, and the whole earth marveled as they followed the beast.** And they worshiped the dragon, for he had given his authority to the beast, and they worshiped the beast, saying, "Who is like the beast, and who can fight against it?" (Revelation 13:1–4, emphasis added)

The apparently miraculous healing of the Antichrist's head wound will amaze the world and convince millions, if not billions, of his divinity.

And because you're paying close attention, you noticed the chilling parallel here with Jewish eschatology. Mashiach ben Yosef is expected to die in the war with Gog of Magog. Then one of two things happens: Mashiach ben David arrives, kills the enemy leader with the breath of his mouth, and brings Mashiach ben Yosef back to life, or Mashiach ben Yosef is resurrected, *becomes* Mashiach ben David, and destroys Gog to end the war.

Not to put too fine a point on it, but when Mashiach ben Yosef is miraculously healed, it will confirm that Mashiach ben David is the Antichrist.

The sad irony is that the rabbis are partly right, except they missed Mashiach ben Yosef when He arrived. He's already been here—Jesus, son of Mary and Joseph. We're just waiting for His return as the conquering Son of David.

In some Jewish traditions, Mashiach ben David then goes on to purify Jerusalem and Israel. If the Israeli Antichrist theory is correct, this has disturbing implications. Purification includes removing non-Jews from Jerusalem. It is not our intent to cast aspersions on our Jewish brothers and sisters, but the Antichrist's bloody war on the saints, prophesied in Daniel 7:25, Daniel 8:24, and Revelation 13:7–10, will happen at some point. This seems to be the most likely place in the prophetic timeline.

The lessons of history aren't always pleasant, but if we take the time to study and learn, they're usually instructive. The final break between early Christians and their Jewish neighbors in Judea didn't occur in the first century, as we might assume. In spite of the persecution of the early church by the Sanhedrin, Jewish Christians, which is to say *most* Christians for the first hundred years or so after the Resurrection, considered themselves part of Jewish society. Many were still members of their local synagogues, differing from their friends and neighbors only in that they knew that Messiah had come, and was coming back.

That all changed during the rebellion against Rome led by Simon bar Kokhba.

The Bar Kokhba revolt began in AD 132. Bar Kokhba was hailed as the *mashiach* by the prominent Rabbi Akiva, still considered one of the most heroic and beloved figures in Jewish history. Bar Kokhba's name was actually Simon ben Kosiba; bar Kokhba ("son of the star") was a messianic claim based on his supposed fulfillment of the prophecy of Balaam, son of Beor:

> I see him, but not now;
> I behold him, but not near:
> a star shall come out of Jacob,
> and a scepter shall rise out of Israel;
> it shall crush the forehead of Moab
> and break down all the sons of Sheth. (Numbers 24:17)

Christians in Judea wouldn't acknowledge a mortal man as the Messiah and refused to fight for bar Kokhba. He punished them with confinement and death. And that led to a break between Jews and the church that hasn't healed to this day.

In the aftermath of his disastrous rebellion, he was derisively called bar Koziba ("son of the lie"). Despite some stunning early success against Rome, once the emperor Hadrian got serious and sent his best generals to put down the rebellion, more than half a million Jews were killed. Judea was depopulated, Jerusalem was destroyed, and the land was renamed Syria Palaestina—Palestine. The net result of bar Kokhba's rebellion was the end of hope for an independent Jewish state in the Holy Land for nearly two thousand years.

In recent years, a surge in Zionist sentiment among Israelis is rehabilitating the reputation of Simon bar Kokhba, who's celebrated as a national hero. Bonfires are lit on Lag Ba'Omer to celebrate his short-lived Jewish state, and Rabbi Akiva's definition of the *mashiach* is still the standard by which many Jews evaluate claimants to the title.

Anyone who's visited Israel can understand the national pride Jews feel. They have survived against tremendous, almost unimaginable odds since declaring independence in 1948. The desert blooms, and Israelis are justifiably proud of their achievements in academia, medicine, and high technology.

But this nationalist sentiment will be manipulated by the supernatural Man of Lawlessness, who will twist it to deceive Jews into following him as their *mashiach*. He may even cite the example of bar Kokhba as he marks Christians still on earth for destruction.

This is not a criticism of Jews. God knows that there are far too many examples of Christians who've been deceived by the Enemy into persecuting Jews in Jesus' name, forgetting that the founder of our faith is the only Jew who ever fulfilled the Law perfectly. Prophecy tells us that the faithful will be persecuted during the period called the Great Tribulation. The Antichrist is of his father, the father of lies, and he will use any tactic that works. Hatred of outsiders is time-tested. Those fooled into supporting the Antichrist's reverse pogrom will believe they're doing God's work—until "Mashiach ben David" stops the daily sacrifices, sits down in the Third Temple, and declares himself to be God.[472]

Then Jews will realize that they've been had.

Summing up: Muslims are waiting for the Mahdi, but what he looks like depends on whether you ask a Sunni or a Shia, and which sect they belong to within those sects. Sunni Islam, specifically radical Mahdism, is probably the tool Allah, Inc., will use to lure Jews and Christians, if the church is still on the earth, into fighting for the Antichrist.

It's easy to tell ourselves that we won't be fooled, that we'll see through the Enemy's deception. Jesus warned against that kind of spiritual pride. As He told the people of Judea two thousand years ago, "I have come in my Father's name, and you do not receive me. If another comes in his own name, you will receive him."[473]

But the victory of Allah, Inc., will be short-lived. Reckoning is coming. As Paul wrote, "Vengeance is mine, I will repay, says the Lord."[474]

And payback is nothing less than the death of the gods.

30

Death of the Gods

We know when judgment against the gods will be executed. Well, not *when*, exactly, as in a date and year; Jesus said that it's not for us to know the times or seasons,[475] but to watch for the signs of the changing of the seasons.[476] (Hence, this book.)

We do know the name of the day when time expires on the temporary dominion of Satan and his colleagues.[477] It's called the Day of the Lord, or the Day of Yahweh, a phrase used by the Hebrew prophets for the time of God's judgment on an unrepentant world.

> Behold, the day of the LORD comes,
> cruel, with wrath and fierce anger,
> to make the land a desolation
> and to destroy its sinners from it.
> For the stars of the heavens and their constellations
> will not give their light;
> the sun will be dark at its rising,
> and the moon will not shed its light.

I will punish the world for its evil,
and the wicked for their iniquity;
I will put an end to the pomp of the arrogant,
and lay low the pompous pride of the ruthless.
I will make people more rare than fine gold,
and mankind than the gold of Ophir.
Therefore I will make the heavens tremble,
and the earth will be shaken out of its place,
at the wrath of the LORD of hosts
in the day of his fierce anger. (Isaiah 13:9–13)

The Day of the Lord, also referred to by the phrase "on that day," is the judgment on an unrepentant world that's been described by many of the prophets. Specifically, Ezekiel, in the aftermath of the Gog-Magog war; John, following Armageddon; Jesus (of course), in the promises of His return in the clouds with glory; and others, such as:

- Isaiah 13:4–13; 27:1, 12–13
- Jeremiah 30:5–9; 46:10
- Zechariah 14
- Joel 2 and 3
- Amos 5
- Obadiah 1:15–18
- Zephaniah 1:7–18
- Malachi 4
- Paul (1 Thessalonians 5:1–11)
- Peter (2 Peter 3:10)

The descriptions of the Day of Yahweh are consistent: When God's patience runs out, sinners pay a heavy price for their rebellion against His authority. But there's an aspect of that day usually not discussed by prophecy teachers—the death of the gods.

Sure, the Bible prophesies the final defeat of Satan, the beast, and the false prophet after God's thousand-year reign on earth,[478] but the gods we've been discussing throughout this book are generally overlooked.

As we noted in the introduction, these gods are already under a death sentence. We're just waiting for sentence to be carried out.

> God has taken his place in the divine council;
> in the midst of the gods he holds judgment: …
> I said, "You are gods,
> sons of the Most High, all of you;
> nevertheless, like men you shall die,
> and fall like any prince." (Psalm 82:1, 6–7)

Bible commentators over the years have suggested that the "gods" of Psalm 82 were the ruling class of Israel—human princes, judges, and magistrates. This is another example of the bias against "g-o-d" meaning anything except Yahweh. That's not how the Jewish prophets, psalmists, and apostles understood the word *elohim*. In singular form, it can mean Yahweh, but in plural form, it refers to the other denizens of the spirit realm. Psalm 82:1 clearly refers to both, since Elohim ("God") would not be in the midst of Himself.

In short, the gods are real, and Psalm 82 describes a heavenly courtroom with God as judge.

So, what does punishment of the gods look like?

> On that day the LORD will punish
> the host of heaven, in heaven,
> and the kings of the earth, on the earth.
> They will be gathered together
> as prisoners in a pit;
> they will be shut up in a prison,
> and after many days they will be punished.

Then the moon will be confounded
and the sun ashamed,
for the LORD of hosts reigns
on Mount Zion and in Jerusalem,
and his glory will be before his elders. (Isaiah 24:21–23)

That's a clear picture of the aftermath of the final battle described by Ezekiel, John, Zechariah, Joel, and others. Isaiah prophesied that this reckoning takes place "on that day," the day of the Lord.

When reading that God would punish the host of heaven, and that "the moon will be confounded and the sun ashamed," it's understandable that many Christians assume the prophet was engaging in a little hyperbole, exaggerating to make a point. I don't think so. When Moses reminded Israel that they were not to worship the gods Yahweh allotted to the rest of the nations, he used exactly the same terms Isaiah used seven hundred years later.

And beware lest you raise your eyes to heaven, and when you see
the sun and the moon and the stars, all the host of heaven, you
be drawn away and bow down to them and serve them, things
that the LORD your God has allotted to all the peoples under the
whole heaven. (Deuteronomy 4:19)

God identified the gods of the nations as the sun (Shemesh, Hebrew name for the sun-god), the moon (Yerakh, Hebrew name for the moon-god), and the host of heaven. Isaiah really meant that these supernatural entities—fallen angels, if you prefer—who conned the nations into worshiping them as the sun, moon, and stars will be imprisoned on the Day of the Lord. Their ultimate destiny is the sentence that was handed down during the courtroom scene described in Psalm 82—death.

There is precedent in the Bible for gods under the judgment of Yahweh. The angels who sinned at Mount Hermon, whom we've identified as the Hebrew Watchers and Greek Titans, were *tartaro* ("thrust down to Tartarus"), where they're chained "under gloomy darkness until the judgment of the great day."[479]

The angels who created the Nephilim are called Watchers in the Book of First Enoch. You'd be forgiven for assuming that that those were *the* Watchers—the only ones, ever, because we never hear about Watchers in church. Not so. Watcher-class angels were still active in human affairs in the time of Daniel, because one of them delivered a message in a dream to Nebuchadnezzar.

> I saw in the visions of my head as I lay in bed, and **behold, a watcher, a holy one, came down from heaven.** He proclaimed aloud and said thus: "Chop down the tree and lop off its branches, strip off its leaves and scatter its fruit. Let the beasts flee from under it and the birds from its branches. But leave the stump of its roots in the earth, bound with a band of iron and bronze, amid the tender grass of the field. Let him be wet with the dew of heaven. Let his portion be with the beasts in the grass of the earth. Let his mind be changed from a man's, and let a beast's mind be given to him; and let seven periods of time pass over him. **The sentence is by the decree of the watchers, the decision by the word of the holy ones,** to the end that the living may know that the Most High rules the kingdom of men and gives it to whom he will and sets over it the lowliest of men."
> (Daniel 4:13–17, emphasis added)

Not only did a Watcher deliver the message of punishment for the king's pride, it was *decreed* by the Watchers.

As in Enoch, this brief mention in Daniel suggests that Watchers have power and authority. This authority comes from God, and it seems that the Watchers in Daniel were faithful in carrying out His will. We've seen what happens to those who rebel—chains and gloomy darkness.

So, OK. We've found the only other Watchers in the Bible, then, right?

Not exactly. Hang on, because we're going to examine some prophecies of the destruction of the rebellious sons of God that have been hiding in plain sight for more than two thousand years.

First, some background. We need to take a step back for a quick look at the origin of the word *nephilim*, the giants created by the angels who sinned in the Genesis 6 incident.

Dr. Michael S. Heiser, author of the highly recommended books *The Unseen Realm* and *Reversing Hermon*, makes a good case for the derivation of the word "Nephilim" from an Aramaic noun, *naphil(a)*, which means "giant."[480] It's similar to the Hebrew word *naphal*, "to fall," which has led many scholars to the conclusion that *nephilim* means "fallen ones."

While they certainly were that, Heiser points out that the rules of Hebrew would make the plural form *nephulim*, while "those who fall away" would be *nophelim*.[481] In other words, "Nephilim" is based on an Aramaic word that's been "Hebrew-ized" with the *-im* plural suffix replacing the Aramaic *-in*.[482]

The point is this: A similar cross-pollination of Hebrew and Aramaic might reveal a more intriguing reading of the end of Isaiah 14, the famous chapter condemning the king of Babylon by comparing him to the divine rebel from Eden:

> May the offspring of evildoers nevermore be named!
> Prepare slaughter for his sons
> because of the guilt of their fathers,
> lest they rise and possess the earth,
> and fill the face of the world with cities. (Isaiah 14:20b–21)

Here's the key: the Hebrew word for "city" is *'iyr*. In Aramaic, the very same word means "Watcher." The connection between the two is that cities in the ancient world were generally surrounded by walls and guarded by—you guessed it—watchmen.[483] The plural forms are *iyrim* and *iyrin*, respectively. Thanks to Dr. Heiser, we have a good example of an Aramaic word that was imported into the Bible and then "corrected" with the *-im* plural suffix, which transformed Aramaic *naphil(a)* into the Bible's *nephilim*.

While you wouldn't want to live in a world covered with cities full of evildoers, urban centers are not inherently evil. The verse doesn't make a lot of sense on its face.

However, in the full context of the chapter, it's possible that another reading fits better. English translators, lacking the worldview of the Hebrew prophets, missed it by assuming that every instance of *'iyr* in the Old Testament must mean "city" (except in Daniel 4, where the context makes it impossible to read *'iyr* as anything but a supernatural entity).

You can see how substituting "Watchers" for "cities" changes the passage in an important way:

> Prepare slaughter for his sons
> because of the guilt of their fathers
> lest they rise and possess the earth,
> and fill the face of the world with [Watchers].
> (Isaiah 14:21, modified)

Isaiah apparently intended to record God's judgment against the off-spring of the rebel angels on Hermon, the Watchers, and their progeny, the Nephilim. In the context of the chapter, this reading isn't much of a stretch, but it isn't the only place in Isaiah where a Watchers-for-cities swap makes sense.[484]

> Behold, their heroes cry in the streets;
> the envoys of peace weep bitterly.
> The highways lie waste;

the traveler ceases.
Covenants are broken;
cities are despised;
there is no regard for man.
The land mourns and languishes;
Lebanon is confounded and withers away;
Sharon is like a desert,
and Bashan and Carmel shake off their leaves. (Isaiah 33:7–9)

The word rendered "heroes" in verse 7 is the Hebrew *'er'el*. Elsewhere in the Bible, *'er'el* is transliterated into English as "Ariel," which means "lion of God." While we don't want to follow unbiblical notions too far, later Jewish tradition was that the Arielites were angels.[485] The "ariels" in verse 7 are paralleled by "envoys," which in Hebrew is *malakim* ("messengers"), which often refers to the lowest class of angel. So, reading "ariels" as "angelic beings" here actually fits.

The context of Isaiah 33 is a warning to Assyria, the neighborhood bully in the Near East in the eighth century BC. God had used them to chastise the kingdoms of Israel and Judah, but a reckoning was in Assyria's future. A surface level reading of the verses fits the political situation of that time; the Assyrian army was marching toward Jerusalem and the envoys sent to Egypt by King Hezekiah had returned to report that no help was coming. Considering that Assyria had steamrolled every other nation in the region, one can imagine the warriors of Judah, its "heroes," weeping at the prospect of a futile battle that would almost certainly end in death, followed by the destruction of everyone and everything they loved.

But a deeper analysis of the verses reveals a prophecy of God's retribution against Assyria.

Ah, you destroyer,
who yourself have not been destroyed,
you traitor,

whom none has betrayed!
When you have ceased to destroy,
you will be destroyed;
and when you have finished betraying,
they will betray you. (Isaiah 33:1)

Of course, the Bible records the fulfillment of this promise when the Assyrians camped outside the walls of Jerusalem were destroyed, but not by human hands.[486] Fittingly, the context of the chapter suggests that the *ariels*, the "heroes" of verse 7, were more than human. Besides pairing the *ariels* with the *malakim* of peace, the references to Lebanon, Bashan, home of the kingdom of Og and Mount Hermon, and Carmel, a mountain known as a holy site for centuries before Isaiah,[487] suggest that Isaiah 33 is either a lament for a supernatural event that had just occurred or dread of something that was about to.

That, of course, makes the substitution of Watchers for cities not only plausible, but logical:

The highways lie waste;
the traveler ceases.
Covenants are broken;
[Watchers] are despised;
there is no regard for man. (Isaiah 33:8, modified)

There is something else to note in that verse: A "traveler" in this context may well be someone on a journey, but it's also a word used by Amorites for the spirits of the divinized dead kings of old, the Rephaim.[488]

And that points us back to another aspect of end-times prophecy that's often overlooked—the return of the Nephilim.

31

Return of the Rephaim

In the Canaanite Rephaim Texts, "Travelers" are spirits who "travel" or "cross over" from one plane of existence to another, from the realm of the dead to the land of the living—in other words, demons, the spirits of the Nephilim destroyed in the days of Noah. It's significant because "Traveler" can be interpreted as a divine name in Ezekiel's prophecy of the Gog-Magog war.[489]

> On that day I will give to Gog a place for burial in Israel, the Valley of the Travelers, east of the sea. It will block the travelers, for there Gog and all his multitude will be buried. It will be called the Valley of Hamon-gog. (Ezekiel 39:11)

These Travelers, the Rephaim, were also called "warriors of Baal" in the Rephaim Texts at Ugarit.[490] The reference to them in Ezekiel 39 is not just significant, but critical. The Amorite pagans of Canaan venerated spirits of the dead for centuries before Israel arrived. That's why God prohibited consulting with mediums and necromancers,[491] and why He sent a plague against Israel for eating sacrifices offered to the dead.[492]

Ezekiel places the Valley of the Travelers east of the Dead Sea, an area where the veil between the worlds was believed to be thin. Place names along the route of the Exodus in Moab include Oboth ("Spirit of the Dead"), Peor ("cleft" or "gap," which in this context refers to the entrance to the netherworld),[493] and Iye-Abarim ("Ruins of the Travelers").[494] Mount Nebo, across the Jordan from Jericho, is called the "mountain of the Abarim (Travelers)."[495]

Archaeologists working at Tall el-Hammam, a site about seven and a half miles northeast of the Dead Sea, have uncovered physical evidence that strongly suggests it was the site of Sodom.[496] A thriving city with massive defensive walls appears to have been leveled around 1700 BC in a single, cataclysmic event that left it and the fertile plain around it uninhabited for the next six to seven hundred years, until the time of Saul, David, and Solomon.[497]

Just southeast of the city is a cluster of about five hundred dolmens, megalithic funerary monuments that scholars date to the Early Bronze Age, possibly as old as 3300 BC.[498] It's estimated that as many as fifteen hundred once stood there, along with menhirs (standing stones), henges, and stone circles, the largest such collection of megalithic structures in the Levant.[499]

The site rises 75 to 150 feet above the plain. So, the stone monuments and the ruined, still-deserted city would have been easily visible to the Israelites who camped on the plains of Moab. It's even possible that their stop at Iye-Abarim, "Ruins of the Travelers," was among the rubble of the city that God destroyed with fire from the sky.

Dr. Phillip Silvia, the director of scientific analysis for the Tall el-Hammam Excavation Project, told me in a 2019 interview that the dolmens, unlike some others in the Jordan valley, don't appear to be aligned with any astronomical features. Instead, they appear to be oriented toward what project archaeologists believe was the temple of Tall el-Hammam.[500]

We're eagerly waiting to see what the ongoing dig turns up, but this is a tantalizing bit of information. Consider: The east side of the Jordan valley is where the Bible places the Rephaim tribes in the days of Abraham.[501] Some twenty-five thousand dolmens have been found along the Jordan from the Golan Heights (ancient Bashan) to the Dead Sea, with the largest concentration of them just outside the walls of Sodom—the largest and most influential city in the Transjordan until the time of Abraham and Lot. Scholars date the construction of the dolmens to time of the Rephaim, the Early and Middle Bronze Ages (roughly 3300–1800 BC),[502] which coincides almost exactly with the period that Sodom dominated the region.[503] Those dolmens apparently faced the city's temple.

That begs the question: Which of the Fallen was worshiped in that temple? Why was God compelled to destroy the city and those around it? His judgment was about more than just their choice of lifestyle.

Anyway, the Hebrew prophets, especially Isaiah and Ezekiel, were clearly familiar with the pagan cult of the dead. References to the Rephaim are there in the original Hebrew, but they've been obscured by translators who may not have understood the historical and religious milieu of the ancient Near East. It doesn't help that we modern Christians have been taught to de-supernaturalize the Bible. A diverse cast of characters possessing free will—including Satan, a handful of major pagan deities, and an army of minor players in the spirit realm like the host of heaven, the "shades" (Rephaim), and demons—has been flattened into the devil and some minions. And most of us have never been taught that those minions are real, much less that they have a role to play in the end-times prophecy.

On the contrary. The prophets knew that demons and the gods who created them are real, and that they're working toward a final confrontation with God that will draw in the entire world.

Let's start with Ezekiel, who prophesied the return of the Nephilim at Armageddon. The spirits of the Rephaim are the Travelers, the demon warriors of Baal (Satan) who make up the army of Gog (Antichrist) at the final battle for Zion.

That may sound crazy, but consider: Since this happens on the Day of the Lord, the day of His terrible judgment on the world, the church won't be here. We are not destined to suffer His wrath.[504] With Christians gone, those still on the earth will not be protected by the Holy Spirit from this demonic army. What the people of Jerusalem face in that final battle is an attacking force possessed by the demonic spirits of the "mighty men who were of old," the Nephilim, following their spirit fathers into battle for one final assault on the holy mountain of God.

It will quite literally be an army of the evil dead.

This brings us back full circle to Isaiah 14, where we find the Rephaim, translated into English as "shades," welcoming the divine rebel upon his fall from Eden.

Sheol beneath is stirred up
to meet you when you come;
it rouses the shades [*Rephaim*] to greet you,
all who were leaders of the earth;
it raises from their thrones
all who were kings of the nations. (Isaiah 14:9)

The description by Isaiah matches the sense of the term in Ugaritic texts from five hundred years earlier: Dead kings of old who now inhabit the netherworld. The main difference is that the Amorites believed that those spirits of the dead would bless and protect their kings, while Isaiah described them as "weak," sleeping beneath worms on a bed of maggots.[505]

Isaiah 14 is, without a doubt, one of the most important chapters in the Bible for understanding this long supernatural war in which you and I are deployed. It tells us about the divine rebel, Day Star (Lucifer), son of Dawn, and his fall from Eden. The five "I wills" that illustrate his destructive pride and ambition give us insight into what drives one of the key members of Allah, Inc. He may even be the mastermind of the plot.

But as often as we've read this chapter of the Bible, Isaiah's report on Lucifer's fall is even more fascinating that we've been taught.

First, as we noted earlier, because Isaiah identified Lucifer's mount of assembly as Zaphon, the mountain sacred to Baal (whom Jesus identified as Satan), we can be pretty sure that Satan is in view here.

Second, the prophet, who is known for his love of wordplay,[506] used an Egyptian loanword to reveal more about the final destiny of the rebel god.

> All the kings of the nations lie in glory,
> each in his own tomb;
> **but you are cast out, away from your grave,**
> **like a loathed branch,**
> clothed with the slain, those pierced by the sword,
> who go down to the stones of the pit,
> like a dead body trampled underfoot.
> (Isaiah 14:18–19, emphasis added)

What did Isaiah mean by calling the rebel from Eden "a loathed branch?"

Most English translations agree that the Hebrew word *netser* means "branch." The range of adjectives chosen by translators includes "loathed," "repulsive," "rejected," "worthless," and "abominable," but they convey the same sense—something utterly detestable. The adjective translated "abhorred" or "abominable," Hebrew *ta'ab*, is significant. It modifies the noun *netser*, which would normally have a positive connotation. In this context, *ta'ab* means something like "unclean," or "ritually impure."[507]

Still, even trying to allow for differences in cultures over the last twenty-seven hundred years, calling someone an "unclean branch" is puzzling. But there is a likely explanation: Isaiah meant something other than "branch" because the Hebrew *netser* wasn't the word he used at all.

[The] term is best explained as a loanword from the common Egyptian noun *ntr*. **Ntr is generally translated "god," but is commonly used of the divinized dead and their physical remains.** It originally came into Hebrew as a noun referring to the putatively divinized corpse of a dead king, which is closely related to the Egyptian usage.[508] (Emphasis added)

"Divinized dead" is a description of the Rephaim, the Nephilim spirits venerated by the Amorites of Canaan, whom the prophet mentioned above, in verse 9. Isaiah used an Egyptian word that *sounds* like the Hebrew word for "branch" to connect the rebel from Eden to the Rephaim by calling Satan an abhorrent dead god.

It fits the context of the chapter. Satan was thrown down from Eden to the netherworld, kicked out of heaven, and demoted to lord of the dead. What humiliation.

Then Isaiah delivered God's final verdict:

You will not be joined with them in burial,
because you have destroyed your land,
you have slain your people.
"May the offspring of evildoers
nevermore be named!
Prepare slaughter for his sons
because of the guilt of their fathers,
lest they rise and possess the earth,
and fill the face of the world with [Watchers]." (Isaiah 14:20–21, modified)

These verses come into clearer focus when they're read with the worldview of the prophet in mind. Associating the rebel from Eden with the dead in Sheol wasn't symbolic; Baal/Satan was ejected from God's holy mountain, Eden, the same way the spirits of the Nephilim had been condemned to wander the earth until the judgment.[509] The place of this unclean, dead god would forevermore be with the spirits of the dead, the "leaders of the earth" and "kings of the nations"—in other words, the "mighty men who were of old." That's who the Amorites believed were their ancestors, the Rephaim and the council of the Didanu—the Titans, the Watchers of Genesis 6.

Isaiah 14 is a record not just of the fall and judgment of Satan; it prophesies the ultimate slaughter of the demonic Rephaim/Nephilim, the warriors of Baal, "lest they rise and possess the earth."

But wait—there's more!

We need to reexamine a prophecy mentioned earlier, one that was interpreted in the second century AD as heralding the would-be *mashiach*, Simon bar Kokhba. It's been interpreted as a messianic prophecy, at least by Jewish scholars, for more than two thousand years.

What scholars have missed is that it foretells not only the coming of Messiah, but of His final victory over the rebel gods and their offspring.

> I see him, but not now;
> I behold him, but not near:
> a star shall come out of Jacob,
> and a scepter shall rise out of Israel;
> it shall crush the forehead of Moab
> and break down all the sons of Sheth.
> Edom shall be dispossessed;
> Seir also, his enemies, shall be dispossessed.
> Israel is doing valiantly. (Numbers 24:17–18)

Scholars have argued for literally thousands of years about the exact meaning of this passage. Some reject a messianic application of Balaam's prophecy. For example, Martin Luther couldn't accept that God would use a devious pagan like Balaam that way. But since Numbers 24:2 tells us that "the Spirit of God came upon him," we assume that Balaam was, in fact, speaking truth.

Moab and Edom, we understand. They were ancient enemies of Israel. Seir is another reference to Edom, taken from the Shara mountains in southern Jordan, which belonged to Edom through most of the Old Testament period.[510]

But who, exactly, are the sons of Sheth?

Some translations render the name "Seth," and a few read "sons of tumult" instead of Seth or Sheth. Which Seth are we talking about here? Seth, the son of Adam? Seth (also called Set or Sutekh), the Egyptian god of chaos?

Allow me to put forward a possibility you probably haven't heard before.

Scholar Amar Annus has linked the name Sheth/Seth to an Amorite tribe called the Suteans. (Surprise—Amorites again.) The Suteans were notorious in ancient Mesopotamia, considered violent, dangerous, and a threat to civilized society. The word "Sutean" eventually became a Mesopotamian synonym for a witch.[511]

Annus notes that the Egyptian term for the Suteans, *Šwtw* ("Shutu"), a form of the Akkadian name for the tribe, appears in one of the Execration Texts from the nineteenth or eighteenth centuries BC, about the time of Abraham, Isaac, and Jacob.[512]

> The Ruler of Shutu, Ayyabum, and all the retainers who are with him; the Ruler of Shutu, Kushar, and all the retainers who are with him; the Ruler of Shutu, Zabulanu, and all the retainers who are with him.[513]

The relevant fact is that "Sheth," "Shutu," and "Sutean" are the same name processed through different languages and types of writing.[514] Other Egyptian texts place the Shutu/Suteans/Sheth in the central and northern Transjordan, which is precisely where the Bible places the Rephaim.[515]

Here's the link: An Akkadian lexical list (that's like an ancient clay tablet version of Google Translate) specifically equates *su-tu-u* and *ti-id-nu*—Sutean and Tidanu. Remember, Tidanu (or Ditanu) was the tribe from which the kings of the Amorites traced their bloodline, and it was the origin of the name of the elder gods of the Greeks, the Titans.

We also find this connection in texts from the Amorite kingdom of Ugarit.

> In Ugaritic literature Suteans are mentioned in the epic of Aqhatu, where the antagonist of the *mt rpi* ["man of the Rephaim"] Dnil is a nomadic Ytpn, *mhr št*—"warrior of the Sutû, Sutean warrior." … In the epic of Keret Suteans are mentioned as *dtn*, spelled also as *ddn*, and it "must be understood as the Di/Tidanu tribe, a part of common Amorite stock. It is even likely that this term was used in Mesopotamia at the end of the 3rd millennium to designate tribes later known as Suteans.[516]

The bottom line: Texts from various places across the ancient Near East, from Egypt and Canaan in the west to Akkad (modern Iraq) in the east, and from the time of Abraham down to the days of the judges, connect the Suteans, the Egyptian Shutu, and the biblical "sons of Sheth" with the ancient Tidanu—the *Titans*.

As the Israelites prepared to invade Canaan, the prophet Balaam foresaw a messianic figure, "a star," who would come out of Jacob to "break down all the sons of Sheth." These were the Suteans, Amorite nomads living in Rephaim country east of the Jordan. The Suteans were known in former days throughout Mesopotamia as the Ditanu/Didanu or Tidanu, dead kings of old who were linked to the Rephaim. And the Dit/Did/Tidanu was the tribe from which the Greeks got the name of their old gods, the Titans.

Here's the short equation:
Sheth = Shutu = Suteans = Ditanu/Tidanu = Titans.

Since the Greek Titans were the angels God imprisoned in Tartarus for their sin at Mount Hermon, they were the Watchers of Hebrew Scripture. The sons of Sheth were the Nephilim—the Rephaim spirits venerated and summoned through rituals by the pagan Canaanites of Moses' day.

So, the pagan prophet Balaam didn't just prophesy the conquest of Israel's old enemies, Edom and Moab; he foretold the Messiah's ultimate destruction of the sons of the Titans—the Nephilim, also called the "warriors of Baal," and the Travelers of Ezekiel 39.

But it gets better. Read a little more of Balaam's prophecy:

And one from Jacob shall exercise dominion
and destroy the survivors of cities! (Numbers 24:19)

You already see where this is going. The root behind the word translated "cities" is the same one rendered "Watchers" in Daniel 4, the same word that we suggest should read "Watchers" in Isaiah 14:21 and Isaiah 33:8.

In the context of this prophecy, which is so clearly messianic that it may have inspired the ill-starred Jewish rebellion against Rome in the second century AD, it's logical to read it as a prophecy of the Messiah's final victory over the rebel gods.

And one from Jacob shall exercise dominion
and destroy the survivors of [the Watchers]! (Numbers 24:19, modified)

Balaam, the pagan prophet for hire, foretold the Messiah's destruction of the Fallen, the sons of God He judged and sentenced in Psalm 82. Judgment comes on the Day of the Lord, when God Himself takes the field to defend His *har mô'ēd*, Zion, at the Battle of Armageddon.

The army of the Antichrist, a demonic force from all the nations of the world, will be destroyed in what Ezekiel called the Valley of the Travelers, a reference to the Rephaim spirits worshiped by the pagan neighbors of ancient Israel. They are the demons who will possess the soldiers who fight against the Most High on that day. It will be the end of the spirits behind Allah, Inc.

The road ahead for planet earth is not an easy one. To paraphrase our friend, the late (and sorely missed) Patrick "Paddy" Heron: The bad news is we're all riding on the planetary equivalent of the Titanic. The good news is it's easy to get a seat on a lifeboat. All you need to do is believe that Jesus Christ died for your sins and was raised again on the third day, in accordance with the Scriptures.[517]

It really is that simple, and that profound.

32

Conclusion

This been a long journey through history and theology, with a little Greek and Hebrew thrown in for spice. Hopefully, we can get back home by a path that pulls it all together.

First and foremost, we Christians must try to understand the world-view of the prophets and apostles. They knew that the gods of their pagan neighbors were real, not the divine equivalent of imaginary friends. God called them gods, and His Law prohibited consulting with necroman-cers and mediums for a reason. The spirits are real, not all are loyal to Him, and they're really deceptive—even appearing as angels of light.

The first rebellion against God took place in Eden. The *nachash* ("serpent"), a supernatural being described by Ezekiel as an "anointed guardian cherub," was kicked out of Eden, the original mountain of God,[518] to become lord of the dead.[519] This rebel was the ancient Near Eastern storm-god known to us as Baal,[520] whom Jesus identified as Satan.

After the fall of Baal/Satan, the Watchers sinned by descending to Mount Hermon and pursuing "strange flesh,"[521] human women. This unholy union produced the Nephilim.[522] The destruction of those "mighty men who were of old" produced demons, hybrid spirits condemned to wander the earth until the Day of the Lord.[523] In turn, they inspired the pagan nations of the ancient world to worship the dead,[524] in particular, the Amorites, who believed their kings descended from an ancient tribe called the Ditanu or Tidanu, whom they summoned through necromancy rituals.[525] This tribe gave its name to the old gods of the Greeks, the Titans, and the Amorites' veneration of what they thought were the spirits of their royal ancestors, the Rephaim, developed into the hero cults of the Greeks. Those demonic spirits haunt the earth to this day.

While the Bible doesn't tell us much about the rebel Watchers (who were the actual Titans), we do know they were imprisoned in the abyss, Tartarus, at the time of the Flood.[526] They're waiting for one final opportunity to challenge God and destroy His creation. Some time in the future, they'll be released from the pit for five months[527] before they and their demonic offspring are destroyed at Armageddon.

This doom has been foretold in a number of prophecies, but we've highlighted several in this book that specifically prophesy the death of the gods, prophecies that have been veiled by translators and/or a bias against belief in the literal existence of these entities:

- Numbers 24:17–19
- Psalm 82:6–8
- Isaiah 14:18–21
- Isaiah 24:21–23
- Ezekiel 39:11

The leader of this group, named Shemihazah in the extrabiblical Book of First Enoch, is probably the same entity identified by later cultures as Enlil (Sumer), Dagan (Amorites and Philistines), El (Canaan), Kumarbi (Hurrians and Hittites), Baal-Hammon (Phoenicia), Kronos

(Greece), and Saturn (Rome). Stories about this god vary from culture to culture, but consistent threads run through all of them: He deposed the older sky-god and was in turn replaced or overthrown by the storm-god; he has a strong connection to the underworld, and was, in some cases, banished there (notably Kronos, Saturn, and Kumarbi); and he's often connected to child sacrifice (especially Baal-Hammon, Kronos, and Saturn).

The third major rebellion in the spirit realm, following Eden and Mount Hermon, occurred after the Tower of Babel incident. That was an attempt by Nimrod to build an artificial cosmic mountain, an "abode of the gods."[528] God's punishment on the nations was to divide them, confusing the speech of the people and allotting *bənê hā 'ĕlōhîm* to them as their gods.[529] Humanity had made it clear that we preferred dealing with other gods, so Yahweh initiated a new plan, calling Abraham from northern Mesopotamia to become the father of a nation that would produce the Messiah.

The rebellious "sons of God" didn't take this lying down. Pagan worship was the norm in the days of the patriarchs, with all manner of detestable practices passing for worship. Today's so-called progressive ideas about sexuality were very old by the time Moses came down from Mount Sinai with the Law. It makes one wonder whether the plan of the gods was to lure humanity into becoming so offensive to God that He destroyed us all in disgust.

That didn't go well for them. The courtroom scene of Psalm 82 tells us how God decreed that these rebels, who had perverted divine law and justice, will one day die like men.

Still they persisted in their rebellion. This is why the Old Testament reads like a chronicle of the world's attempts to destroy Israel. But despite the destruction of the northern kingdom of Israel by Assyria in 722 BC and the sack of Jerusalem by Nebuchadnezzar in 587 BC, God's divine punishment on a disobedient Israel, He returned His people to the land. They ruled themselves for a short time in the second and first centuries before Christ. Meanwhile, the small-*g* gods continued attacking Israel from without and dividing it from within, in the same way they stirred up divisions in the Christian church before the apostles had even finished writing the New Testament.

Through all of this, it appears that the spirits who convinced humans to worship them competed with each other even as they stood together in rebellion against the Most High. This is suggested by the wars between nations that followed different gods—the Amorite kingdoms in the east, especially Babylon, were led by dynasties that worshiped the moon-god, while Western Amorites in Canaan and Syria served the storm-god; Assyrians to the north followed their chief god, Ashur; Egyptians to the southwest elevated the sun-god to the top of the pantheon; and smaller nations each had their own patron god, like Milcom of Ammon, Chemosh of Moab, and Qôs of Edom.

Popular regional gods included Inanna/Ishtar/Astarte, the gender-fluid goddess of sex and war; the warrior plague-god Nergal/Resheph/Apollo; the mother-goddess Asherah, called the Dragon Lady; and the dead, who compelled families to set out necromantic meals for what they believed were their deceased ancestors, a cult that developed into veneration of the royal dead—the Rephaim/Nephilim—which ensnared even the people of Israel and Judah.

Time passed and the Amorites gave way to their descendants, the Aramaeans (Baal) and Phoenicians (Baal-Hammon/Kronos), while the Greeks and Romans emerged to the west as political powers under their versions of the storm-god and "the" god, Zeus/Jupiter and Kronos/Saturn.

Then the Messiah arrived and everything changed.

He was rejected by Jewish religious authorities, who expected a geopolitical savior. Even His disciples didn't get it. But the crucial point is that the Fallen missed the purpose of Christ's mission, too.[530] To add insult to injury, Jesus spent the time between His death and return to earth lecturing the spirits "in prison."[531] Since Peter identified those spirits as the ones who disobeyed in the days of Noah, they can only have been the Watchers from Genesis 6. Most Bible teachers see those spirits as human, but the Greek word for "spirit," in the context of 1 Peter 3:19–20, almost certainly refers to supernatural beings.[532] Jesus, in other words, proclaimed his victory to the rebel Watchers before His glorious Resurrection.

Talk about rubbing salt into a wound.

And that, I believe, is what led to an unprecedented event in the spirit realm: A coalition of the most prominent and powerful *banê hā'ĕlōhîm*, the gods of the ancient Near East, banded together to create a new religion to counter the growing movement of Christ followers.

It's my belief that the rebel gods, completely outmaneuvered and aware that their time was growing short, realized their only hope of surviving the judgment decreed by God was to work together. They created a new religion in the early seventh century through the agency of a charismatic spiritual leader and brilliant military tactician, Muhammad ibn Abdullah.

Muhammad was exactly what the Fallen needed.

Christians who try to identify the spiritual force behind Islam tend to look for an individual entity, usually Satan, or they categorize it as a pagan religion based on an imaginary moon-god because of the prominent use of the crescent moon in Islamic symbols.

Here is where I differ: While I agree that Satan is involved, I contend that the moon-god is real and a key member of the coalition behind Islam. Call it Allah, Inc.

When Christianity began to spread, it grew to become the dominant religion in nearly all of the lands of the Bible. From Mesopotamia to Britain, the followers of Christ were the majority religion by the early seventh century.

Except in Arabia. Of all the places featured prominently in the Bible, Arabia was the only region where the gospel never took deep root. Why? We can't say with certainty, of course, but the most logical explanation is that the rebel gods, faced with the spread of the Christian faith, used Arabia as a base to launch a counterattack.

Please understand: This is not a claim that the Roman empire's adoption of Christianity chased the pagan gods to Arabia. There is more than enough historical evidence of bad behavior by "Christian" kings, queens, and churchmen to question whether any government on earth has ever been Christian in the true sense of the word.

But the presence of the Holy Spirit among so many believers in lands touched by the gospel must have been a real hindrance to the Fallen. So, they withdrew to Arabia—and waited for the right man to come along to run their new venture.

The history of Islam reflects the character of the entities behind it: Conquest, slavery, and death in the service of Allah, Inc., *jihad* waged by faithful warriors who were motivated by the promise of an eternity of perverse carnal delights—a paradise filled with an endless supply of wine, women, and willing young boys. Even the heavenly rewards offered to Muslims, the faith created by this supernatural corporate merger, are the opposite of what Jesus Christ promised His followers. He made it clear that His kingdom was not of this world.

Not then, anyway.

But a day is coming when the old gods and their demon spawn die like men as they try to storm the mountain of God. When the Messiah returns, He won't be a baby in a barn. He's coming back as a warrior—Messiah ben David.

The future of earth won't be peaceful. The old gods are vicious, vengeful, and willing to do anything to destroy what God created and called good. Tragically, that includes what may be the deaths of literally billions of humans before the end.

You see, the tragedy of this story is that Muslims have been duped. They believe they're following the will of God when they're actually working for the Enemy. But the Fallen care no more for them than they do for you or me. Islam was created, in my view, to set up the most diabolical double-cross in history, when the Fallen willingly sacrifice millions of their own followers to lure Jews, and perhaps Christians, into welcoming and worshiping a false *mashiach*, the Antichrist.

A frontal assault is too obvious. The Enemy is far cleverer than that. This deception will play on the hopes and dreams of those who long for the arrival of Emmanuel—"God with us," the Messiah.

As Christians, we must remember that our struggle is not with human opponents. The cosmic powers over this present darkness are the true Enemy. Jesus Christ died for Muslims, too, even if they don't believe it.

This doesn't mean being foolish, or blind to what Islam is. After more than seventy-five thousand words, I hope you know that I believe that Islam is a religion created by a coalition of ancient, extremely powerful, and indescribably evil entities who move in dimensions we cannot imagine, much less perceive. Worse, they hate us and everyone we love.

But their human foot soldiers—they're the symptom, not the disease.

Witnessing to a hostile camp isn't easy. If it was, we'd all be doing it. We wouldn't need Jesus' command to love our enemies. You and I may not be called to serve as missionaries to the Muslim world, but we can pray for and support those who are. We can also be careful not to make ourselves into additional stumbling blocks between people who are already in spiritual chains and the saving gospel of Jesus Christ.

Islam is a powerful weapon forged by an infernal council to strike at the heart of God's creation—His people, and His holy mountain, Zion.

It will fail. And with that failure comes the death of the gods.

It's been many years since Yahweh Himself led His heavenly host into battle. On that day, when the battle rages at Jerusalem, the army of Antichrist will be absolutely and completely destroyed.

Then the nations will know that Yahweh is the Holy One *in* Israel. Hallelujah!

Notes

1. Deuteronomy 4:19, 29:26.
2. Edward Lipiński, "El's Abode: Mythological Traditions Related to Mount Hermon and to the Mountains of Armenia." *Orientalia Lovaniensa Periodica II* (Leuven: Peters, 1971).
3. Noga Ayali-Darshan, "The Seventy Bulls Sacrificed at Sukkot (Num 29:12-34) in Light of a Ritual Text from Emar (Emar 6, 373)," *Vetus Testamentum* 65:1 (2015), 9–19.
4. Numbers 29:12–34.
5. Ibid.
6. Dr. Michael S. Heiser, "The 70 Bulls of the Feast of Tabernacles," *Naked Bible Podcast*, March 13, 2018 (Transcript: http://www.nakedbiblepodcast. com/wp-content/uploads/2018/03/NB-206-Transcript.pdf), retrieved 8/18/18.
7. Ephesians 6:12.
8. 1 Corinthians 2:6–8.
9. Daniel Bodi, "Is There a Connection Between the Amorites and the Arameans?" *Aram Twenty Eighth International Conference: Zoroastrianism in the Levant; 05-07 July 2010, The Oriental Institute* (Aram Society for Syro-Mesopotamian Studies, 2014), 385.

10. His conclusion has been endorsed by Nicolas Wyatt of the University of Edinburgh.

11. 2 Peter 2:4.

12. Jude 6–7.

13. Amar Annus, "On the Origin of Watchers: A Comparative Study of the Antediluvian Wisdom in Mesopotamian and Jewish Traditions." *Journal for the Study of the Pseudepigrapha* 19.4 (2010), 277–320.

14. Based on their mutual oath to go ahead with their plan so that no one Watcher would take the fall when God found out. See 1 Enoch 6:3–6.

15. See chapter 5 of my book, *Last Clash of the Titans: The Second Coming of Hercules, Leviathan, and the Prophesied War Between Jesus Christ and the Gods of Antiquity.*

16. Brian B. Schmidt, *Israel's Beneficent Dead: Ancestor Cult and Necromancy in Ancient Israelite Religion and Tradition* (Winona Lake, In.: Eisenbrauns, 1996), 127.

17. Samuel N. Kramer, "Lamentation Over the Destruction of Sumer and Ur," *Ancient Near Eastern Texts Relating to the Old Testament. Edited by James B. Pritchard. Third Edition with Supplement* (Trenton: Princeton University Press, 1969), 616.

18. For example, see Albert Tobias Clay, *The Empire of the Amorites* (New Haven: Yale University Press), 1919.

19. Piotr Michalowski, "The Men from Mari." *Immigration and Emigration Within the Ancient Near East*, K. van Lerberghe and A. Schoors (eds.) (Leuven: Peeters, 1995), 182.

20. Madeleine Andre Fitzgerald, *The Rulers of Larsa* (Yale University dissertation, 2002), 20.

21. Which is one of the reasons I argued in *The Great Inception* that the Tower of Babel, which must have been built at the peak of the Uruk kingdom more than a thousand years earlier, could not have been at Babylon.

22. Sara Tricoli, "The Ritual Destruction of the Palace of Mari by Hammurapi under the Light of the Cult of the Ancestors' Seat in Mesopotamian Houses and Palaces." In *Krieg und Frieden im Alten Vorderasien* (Münster: Ugarit-Verlag, 2014), 795–836.

23. Schmidt, op. cit., 158–159. Also Derek P. Gilbert, *Last Clash of the Titans* (Crane, Mo.: Defender, 2018), 84.

24. Nicolas Wyatt, "À la Recherche des Rephaïm Perdus." In *The Archaeology of Myth*, ed. Nicolas Wyatt (London: Equinox, 2010), 595.

25. Ibid.

26. KTU 1.161, which was apparently a ritual performed at the coronation of the last king of Ugarit, Ammurapi III. Note that he shared the same name as his more famous predecessor, Hammurabi of Babylon, who lived more than five hundred years earlier.

27. Jordi Vidal, "The Origins of the Last Ugaritic Dynasty." In *Altorientalishce Forschungen* 33 (2006), 169.

28. James B. Pritchard (ed.), *Ancient Near Eastern Texts Relating to the Old Testament* (Princeton: Princeton University Press, 1969), 253.

29. Niv Allon, "Seth is Baal: Evidence from the Egyptian Script." In *Egypt and the Levant*, Manfred Bietak (ed.) (Wien: Österreichische Akademie der Wissenschaften, 2007), 15–21.

30. Exodus 14:1–2.

31. Deuteronomy 12:11.

32. Bodi, op. cit., 383–409.

33. Georges Roux, *Ancient Iraq*. London: Penguin Books, 1992, 281.

34. Edward the Elder, son of Alfred the Great, in case you're wondering.

35. Ephesians 6:12.

36. Wu Yuhong and Stephanie Dalley, "The Origins of the Manana Dynasty at Kish, and the Assyrian King List." *Iraq, 52* (1990), 160.

37. Mark G. Hall, *A Study of the Sumerian Moon-God, Nanna/Suen* (Ann Arbor, Mich.: University Microfilms International, 1985), 33.

38. Derek P. Gilbert, *The Great Inception: Satan's PSYOPs from Eden to Armageddon* (Crane, Mo.: Defender, 2017), 59.

39. Tallay Ornan, "The Bull and Its Two Masters: Moon and Storm Deities in Relation to the Bull in Ancient Near Eastern Art." *Israel Exploration Journal*, Vol. 51, No. 1 (2001), 3.

40. Jane R. McIntosh, *Ancient Mesopotamia: New Perspectives* (Santa Barbara, Calif.; Denver; London: ABC-CLIO, 2005), 223.

41. Mark E. Cohen, *The Cultic Calendars of the Ancient Near East*. (Bethesda, Md.: CDL Press, 1993), 401.

42. J. A. Black, "The New Year Ceremonies in Ancient Babylon: 'Taking Bel by the Hand' and a Cultic Picnic," *Religion*, 11:1 (1981), 40.

43. Hall, op. cit., 336.

44. Ibid., 336.

45. Cohen, op. cit., 402.

46. Ibid., 403.

47. Ibid., 404.

48. Beate Pongratz-Leisten, "Akitu." *The Encyclopedia of Ancient History, First Edition*, edited by Roger S. Bagnall, et al. (Hoboken, NJ: John Wiley and Sons, 2013), 265–266.

49. "The History of the PEF." (https://www.pef.org.uk/history/), retrieved 10/14/18.

50. George W. E. Nickelsburg, *1 Enoch 1: A Commentary on the Book of 1 Enoch, Chapters 1–36* (Minneapolis: Fortress, 2001), 81–108.

51. George W.E. Nickelsburg, *1 Enoch: The Hermeneia Translation* (Kindle edition) (Minneapolis: Fortress Press, 2012), 23–24.

52. Lipiński, op. cit., 29.

53. Charles Warren, R. E., "The Summit of Hermon, With an Illustration." *Palestine Exploration Fund Quarterly Statement 2.5* (Jan. 1 to March 31, 1870), 212.

54. Jeremiah Peterson, "Nanna/Suen Convenes in the Divine Assembly as King," *Aula Orientalis* 29 (2011), 279.

55. Ibid., 284–285.

56. Inscription found at Nippur. Amélie Kuhrt, *The Ancient Near East C. 3000–330 B.C.: Vol. 1* (London: Routledge, Taylor & Francis Group, 2009), 49.

57. "Saddam Does Battle with Nebuchadnezzar." *The Guardian*, January 4, 1999 (https://www.theguardian.com/world/1999/jan/04/iraq1), retrieved 2/7/19.

58. Cyrus H. Gordon, "Abraham and the Merchants of Ura." *Journal of Near Eastern Studies*, Vol. 17, No. 1 (Jan. 1958), 28–31.

59. Mark Chavalas, "Genealogical History as 'Charter': A Study of Old Babylonian Period Historiography and the Old Testament." In *Faith,*

Tradition, and History: Old Testament Historiography in Its Near Eastern Context (Winona Lake, Ind.: Eisenbrauns, 1994), 122.

60. Gordon, op. cit., 31.

61. Tamara M. Green, *The City of the Moon God: Religious Traditions of Harran* (Leiden; New York: E. J. Brill, 1992), 20.

62. Minna Silver, "Equid Burials in Archaeological Contexts in the Amorite, Hurrian, and Hyksos Cultural Intercourse." *Aram* 26:1&2 (2014), 342.

63. Kenneth C. Way, "Assessing Sacred Asses: Bronze Age Donkey Burials in the Near East." *Levant* 42:2 (2010), 214.

64. Jack M. Sasson, "Thoughts of Zimri-Lim," *Biblical Archaeologist* (June 1984), 118–119.

65. Raphael Greenberg, Sarit Paz, David Wengrow, and Mark Iserlis, "Tel Bet Yerah: Hub of the Early Bronze Age Levant," *Near Eastern Archaeology* 75:2 (2012), 90.

66. Ibid., 95–96.

67. Sarit Paz, "A Home Away from Home? The Settlement of Early Transcaucasian Migrants at Tel Bet Yerah," *Tel Aviv* Vol. 36 (2009), 196–216.

68. "5,000-year-old Moon-shaped Stone Structure Identified in Northern Israel," *Haaretz*, September 16, 2014 (https://www.haaretz.com/archaeology/5-000-year-old-monument-identified-in-north-1.5301928), retrieved 3/18/17.

69. Deuteronomy 32:8.

70. Deuteronomy 32:9.

71. Genesis 22:17, 26:4. It's probable that God meant more than just the number of Abraham's offspring, since "stars" is frequently used to describe the host of heaven. However, we'll have to leave it there as we don't have time to unpack that aspect of God's covenant with Abraham in this book.

72. Genesis 9:5–6

73. See Leviticus 18:21 and 20:2–5.

74. For example, Umm el-Marra in western Syria, near Aleppo. Glenn M. Schwartz, "Memory and its Demolition: Ancestors, Animals and Sacrifice at Umm el-Marra, Syria." *Cambridge Archaeological Journal*, 23 (2013), 495–522.

75. Genesis 22:4.

76. Colin J. Humphreys, *The Miracles of Exodus: A Scientist's Discovery of the Extraordinary Natural Causes of the Biblical Stories* (London [etc.]: Continuum, 2004), 297.

77. Exodus 16:4–36.

78. Joseph Jacobs, M. Seligsohn, Wilhelm Bacher, "Sinai, Mount," *Jewish Encyclopedia* (http://www.jewishencyclopedia.com/articles/13766-sinai-mount), retrieved 10/28/18.

79. Lloyd R. Bailey, "Israelite 'Ēl Šadday and Amorite Bêl Šadê." *Journal of Biblical Literature*, Vol. 87, No. 4 (Dec., 1968), 435.

80. *Lipiński*, op. cit., 13–69.

81. Bailey, op. cit. 436.

82. Ibid, 437.

83. See Ezekiel 28:2, 13–14.

84. Deuteronomy 32:8.

85. Deuteronomy 4:19.

86. See my book, *Last Clash of the Titans,* for a more thorough treatment of the connections between bovid imagery and pagan gods. The old gods of Greece, the Titans, derived their name from an ancient Amorite tribe, which in turn appears to have been named for the Akkadian word for "bison" or "aurochs," an extinct breed of wild cattle that was huge—up to 72" at the shoulders—and very dangerous.

87. See, for example, Exodus 33:11; Numbers 12:6–8; Deuteronomy 34:10–12.

88. For example, Judges 2:1–3: "I brought you up from Egypt…. I said, 'I will never break my covenant with you'…. But you have not obeyed my voice. What is this you have done? So now I say, I will not drive them out before you."

89. Total population about 9.5 million.

90. Numbers 21:21–22.

91. Ugaritic text KTU 1.108. Nicolas Wyatt, "After Death Has Us Parted." In *The Perfumes of the Seven Tamarisks: Studies in Honor of Wilfred G. E. Watson* (Münster: Ugarit-Verlag, 2012), 272.

92. KTU 1.100, line 41.

93. From Ugaritic *bṯn* ("serpent"). Lete, del O. G., "Bashan." In K. van der Toorn, B. Becking, & P. W. van der Horst (Eds.), *Dictionary of Deities and Demons in the Bible (2nd extensively rev. ed)* (Leiden; Boston; Köln; Grand Rapids, MI; Cambridge: Brill; Eerdmans, 1999), 161.

94. Derek P. Gilbert, *Last Clash of the Titans: The Second Coming of Hercules, Leviathan, and the Prophesied War Between Jesus Christ and the Gods of Antiquity* (Crane, Mo.: Defender, 2018), 170–173.

95. Deuteronomy 3:11.

96. Timo Veijola, "King Og's Iron Bed (Deut 3:11): Once Again," *Studies in the Hebrew Bible, Qumran, and the Septuagint* (ed. Peter W. Flint et al. VTSup 101 (Leiden: Brill, 2003), 63.

97. Wolfgang Heimpel, *Letters to the King of Mari: A New Translation, with Historical Introduction, Notes, and Commentary* (Winona Lake, In.: Eisenbrauns, 2003), 16.

98. Daniel E. Fleming, *Democracy's Ancient Ancestors: Mari and Early Collective Governance* (Cambridge: Cambridge University Press, 2004), 9–10.

99. Daniel E. Fleming, "Mari and the Possibilities of Biblical Memory." *Revue d'Assyriologie et d'archéologie orientale*, Vol. 92, No. 1 (1998), 61–62.

100. Pongratz-Leisten, op. cit., 265–266.

101. Joshua 6:1.

102. Cohen, op. cit., 405.

103. Daniel 10:13.

104. Adam Zertal, *Sisera's Secret.* (Haifa: Seker Publishing, 2016).

105. See Judges 6:1–6.

106. Dr. Michael S. Heiser, "Deuteronomy 32:8–9 and the Old Testament Worldview" (http://www.thedivinecouncil.com/Deuteronomy32OTWorldview.pdf), retrieved 11/5/18.

107. E. Tully, "Asherah." In J. D. Barry, D. Bomar, D. R. Brown, R. Klippenstein, D. Mangum, C. Sinclair Wolcott, … W. Widder (Eds.), *The Lexham Bible Dictionary* (Bellingham, WA: Lexham Press, 2016).

108. 2 Kings 21:1–9.

109. His last dated prophecy is in Ezekiel 29:17, "the twenty-seventh year, in the first month, on the first day of the month," which was April 26, 571 BC.

110. Mark B. Garrison, "Antiquarianism, Copying, Collecting." In *A Companion to Archaeology in the Ancient Near East*, D. T. Potts, ed. (Chichester, West Sussex: Wiley-Blackwell, 2012), 44–46.

111. Also called Tema or Teman in the Bible.

112. Genesis 25:15.

113. Humphreys, op. cit., 300.

114. Arnulf Hausleiter, "North Arabian Kingdoms." *A Companion to Archaeology in the Ancient Near East*, D.T. Potts, ed. (Chichester, West Sussex: Wiley-Blackwell, 2012), 828.

115. Jin Yang Kim, "F. M. Cross' Reconstruction of 4Q242." *Old Testament Story* (https://otstory.wordpress.com/2008/02/22/f-m-cross-reconstruction-of-4q242/), retrieved 11/8/18.

116. Humphreys, op. cit., 300.

117. Paul-Alain Beaulieu. *The Reign of Nabonidus, King of Babylon, 556–539 B.C.* (New Haven: Yale University Press, 1989), 150.

118. Al Wolters, "Belshazzar's Feast and the Cult of the Moon God Sîn," *Bulletin for Biblical Research* 5 (1995), 201-202.

119. 1 Corinthians 2:8.

120. Rients de Boer, "Amorites in the Early Old Babylonian Period." Dissertation, Leiden University (2014), 69. http://hdl.handle.net/1887/25842, retrieved 11/8/18.

121. Ibid.

122. Lluis Feliu and Wilfred G. E. Watson. *The God Dagan in Bronze Age Syria*. (Leiden: Brill, 2003), 299.

123. Michael C. Astour, "Semitic Elements in the Kumarbi Myth." *Journal of Near Eastern Studies*, Vol. 27, No. 3 (July, 1968), 172.

124. Feliu, op. cit., 303.

125. Lluis Feliu, "Concerning the Etymology of Enlil: the An=Anum Approach." *Aula Orientalis-Supplementa* 22 (2006), 229.

126. Ibid., 246.

127. Ibid.

128. Ibid., 230.

129. Frank Moore Cross, *Canaanite Myth and Hebrew Epic: Essays in the History of the Religion of Israel* (Cambridge: Harvard University Press, 1973), 41.

130. Lipiński, op. cit., 64.

131. Cross, op. cit., 26.

132. "Calneh" in Genesis 10:10 may be a mistranslation of a Hebrew word meaning "all of them," resulting in the translation "all of them in the land of Shinar" (RSV). See W. A. Elwell & B. J. Beitzel, B. J., "Calneh." *Baker Encyclopedia of the Bible Vol. 1* (Grand Rapids, MI: Baker Book House, 1988), 405.

133. Shirly Ben-Dor Evian, "Ramesses III and the 'Sea-Peoples': Towards a New Philistine Paradigm." *Oxford Journal of Archaeology* 36(3) (2017), 278.

134. Ibid.

135. Jenny Strauss Clay and Amir Gilan, "The Hittite 'Song of Emergence' and the *Theogony*." *Philologus* 58 (2014), 1–9.

136. "The Epic of Atrahasis." *Livius* (http://www.livius.org/sources/content/anet/104-106-the-epic-of-atrahasis/), retrieved 11/9/18.

137. Ausonius, *Eclogue 23*.

138. Macrobius, *Saturnalia* 1.7.31.

139. Jan N. Bremmer, *The Strange World of Human Sacrifice.* (Leuven: Peeters, 2007), 57–58. See also Diodorus Siculus, *Library of History, XX. 14.4-7* (ed. Loeb).

140. Cross, op. cit., 26.

141. Jan N. Bremmer, "Remember the Titans!" In *The Fall of the Angels*, C. Auffarth and L. Stuckenbruck, eds. (Leiden; Boston: Brill, 2004), 46.

142. Alfonso Archi, "The West Hurrian Pantheon and Its Background." In *Beyond Hatti: A Tribute to Gary Beckman*, Billie Jean Collins and Piotr Michalowski (eds.) (Atlanta: Lockwood Press, 2013), 12.

143. Ibid., 1.

144. Brian B. Schmidt, "Israel's Beneficent Dead: The Origin and Character of Israelite Ancestor Cults and Necromancy." Doctoral thesis: University of Oxford (1991), 158–159.

145. Wyatt (2010), op. cit., 600.

146. Deuteronomy 3:11.

147. Robert D. Miller II, "Baals of Bashan." *Revue Biblique*, Vol. 121, No. 4 (2014), 506–515.

148. Wyatt (2010), op. cit., 598.

149. Ibid., 595.

150. Daniel Schwemer, "The Storm-gods of the Ancient Near East." *JANER* 7.2 (2008), 128.

151. Ibid.

152. Wolfgang Herrmann, "Baal." In K. van der Toorn, B. Becking, & P. W. van der Horst (Eds.), *Dictionary of Deities and Demons in the Bible (2nd extensively rev. ed.).* (Leiden; Boston; Köln; Grand Rapids, MI; Cambridge: Brill; Eerdmans, 1999), 134.

153. Ibid., 135–136.

154. Interestingly, per KTU 1.4:vi:30-38, the process took seven days. Nicolas Wyatt, *Religious Texts from Ugarit* (2nd ed.). (London; New York: Sheffield Academic Press, 2002), 106.

155. Lipiński, op. cit., 64.

156. Manfred Bietak, "The King and the Syrian Weather God on Egyptian Seals of the Thirteenth Dynasty." *Studies in Honor of Ali Radwan*, Preface by Z. Hawass, ed. by K. Daoud, S. Bedier, Sawsan Abd el Fatah, SASAE 34/I, (Cairo: Egyptian Supreme Council of Antiquities, 2006), 201–212.

157. Revelation 2:13.

158. Nicolas Wyatt, *Religious texts from Ugarit (2nd ed.).* (London; New York: Sheffield Academic Press, 2002), 78.

159. 1 Kings 20:42.

160. Dr. Michael S. Heiser, "What's Ugaritic Got to Do with Anything?" *Logos.com*, https://www.logos.com/ugaritic, retrieved 11/23/18.

161. For example, KTU 1.2:iv:8, 1.2:iv:29, 1.3:ii: 40, 1.3:iv:4, 1.4:v:60, 1.10:i:7, and elsewhere.

162. The pillar of cloud that went before the Israelites (see Exodus 13:21—22, 14:19–20, and others) and the glory of the Lord over the tent of meeting (for example, Exodus 33:9–10 and 40:34–38).

163. His famous wheel-within-a-wheel vision; see Ezekiel 1:4.

164. Matthew 17:5, Mark 9:7, Luke 9:34–35.

165. Hermon is the only "high mountain" near Caesarea Philippi (Matthew 16:13).

166. Matthew 24:30; also Mark 13:26 and Luke 21:27.

167. Isaiah 14:11.

168. For a more detailed treatment of this topic, see my previous book, *Last Clash of the Titans.*

169. Herrmann, op. cit., 135.

170. Ezekiel 28:11.

171. See 2 Peter 2:4–10 and Jude 6–7.

172. 1 Enoch 15:8–11.

173. Derek P. Gilbert, *Last Clash of the Titans: The Second Coming of Hercules, Leviathan, and the Prophesied War Between Jesus Christ and the Gods of Antiquity.* (Crane, Mo.: Defender, 2018), 86–87.

174. K. van der Toorn and P. W. van der Horst, "Nimrod Before and After the Bible." *Harvard Theological Review* 83:1 (1990), 8–15.

175. Derek P. Gilbert, "The Double-Headed Eagle: Scottish Rite Freemasonry's Veneration of Nimrod." https://www.academia.edu/9062169/The_Double-Headed_Eagle_Scottish_Rite_Freemasonrys_Veneration_of_Nimrod.

176. Ian Shaw (ed.), *The Oxford History of Ancient Egypt.* (Oxford: Oxford University Press, 2000), 482.

177. At this point in history, Set was still one of the good guys in Egyptian religion. It was about a thousand years later, after Egypt had been invaded and/or conquered by Nubians, Assyrians, Babylonians, and Persians that Set—the god of foreigners, remember—became the villain who killed his brother Osiris and cut him into fourteen pieces.

178. Orly Goldwasser, "King Apophis of Avaris and the Emergence of Monotheism." In: *Timelines*, ed. E. Czerny et al., vol. II, *Orientalia Lovaniensia Analecta* 149/II (Peeters: Leuven, 2006), 129–133.

179. Samuel Noah Kramer, *The Sumerians: Their History, Culture, and Character* (Chicago: University of Chicago Press, 1963), 339.

180. 1 Timothy 2:2.

181. Joshua 10:14.

182. Eiko Matsushima, "Ištar and Other Goddesses of the So-Called 'Sacred Marriage' in Ancient Mesopotamia." In David T. Sugimoto (Ed.), *Transformation of a Goddess: Ishtar - Astarte - Aphrodite* (Fribourg: Academic Press; Göttingen: Vandenhoeck & Ruprecht, 2014), 1.

183. Black, J. A., Cunningham, G., Fluckiger-Hawker, E, Robson, E., and

Zólyomi, G. "Enmerkar and the Lord of Aratta." *The Electronic Text Corpus of Sumerian Literature* (http://etcsl.orinst.ox.ac.uk/cgi-bin/etcsl. cgi?text=t.1.8.2.3#), retrieved 12/17/16.

184. Although the Sumerian word *kur* also meant "underworld," an interesting dual meaning given "the" god's links to the underworld, as discussed in chapter 8.

185. Matsushima, op. cit., 3.

186. Herodotus I 199, cited in Jerrold S. Cooper, "Sex and the Temple." Kai Kaniuth, Anne Löhnert, Jared L. Miller, Adelheid Otto, Michael Roaf and Walther Sallaberger (Eds.), *Tempel im Alten Orient* (Wiesbaden: Harrassowitz Verlag, 2013), 49–50.

187. Contrary to popular history, Leonidas had more than three hundred men. Herodotus estimated about five thousand; modern scholars put his forces at around seven thousand. Although it wasn't as impressive as what Gideon did with the *original* three hundred, Leonidas and his men were still outnumbered at least twenty-to-one.

188. Designated AO 3065 and housed at the Louvre in Paris.

189. Michael P. Streck and Nathan Wasserman, "The Man Is Like a Woman, the Maiden Is a Young Man: A New Edition of Ištar-Louvre (Tab. I-II)." *Orientalia* 87 (2018), 5–6.

190. Black, J. A., Cunningham, G., Fluckiger-Hawker, E, Robson, E., and Zólyomi, G., "A *cir-namcub* to Inana (Inana I)," *The Electronic Text Corpus of Sumerian Literature* (http://etcsl.orinst.ox.ac.uk/cgi-bin/etcsl. cgi?text=t.4.07.9&charenc=j#), retrieved 12/17/16.

191. A. W. Sjoberg, "In-nin Sa-gur-ra: A Hymn to the Goddess Inanna," *Zeitschrift fur Assyriologie* 65, no. 2 (1976), 225.

192. Streck and Wasserman, op. cit., 17–19.

193. Christopher E. Ortega, "Inanna: Reinforcer of Heteronormativity, or Legitimizer of Non-Heteronormativity?" Paper presented at the Spring 2015 Western Regional Conference of The American Academy of Religion (Long Beach: California State University, 2015), 2–3.

194. Rivkah Harris, "Inanna-Ishtar as Paradox and a Coincidence of Opposites." *History of Religions*, Vol. 30, No. 3 (Feb. 1991), 277.

195. For example, Ortega (cited above) points out that some of Inanna's temple personnel were cross-dressing priests called *gala*. The Sumerian word *gala* was formed by the symbols for "penis" and "anus."

196. 2 Kings 23:7.

197. 2 Kings 18:5.

198. Harris, op. cit., 261.

199. Ezekiel 8:14.

200. Akio Tsukimoto, "'In the Shadow of Thy Wings': A Review of the Winged Goddess in Ancient Near Eastern Iconography." In David T. Sugimoto (Ed.), *Transformation of a Goddess: Ishtar - Astarte - Aphrodite* (Fribourg: Academic Press; Göttingen: Vandenhoeck & Ruprecht, 2014), 15–16.

201. Matsushima, op. cit., 3.

202. Ilona Zsolnay, "Ištar, 'Goddess of War, Pacifier of Kings: An Analysis of Ištar's Martial Role in the Maledictory Sections of the Assyrian Royal Inscriptions." *Sumerian and Akkadian Literature and Literary Language* (Winona Lake, In.: Eisenbrauns, 2010), 402.

203. Giovanni Pettinato, *The Archives of Ebla: An Empire Inscribed in Clay.* (Garden City, NY: Doubleday & Company, Inc., 1981), 247.

204. "Erra (god)." *Ancient Mesopotamia Gods and Goddesses,* http://oracc. museum.upenn.edu/amgg/listofdeities/erra/, retrieved 12/14/18.

205. Peter Machinist, "Rest and Violence in the Epic of Erra." *Journal of the American Oriental Society* 103.1 (1983), 221.

206. "Hail" is the Hebrew *Barad*, another entity who was apparently part of God's "company of destroying angels."

207. Paolo Xella, "Resheph." In K. van der Toorn, B. Becking, & P. W. van der Horst (Eds.), *Dictionary of Deities and Demons in the Bible* (2nd extensively rev. ed.). (Leiden; Boston; Köln; Grand Rapids, MI; Cambridge: Brill; Eerdmans, 1999), 702.

208. Ibid., 701.

209. Maciej M. Münnich, *The God Resheph in the Ancient Near East.* (Tübingen: Mohr Siebeck, 2013), 102.

210. Douglas N. Petrovich, "Amenhotep II and the Historicity of the Exodus-Pharaoh." https://www.academia.edu/1049040/_2006_Amenhotep_II_

and_the_Historicity_of_the_Exodus-Pharaoh, retrieved 12/12/18. Also published online at http://www.biblearchaeology.org/post/2010/02/04/Amenhotep-II-and-the-Historicity-of-the-Exodus-Pharaoh.aspx.

211. Pettinato, op. cit., 248.

212. Joshua 8:30–35.

213. Deuteronomy 11:29.

214. Assaf Kamar, "A rare visit to the supposed altar of prophet Joshua." *Ynet News*, August 9, 2016 (https://www.ynetnews.com/articles/0,7340,L-4838962,00.html), retrieved 12/14/18.

215. Genesis 37:12–26.

216. Manfred Hutter. "Abaddon." In K. van der Toorn, B. Becking, & P. W. van der Horst (Eds.), *Dictionary of Deities and Demons in the Bible* (2nd extensively rev. ed.). (Leiden; Boston; Köln; Grand Rapids, MI; Cambridge: Brill; Eerdmans, 1999), 1.

217. Peter Levenda. *The Dark Lord: H. P. Lovecraft, Kenneth Grant, and the Typhonian Tradition in Magic.* (Nicolas-Hays, Inc. Kindle Edition, 2013), 97.

218. "Remembering Kenneth Grant's Understanding of The Necronomicon Tradition." (https://warlockasyluminternationalnews.com/2011/02/18/remembering-kenneth-grants-understanding-of-the-necronomicon-tradition/), retrieved 8/7/17.

219. Levenda, op. cit., 102.

220. Ibid., 104.

221. P. L. Day, "Anat." In K. van der Toorn, B. Becking, & P. W. van der Horst (Eds.), *Dictionary of deities and demons in the Bible* (2nd extensively rev. ed.). (Leiden; Boston; Köln; Grand Rapids, MI; Cambridge: Brill; Eerdmans, 1999), 36.

222. Nicolas Wyatt, "KTU 1.3 ii:12-15." *Religious Texts from Ugarit.* (London; New York: Sheffield Academic Press, 2002), 74.

223. 1 Kings 11:7; 2 Kings 23:13.

224. Pettinato, op. cit., 257.

225. Ibid., 292.

226. Jeremiah 46:2; 2 Chronicles 35:20; Isaiah 10:9.

227. Genesis 19:37.

228. "The Stela of Mesha." Livius.org (http://www.livius.org/sources/content/anet/320-the-stela-of-mesha/), retrieved 12/27/18.

229. Diodorus Siculus, *The Library of History*, Book XX, Chapter 14. *Lacus Curtius* (http://penelope.uchicago.edu/Thayer/E/Roman/Texts/Diodorus_Siculus/20A*.html), retrieved 12/27/18.

230. Anthony J. Spalinger, "A Canaanite Ritual Found in Egyptian Reliefs." *Journal of the Society for the Study of Egyptian Antiquities* 8 (1978), 50.

231. David Flusser, *Judaism of the Second Temple Period: Sages and Literature* (Grand Rapids, Mich.; Cambridge; Jerusalem: William B. Eerdmans Publishing Company: Hebrew University Magnes Press, 2009), 41.

232. 1 Enoch 69:6.

233. Book of Jubilees 10:8, 17:15–16.

234. "Jewish Concepts: Angels and Angelology." *Jewish Virtual Library* (https://www.jewishvirtuallibrary.org/angels-and-angelology-2), retrieved 12/28/18.

235. Houtman, C., "Queen of Heaven." In K. van der Toorn, B. Becking, & P. W. van der Horst (Eds.), *Dictionary of deities and demons in the Bible* (2nd extensively rev. ed.) (Leiden; Boston; Köln; Grand Rapids, MI; Cambridge: Brill; Eerdmans, 1999), 678.

236. Collin Cornell, "What Happened to Kemosh?" *Zeitschrift für die alttestamentliche Wissenschaft* 128(2) (2016), 10.

237. Ibid., 12.

238. Matthew 12:24–28, Mark 3:22–26, and Luke 11:14–18 (Beelzebul = "Baal the prince"); and Revelation 2:12-13 ("Satan's throne" in Pergamum was the Great Altar of Zeus, who, like Baal, was a storm-god.)

239. Daniel 10:13.

240. Daniel 12:1.

241. Lloyd Llewellyn-Jones. *King and Court in Ancient Persia 559 to 331 BCE* (Edinburgh: Edinburgh University Press Ltd., 2013), 24.

242. 1 Corinthians 2:6.

243. See Isaiah 44:24–45:7.

244. "Zoroastrianism." *Adherents.com* (http://www.adherents.com/Religions_By_Adherents.html#Zoroastrianism), retrieved 12/26/18.

245. Joanna Töyräänvuori, "Weapons of the Storm God in Ancient Near Eastern and Biblical Traditions." *Studia Orientalia Vol. 112* (Helsinki: Finnish Oriental Society, 2012), 150.

246. Daniel Bodi, "The Retribution Principle in the Amorite View of History: Yasmah-Addu's Letter to Nergal (ARM13) and Adad's Message to Zimrī-Līm (A. 1968)." *ARAM* 26:1&2 (2014), 290–291.

247. Nicolas Wyatt, "KTU 1.114: The Myth of El's Banquet: A Medical Text." *Religious texts from Ugarit (2nd ed.)* (London; New York: Sheffield Academic Press, 2002), 407-409.

248. Ibid.

249. Robert Wenning, "North Arabian Deities and the Deities of Petra." *Men on the Rocks: The Formation of Nabataean Petra*, M. Mouton and S.G. Schmid (eds.) (Berlin: Logos Verlag Berlin, 2012), 335.

250. "Chronicle Concerning the Reign of Nabonidus." http://www.livius.org/sources/content/mesopotamian-chronicles-content/abc-7-nabonidus-chronicle/?#17, retrieved 12/26/18. Interesting to note that the gods who "did not enter" Babylon were Shamash, the sun-god; Nergal (Resheph/Apollo), the underworld gatekeeper and plague-god; and Nabu, the god of wisdom and Marduk's top assistant.

251. Paul-Alain Beaulieu, "An Episode in the Fall of Babylon to the Persians." *Journal of Near Eastern Studies*, Vol. 52, No. 4 (Oct., 1993), 257.

252. Ibid., 260.

253. Ibid., 261.

254. Ibid., 243.

255. "Subsistence Pastoralism," *Near Eastern Archaeology: A Reader*. Susanne Richard (ed.) (Winona Lake, In.: Eisenbrauns, 2003), 120–121.

256. Neil King, "Saudi Crown Prince Launches Tourism Mega-project in Al Ula." *Gulf Business* (Feb. 11, 2019), https://gulfbusiness.com/saudi-crown-prince-launches-tourism-mega-project-al-ula/, retrieved 2/12/19.

257. Bradley L. Crowell, "Nabonidus, as-Sila , and the Beginning of the End of Edom." *Bulletin of the American Schools of Oriental Research*, No. 348 (2007), 75–88.

258. The conquest of Edom by Nabonidus may have fulfilled prophecies of its destruction in Isaiah 36:5–17 and Amos 1:11–12.

259. Brand, C., Draper, C., England, A., Bond, S., Clendenen, E. R., & Butler, T. C. (Eds.). "Teman." *Holman Illustrated Bible Dictionary* (Nashville, TN: Holman Bible Publishers, 2003), 1560.

260. Wenning, op. cit., 336. Note that scholars don't all agree on this point; some believe Salm was the moon-god (which would be consistent with the bull imagery from ancient Mesopotamia) and Sangila was the sun-god.

261. Ibid., 335–336.

262. Eric M. Orlin, *The Routledge Encyclopedia of Ancient Mediterranean Religions* (New York: Routledge, Taylor & Francis Group, 2016).

263. Genesis 25:13.

264. Wenning, op. cit., 336.

265. D. T. Potts, "The Arabian Peninsula, 600 BCE to 600 CE." *Coinage of the Caravan Kingdoms* (New York: The American Numismatic Society, 2010), 42.

266. Christian Julien Robin, "Religions in Pre-Islamic South Arabia." *Encyclopedia of the Quran, Volume Five.* Jane McAuliffe (ed.) (Leiden; Boston: Brill, 2006), 86–87.

267. Ibid., 87.

268. Tom Holland, *In the Shadow of the Sword: The Battle for Global Empire and the End of the Ancient World.* (London: Abacus, 2014), 303.

269. Sura 48:24.

270. Sura 3:96.

271. Oliver Leaman, "Ka'ba." *The Quran: An Encyclopedia.* (London; New York: Routledge, 2006), 337.

272. Sura 48:24 (Pickthall, Shakir, Muhammad Sarwar); al-Bukhari Hadith 3:891.

273. Al-Bukhari Hadith 2:685.

274. Al-Bukhari Hadith 9:337.

275. Al-Tirmidhi Hadith 1535.

276. Holland, op. cit., 303.

277. Ibid., 471.

278. Ibid., 303.

279. Sura 2:142–145.

280. *The History of Al-Tabari: The Foundation of the Community*, Volume VII.

Translated by M. V. McDonald, annotated by W. Montgomery Watt (Albany: State University of New York Press (SUNY), 1987), 24–25.

281. *The Life of Muhammad: A Translation of Ishaq's Sirat Rasul Allah.* Introduction and notes by Alfred Guillaume (Karachi: Oxford University Press, 1995), 258–259.

282. Dan Gibson, *Early Islamic Qiblas* (Vancouver: Independent Scholars Press, 2017), 8.

283. Ibid., 6.

284. Dan Gibson, *Quranic Geography* (Saskatoon: Independent Scholars Press, 2011), 331–332.

285. Holland, op. cit. 373.

286. Ibid., 373–374.

287. Epiphanius, *Panarion* 22, 9–11. Translated by Frank Williams (Leiden; Boston: Brill, 2013), 52.

288. Stephanie Bowers Peterson, "The Cult of Dushara and the Roman Annexation of Petra." Masters Thesis (McMaster University, 2006), 53.

289. http://www.teviscup.org/results/official-results-of-the-tevis-cup-100-miles-one-day-trail-ride, retrieved 1/12/19.

290. Sayyid Muhammad Ibn Alawi al-Maliki and Dr. Gibril Fouad Haddad, *The Prophet's Night Journey and Heavenly Ascent* (United Kingdom: Aqsa Publications, 2010).

291. Lucy Wadeson, "The Funerary Landscape of Petra: Results from a New Study." *Proceedings of the Seminar for Arabian Studies*, Vol. 42, Supplement: The Nabataeans in Focus: Current Archaeological Research at Petra. Papers from the Special Session of the Seminar for Arabian Studies held on 29 July 2011 (2012), 99–125.

292. Robert Wenning, "The Betyls of Petra." *Bulletin of the American Schools of Oriental Research* 324 (2001), 79.

293. Augustine Pagolou, *Patriarchal Religion as Portrayed in Genesis 12–50: Comparison with Ancient Near Eastern and Later Israelite Religions.* PhD thesis (Open University, 1995), 99.

294. Wenning, "The Betyls of Petra," 80.

295. Ibid.

296. Pagolou, op. cit., 100.

297. Wenning, "The Betyls of Petra," 80.

298. Ibid.

299. Jane Taylor, *Petra and the Lost Kingdom of the Nabataeans* (London; New York: I.B. Tauris, 2001), 124.

300. Zeyed Mustafa al-Shorman, "The Assimilation of Dushara - D wšara in Greco-Roman Period." *Arabia, Greece and Byzantium: Cultural Contacts in Ancient and Medieval Times*, ed. Abdulaziz Al-Helabi, Dimitrios Letsios, Moshalleh Al-Moraekhi, Abdullah Al-Abduljabbar (Riyadh: King Saud University, 2012), 43.

301. See also Habakkuk 3:3.

302. Knauf, E. A., "Qôs." In K. van der Toorn, B. Becking, & P. W. van der Horst (Eds.), *Dictionary of deities and demons in the Bible* (2nd extensively rev. ed.) (Leiden; Boston; Köln; Grand Rapids, MI; Cambridge: Brill; Eerdmans, 1999), 674–675.

303. Ibid., 676.

304. Ibid.

305. Timothy W. Dunkin, "Ba'al, Hubal, and Allah." *Study To Answer. net* (https://web.archive.org/web/20180428231312/http://www. studytoanswer.net/islam/hubalallah.html#ha20), retrieved 1/5/19.

306. Karen Armstrong, *Islam: A Short History* (New York: Random House, 2002), 11.

307. *The Life of Muhammad: A Translation of Ishaq's Sirat Rasul Allah.* Translated by A. Guillaume (Oxford; New York; Delhi: Oxford University Press, 1955), 64.

308. Ibid., 37.

309. Ibid., 64.

310. Patricia Crone, *Meccan Trade and the Rise of Islam* (Piscataway, NJ: Gorgias Press), 193.

311. Shaher Rababeh & Rama Al Rabady, "The Crowsteps Motif in Nabataean Architecture: Insights into Its Meaning and Use." *Arabian Archaeology and Epigraphy* 25 (2014), 22–36.

312. 2 Kings 14:7.

313. "Makkah Royal Clock Tower Hotel," *The Skyscraper Center* (https://web.archive.org/web/20140328212835/http://www.skyscrapercenter.com/mecca/makkah-royal-clock-tower-hotel), retrieved 1/7/19.

314. "Scholarly Pursuits: Joseph Lumbard, Classical Islam Professor." *BrandeisNOW*, December 11, 2007 (http://www.brandeis.edu/now/2008/january/JosephLumbardstory.html), retrieved 1/8/19.

315. Jeanny Vorys Canby, "A Monumental Puzzle: Reconstructing the Ur-Nammu Stela." *Expedition* Vol. 29, No. 1 (1987), 54–64.

316. Yulia Ustinova, *The Supreme Gods of the Bosporan Kingdom* (Leiden; Boston: Brill, 1998), 270–274.

317. Vasiliki Limberis, *Divine Heiress: The Virgin Mary and the Making of Christian Constantinople* (London: Routledge, 1994), 126–127.

318. John Denham Parsons, *The Non-Christian Cross: An Enquiry into the Origin and History of the Symbol Eventually Adopted as That of Our Religion* (London: Simpkin, Marshall, Hamilton, Kent & Co., Ltd., 1896), 95.

319. Dr. Fiaz Fazili, "The Untold Story of Crescent Moon and Stars as Symbols, Logos, or Tattoos." *Crescent* (September 2009), 42.

320. Based on a reference by the early Christian apologist Arnobius, who wrote in Book 2 of his work *Against the Pagans*, shortly after AD 300, that the gospel had reached "the Seres," an old Roman name for northern China. English translation at http://www.newadvent.org/fathers/06312.htm, retrieved 1/9/19.

321. Dr. Thomas D. Williams, "Abortion Leading Cause of Death in 2018 with 41 Million Killed." *Breitbart*, December 31, 2018 (https://www.breitbart.com/health/2018/12/31/abortion-leading-cause-of-death-in-2018-with-41-million-killed/), retrieved 1/9/19.

322. Ibid.

323. Feliu (2006), op. cit.

324. Javier Teixidor, *The Pagan God: Popular Religion in the Greco-Roman Near East* (Princeton: Princeton University Press, 1977), 83.

325. "Allah," *Encyclopedia of Islam* (Richard C. Martin, ed.) (New York: Macmillan Reference USA, 2004), 39.

326. Ibid., 40.

327. For example, Psalm 82, Job 1 and 2, and 1 Kings 22:19–22.

328. Actually, "henotheism" is a more accurate term. It's the belief in multiple gods, but only one supreme, transcendent God.

329. E. A. Knauf, "Qos." *Dictionary of Deities and Demons in the Bible (Second Extensively Revised Edition)* (Leiden; Boston: Brill, 1999), 676.

330. Jude 1:6 (KJV).

331. Karen Armstrong, *Islam: A Short History* (New York: Random House. 2002), 18–19.

332. Raymond Ibrahim, *Sword and Scimitar: Fourteen Centuries of War Between Islam and the West* (New York: Da Capo Press, 2018), 2.

333. Ibid.

334. Ibid., 6.

335. The conquest of Canaan was neither. For an excellent treatment of the concept of *kherem*, or "under the ban," see chapter 25 of Dr. Michael Heiser's excellent book *The Unseen Realm*.

336. Matthew 10:14; Mark 6:11; Luke 9:5, 10:11.

337. Pettinato, op. cit., 257.

338. "American Commissioners to John Jay, 28 March 1786." *Founders Online* (https://founders.archives.gov/documents/Jefferson/01-09-02-0315), retrieved 1/19/19.

339. Leon de Winter, "Europe's Muslims Hate the West." *Politico*, March 29, 2016 (https://www.politico.eu/article/brussels-attacks-terrorism-europe-muslims-brussels-attacks-airport-metro/), retrieved 1/19/19.

340. Ibrahim, op. cit., 13.

341. John Hinderaker, "The American Blood Is Best, and We Will Taste It Soon." *Powerline* (https://www.powerlineblog.com/archives/2015/11/the-american-blood-is-best-and-we-will-taste-it-soon.php), retrieved 1/19/19.

342. Ibrahim, op.cit., 296.

343. Ibid., 9.

344. Ibid., 261.

345. Ibid., 267.

346. Ibid.

347. Rory Carroll, "New Book Reopens Old Arguments about Slave Raids on Europe." *The Guardian*, March 11, 2004 (https://www.theguardian.com/uk/2004/mar/11/highereducation.books), retrieved 1/19/19.

348. Ibrahim, op.cit., 280–281.
349. Juliet Eilperin, "Critics Pounce after Obama Talks Crusades, Slavery at Prayer Breakfast." *Washington Post*, February 5, 2015 (https://www.washingtonpost.com/politics/obamas-speech-at-prayer-breakfast-called-offensive-to-christians/2015/02/05/6a15a240-ad50-11e4-ad71-7b9eba0f87d6_story.html), retrieved 1/19/19.
350. Magdi Abdelhadi, "Arab Journalist Attacks Radical Islam." *BBC News*, September 7, 2004 (http://news.bbc.co.uk/2/hi/middle_east/3632462.stm), retrieved 1/23/19.
351. Joseph Goldstein, "U.S. Soldiers Told to Ignore Sexual Abuse of Boys by Afghan Allies." *The New York Times*, September 20, 2015 (https://www.nytimes.com/2015/09/21/world/asia/us-soldiers-told-to-ignore-afghan-allies-abuse-of-boys.html), retrieved 1/18/19.
352. Ibid.
353. Kyle Jahner, "Green Beret Who Beat Up Accused Child Rapist Can Stay in Army." *Army Times*, April 28, 2016 (https://www.armytimes.com/news/your-army/2016/04/29/green-beret-who-beat-up-accused-child-rapist-can-stay-in-army/), retrieved 1/18/19.
354. Craig S. Smith, "Kandahar Journal; Shh, It's an Open Secret: Warlords and Pedophilia." *The New York Times*, February 21, 2002 (https://www.nytimes.com/2002/02/21/world/kandahar-journal-shh-it-s-an-open-secret-warlords-and-pedophilia.html), retrieved 1/18/19.
355. Special Inspector General for Afghanistan Reconstruction, "Child Sexual Assault in Afghanistan: Implementation of the Leahy Laws and Reports of Assault by Afghan Security Forces." PDF document (https://www.sigar.mil/pdf/inspections/SIGAR%2017-47-IP.pdf), retrieved 1/18/19.
356. Ibid., 3.
357. Rod Nordland, "Afghan Pedophiles Get Free Pass From U.S. Military, Report Says." *The New York Times,* January 23, 2018 (https://www.nytimes.com/2018/01/23/world/asia/afghanistan-military-abuse.html), retrieved 1/18/19.
358. Special Inspector General for Afghanistan Reconstruction, op. cit., 2.
359. Nordland, op. cit.

360. Ibid.

361. Clinton Bailey, *Bedouin Culture in the Bible* (New Haven; London: Yale University Press, 2018), 113.

362. Ibid., 219–220.

363. James Neill, *The Origins and Role of Same-Sex Relations in Human Societies* (Jefferson, NC; London: McFarland & Co., 2009), 301.

364. Ibid., 303.

365. Jan Willem de Lind van Wijngaarden & Bettina T. Schunter, "'Part of the job': Male-to-male Sexual Experiences and Abuse of Young Men Working as 'Truck Cleaners' along the Highways of Pakistan." *Culture, Health & Sexuality*, 16:5 (2014), 562–574.

366. Ruth Styles, "The Bus Driver Who Has Raped 12 Little Boys (and Doesn't Think He's Done Anything Wrong): Why Thousands of Pakistani Children Are Falling Prey to Paedophiles." *Daily Mail*, September 1, 2014 (https://www.dailymail.co.uk/femail/article-2739799/Why-millions-Pakistani-children-falling-prey-vicious-paedophiles.html), retrieved 1/18/19.

367. Raymond Ibrahim, "'It Is Permissible for the Mujahid to Enjoy Young Boys in the Absence of Women.'" *Jihad Watch*, June 2, 2015 (https://www.jihadwatch.org/2015/06/it-is-permissible-for-the-mujahid-to-enjoy-young-boys-in-the-absence-of-women), retrieved 1/19/19.

368. Shabnam Mahmood. "Yorkshire Muslim Girl Speaks of Grooming Ordeal." *BBC*, November 24, 2014 (https://www.bbc.com/news/uk-30152240), retrieved 1/19/19.

369. Frances Perraudin, "Judges Uphold Decision to Strip Grooming Gang Members of Citizenship." *The Guardian*, August 8, 2018 (https://www.theguardian.com/uk-news/2018/aug/08/judges-uphold-decision-to-strip-rochdale-grooming-gang-members-of-citizenship), retrieved 1/19/19.

370. James Novogrod and Richard Engel, "ISIS Terror: Yazidi Woman Recalls Horrors of Slave Auction." *NBC News*, February 13, 2015 (https://www.nbcnews.com/storyline/isis-uncovered/isis-terror-yazidi-woman-recalls-horrors-slave-auction-n305856), retrieved 1/19/19.

371. Ibrahim, *Sword and Scimitar*, 49.

372. Nina Shea, "The Islamic State's Christian and Yizidi Sex Slaves." *Hudson Institute*, July 31, 2015 (https://www.hudson.org/research/11486-the-islamic-state-s-christian-and-yizidi-sex-slaves), retrieved 1/19/19.

373. This is recorded in a number of hadiths. For example, *Sahih al-Bukhtari*, Volume 5, Book 58, Nos. 234, 236; Volume 7, Book 62, No. 64.

374. Raymond Ibrahim, "Islamic Necrophilia: Or, "Every Hole Is a Goal." *RaymondIbrahim.com*, February 15, 2019 (https://www.raymondibrahim.com/2019/02/15/islamic-necrophilia-or-every-hole-is-a-goal/), retrieved 2/16/19.

375. Rick Noack, "Leaked Document Says 2,000 Men Allegedly Assaulted 1,200 German Women on New Year's Eve." *Washington Post*, July 11, 2016 (https://www.washingtonpost.com/news/worldviews/wp/2016/07/10/leaked-document-says-2000-men-allegedly-assaulted-1200-german-women-on-new-years-eve/), retrieved 1/19/19.

376. Liam Deacon, "Spate of New Year's Eve Sex Attacks in Berlin and Cologne." *Breitbart News*, January 2, 2018 (https://www.breitbart.com/europe/2018/01/02/spate-new-years-eve-sex-attacks-berlin-cologne/), retrieved 1/19/19.

377. "*The Times*: Breitbart London Brought the Truth About Cologne to the Global Public." January 8, 2016 (https://www.breitbart.com/europe/2016/01/08/the-times-breitbart-london-brought-the-truth-about-cologne-to-the-global-public/), retrieved 1/19/19.

378. Matthew 5:27–28.

379. Ephesians 5:25.

380. Ibrahim, op. cit., 1–2.

381. Ephesians 2:8–9; 1 Corinthians 15:1–4.

382. Romans 3:9.

383. Dr. Timothy Furnish. *Sects, Lies, and the Caliphate: Ten Years of Observations on Islam* (Kindle Edition, 2016), 1540.

384. Sura 4:3, 28.

385. "Temporary Marriage in Islam Part 1." *Al-Islam.org*. https://www.al-islam.org/shiite-encyclopedia-ahlul-bayt-dilp-team/temporary-marriage-islam-part-1, retrieved 1/20/19.

386. Betwa Sharma, "Islam's Sex Licenses." *The Daily Beast*, April 29, 2009. https://www.thedailybeast.com/islams-sex-licenses, retrieved 1/20/19.

387. Ibrahim, op. cit, 203.

388. Raymond Ibrahim, "How Taqiyya Alters Islam's Rules of War." *Middle East Quarterly* (Winter 2010), 3–13.

389. Sura 4:157–158.

390. Holland, op. cit., 233.

391. Armstrong, op. cit., 10.

392. John Lewis Burckhardt, *Travels in Arabia*. London: Henry Colburn, New Burlington Street, 1829 (http://www.gutenberg.org/cache/epub/9457/pg9457-images.html), retrieved 1/12/19.

393. Francis E. Peters, *Muhammad and the Origins of Islam* (Albany: State University of New York Press, 1994), 108.

394. Timothy W. Dunkin, "Ba'al, Hubal, and Allah: A Rebuttal to the *Islamic Awareness* Article Entitled "Is Hubal the Same as Allah?" by M. S. M. Saifullah and 'Abdallah David." *StudyToAnswer.net* (https://web.archive.org/web/20180327233537/http://www.studytoanswer.net/islam/hubalallah.html), retrieved 1/12/19.

395. "Mecca." *Jewish Virtual Library* (https://www.jewishvirtuallibrary.org/mecca#history), retrieved 1/12/19.

396. Armstrong, op. cit., 11.

397. Dunkin, op. cit.

398. Ibid.

399. Knauf, op. cit., 676.

400. Ibid.

401. Mark Smith and Wayne Pitard, *The Ugaritic Baal Cycle: Volume II* (Leiden; Boston: Brill, 2009), 49.

402. Jonathan P. Berkey, *The Formation of Islam: Religion and Society in the Near East 600–1800* (Cambridge: Cambridge University Press, 2003), 42.

403. John Burton, "Those Are the High-Flying Cranes." *Journal of Semitic Studies*, Volume 15, Issue 2 (1970), 246.

404. Abū Ja'far Muhammad b. Jarīr al-Tabarī, *The History of al-Tabari Vol. VI: Muhammad at Mecca*. Translated and annotated by W. Montgomery Watt

and M. V. McDonald (Albany: State University of New York Press, 1988), 108.

405. Ibid.

406. Peters, op. cit, 110–111.

407. Ezekiel 28:11–19. Eden was a garden, but it was also "the holy mountain of God."

408. Charles Warren, R. E., "The Summit of Hermon, With An Illustration," *Palestine Exploration Fund Quarterly Statement* 2.5 (Jan. 1 to March 31, 1870), 214.

409. John Lewis Burckhardt, *Travels in Arabia, Comprehending an Account of Those Territories in Hedjaz Which the Mohammedans Regard as Sacred* (London: H. Colburn, 1829), 172.

410. Ibid., 177–178.

411. Warren, op. cit., 214–215.

412. See pages 87–89 of my book *Last Clash of the Titans*.

413. 1 Corinthians 2:8.

414. Daniel 9:24–27. Artaxerxes issued his decree in 445 B.C. (Nehemiah 2:1–9).

415. Daniel 9:26.

416. Dr. Michael S. Heiser, "September 11: Happy Birthday to Jesus." http://drmsh.com/september-11-happy-birthday-to-jesus/, retrieved 1/23/19.

417. $173,880 / 365.25 = 476$ years, 2 days.

418. This is consistent with the note in Luke 3:23 that Jesus was "about thirty years of age" when He began to preach.

419. 1 Corinthians 13:12.

420. Matthew 24:23–24.

421. Yes, I am aware that Islam is not Abrahamic in the true sense of the word. Jesus is Yahweh and Muslims believe that Allah has no son. I use the term as a convenience and to be polite.

422. Dr. Timothy R. Furnish, "Mahdism (and Sectarianism and Superstition) Rises in the Islamic World." *History News Network*, August 13, 2012 (http://historynewsnetwork.org/article/147714), retrieved 1/23/19.

423. Furnish, 2012.

424. Dr. Timothy R. Furnish, *Ten Years' Captivation with the Mahdi's Camps: Essays on Muslim Eschatology, 2005–2015* (Kindle Edition, 2016), 6.

425. Dr. Timothy R. Furnish, "A Western View on Iran's WMD Goal: Nuclearizing the Eschaton, or Pre-Stocking the Mahdi's Arsenal?" *Institute for Near East & Gulf Military Analysis* (January 2011), 4.

426. Ze'ev Maghen, "Occultation in Perpetuum: Shi`ite Messianism and the Policies of the Islamic Republic," *Middle East Journal*, Vol. 62, No. 2 (Spring 2008), 237 (cited by Furnish).

427. Furnish, *Ten Years' Captivation With the Mahdi's Camps: Essays on Muslim Eschatology, 2005–2015*, 11–12.

428. Matthew 24:24.

429. Ibrahim, *Sword and Scimitar*, 3.

430. 2 Chronicles 25:12; 2 Kings 14:7. The incident possibly took place at Petra, which is called Sela ("Rock") in the Old Testament.

431. Referring to the Thirty Years War. Not to overlook the conflicts between the Irish and English in the seventeenth century, but the wars in Central Europe were considerably bloodier, with some eight million dead.

432. Veronica Neffinger, "Muslims Coming to Christ in Great Numbers Through Dreams and Visions." *Christian Headlines.com*, March 15, 2017 (https://www.christianheadlines.com/blog/muslims-coming-to-christ-in-great-numbers-through-dreams-and-visions.html), retrieved 1/25/19.

433. Ilan Ben Zion, "Jerusalem Mufti: Temple Mount Never Housed Jewish Temple." *The Times of Israel*, October 25, 2015 (https://www.timesofisrael.com/jerusalem-mufti-denies-temple-mount-ever-housed-jewish-shrine/), retrieved 1/25/19.

434. Ezequiel Doiny, "Replace the Waqf." *Israel National News*, July 17, 2017 (http://www.israelnationalnews.com/Articles/Article.aspx/20761), retrieved 1/25/19.

435. Elisabetta Povoledo, "Vatican Formally Recognizes Palestinian State by Signing Treaty." *The New York Times*, June 26, 2015 (https://www.nytimes.com/2015/06/27/world/middleeast/vatican-palestinian-state.html), retrieved 1/25/19.

436. Joel Bainerman, "The Vatican Agenda: How Does the Vatican View the

Legitimacy of Israel's Claims to Jerusalem?" *RedMoonRising.com* (http://www.redmoonrising.com/chamish/vaticanagenda.htm), retrieved 1/25/19.

437. Jerusalem Old City Initiative (http://www.cips-cepi.ca/event/jerusalem-old-city-initiative/), retrieved 12/12/15.

438. Aaron Klein, "International Mandate to Control Sections of Israel's Capital," *WND*, December 15, 2013 (http://www.wnd.com/2013/12/u-s-plan-gives-jerusalem-holy-sites-to-vatican/), retrieved 2/12/19.

439. For example: Bethan McKernan, "Turkish President Erdogan Calls on All Muslims to 'Protect' Jerusalem Holy Site Known as Temple Mount and Noble Sanctuary." *The Independent*, July 25, 2017 (https://www.independent.co.uk/news/world/middle-east/recep-tayyip-erdogan-jerusalem-turkey-president-muslims-temple-mount-mosque-haram-esh-sharif-a7858691.html), retrieved 1/25/19.

440. "Report: State Funds Groups That Advocate Building Third Temple." *Jerusalem Post*, August 31, 2014 (https://m.jpost.com/Diplomacy-and-Politics/Report-State-funds-groups-that-advocate-building-Third-Temple-321990), retrieved 1/25/19.

441. Adam Eliyahu Berkowitz, "Harbinger to Messiah: Red Heifer Is Born." *Breaking Israel News*, September 5, 2018 (https://www.breakingisraelnews.com/113476/temple-institute-certifies-red-heifer/), retrieved 2/19/19.

442. Uri Blau, "Netanyahu Allies Donated to Groups Pushing for Third Temple." *Haaretz*, December 9, 2015 (https://www.haaretz.com/netanyahu-allies-donated-to-groups-pushing-for-third-temple-1.5434678), retrieved 1/25/19.

443. Adam Eliyahu Berkowitz, "Shmittah and the Messiah: Could This Be the Year Before His Arrival?" *Breaking Israel News*, July 12, 2015 (https://www.breakingisraelnews.com/45001/shmitah-messiah-this-year-arrival-jewish-world/), retrieved 1/25/19.

444. Ezekiel 39:22. Note that "pestilence" in this verse is Deber, the patron god of ancient Ebla (c. 2500 BC), who's mentioned in Habakkuk 3:5 alongside Resheph, the plague-god.

445. Zechariah 12:10.

446. Matthew 24:30, Luke 21:27, Mark 13:26, Revelation 1:7.

447. 2 Corinthians 11:14.

448. Matthew 24:24, Mark 13:22.

449. Ezekiel 38:20.

450. Ezekiel 39:7.

451. Ezekiel 39:18.

452. For example, *Benson's Commentary on the Old and New Testaments* (1857), *Matthew Poole's Commentary* (1685), *Heinrich August Wilhelm Mayer's New Testament Commentary* (1880), *Jamieson Fausset and Brown Commentary* (1871), and *The Expositor's Greek Testament* (1891).

453. Daniel I. Block, *The Book of Ezekiel: Chapters 25–48* (Grand Rapids, Mi.; Cambridge: Eerdmans, 1998), 440.

454. Ibid., 434.

455. Matthew 12:24–26; Revelation 2:13.

456. Ezekiel 38:6, 15; 39:2.

457. Acts 11:26.

458. The other being the village of Dabiq, Syria, about twenty-five miles northeast of Aleppo. Sahih Muslim Book 041, Hadith Number 6924.

459. Sharon K. Gilbert, *EIKON*, unpublished presentation script shared via personal correspondence.

460. Bill Salus, *Psalm 83, the Missing Prophecy Revealed: How Israel Becomes the Next Mideast Superpower* (La Quinta, Calif.: Prophecy Depot Publishing, 2013).

461. For example, 1 Kings 21:26, 2 Kings 21:11.

462. "Oil Tanker Firms Scrap Most Ships In Three Decades." *OilPrice.com*, January 1, 2019 (https://oilprice.com/Energy/Energy-General/Oil-Tanker-Firms-Scrap-Most-Ships-In-Three-Decades.html), retrieved 2/27/19.

463. Revelation 17:18.

464. Revelation 17:16.

465. Daniel 9:27.

466. Genesis 15:18–21. This would push Israel's borders to include the Sinai Peninsula and eastward to the Euphrates River, which would take all or parts of Egypt, Lebanon, Syria, Jordan, and Iraq.

467. Irenaeus, *Against Heresies*, 30.2.

468. See the section titled "A Lot of Bull" in my book *Last Clash of the Titans*, pages 97–100.

469. Lipiński, op. cit.

470. This is the so-called Seven Mountains Mandate, which teaches that Christians are commanded to conquer the seven "mountains" of culture or societal influence: Arts and Entertainment, Business, Education, Family, Government, Media, and Religion.

471. For good biblical analysis of the apostolic-prophetic movement, see the books *A New Apostolic Reformation? A Biblical Response to a Worldwide Movement* and *God's Super-Apostles: Encountering the Worldwide Prophets and Apostles Movement*, both by Holly Pivec and Douglas Geivett.

472. 2 Thessalonians 2:4.

473. John 5:43.

474. Romans 12:19, quoting Deuteronomy 32:25.

475. Acts 1:7.

476. Luke 21:29–31.

477. Luke 4:5, which refers to the division of the nations described in Deuteronomy 32:8 (ESV and NET Bibles capture this sense, basing their translations "sons of God" and "heavenly assembly," respectively, rather than "sons of Israel") on the Septuagint and Dead Sea scrolls texts.

478. Revelation 20:7–10.

479. Jude 6.

480. Dr. Michael S. Heiser, "The Nephilim." *SitchinIsWrong.com* (http://www.sitchiniswrong.com/nephilim/nephilim.htm), retrieved 4/16/18.

481. Ibid.

482. Ibid.

483. "*'iyr*." *Blue Letter Bible* (https://www.blueletterbible.org/lang/lexicon/lexicon.cfm?Strongs=H5892), retrieved 1/30/19.

484. Dr. Michael S. Heiser, *The Divine Council in Late Canonical and Non-Canonical Second Temple Jewish Literature*. Doctoral dissertation (University of Wisconsin-Madison, 2004), 227–228.

485. S. Münger, "Ariel." In K. van der Toorn, B. Becking, & P. W. van der Horst (Eds.), *Dictionary of Deities and Demons in the Bible (2nd extensively rev. ed.)* (Leiden; Boston; Köln; Grand Rapids, MI; Cambridge: Brill; Eerdmans, 1999), 89.

486. 2 Kings 18:13–19:37.

487. M. J. Mulder, "Carmel." In K. van der Toorn, B. Becking, & P. W. van der Horst (Eds.), *Dictionary of Deities and Demons in the Bible (2nd extensively rev. ed.)* (Leiden; Boston; Köln; Grand Rapids, MI; Cambridge: Brill; Eerdmans, 1999), 182–183.

488. Ugaritic text KTU 1.22. Nicolas Wyatt, *Religious texts from Ugarit* (2nd ed.) (London; New York: Sheffield Academic Press, 2002), 322.

489. Klaas Spronk, "Travellers." In K. van der Toorn, B. Becking, & P. W. van der Horst (Eds.), *Dictionary of deities and demons in the Bible (2nd extensively rev. ed.)* (Leiden; Boston; Köln; Grand Rapids, MI; Cambridge: Brill; Eerdmans, 1999), 876.

490. Wyatt, op. cit., 321.

491. Leviticus 19:31, 20:7, 20:26; Deuteronomy 18:11.

492. Psalm 106:28–29.

493. Gilbert, *Last Clash of the Titans*, 170–171.

494. Spronk, op. cit.

495. Deuteronomy 32:49.

496. Bruce Bower, "An exploding meteor may have wiped out ancient Dead Sea communities." *ScienceNews* (https://www.sciencenews.org/article/exploding-meteor-may-have-wiped-out-ancient-dead-sea-communities), retrieved 2/15/19.

497. Phillip J. Silvia, "The Geography and History of Tall el-Hammam." Society for Interdisciplinary Studies *Chronology & Catastrophism Workshop* (2014:1), 33–36.

498. Khair Yassine, "The Dolmens: Construction and Dating Reconsidered." *Bulletin of the American Schools of Oriental Research*, No. 259 (Summer, 1985), 63–69.

499. Steven Collins and Latayne C. Scott, *Discovering the City of Sodom* (New York: Howard Books, 2013), 30–31.

500. "Dr. Phillip Silvia: The Science of Finding Sodom." *A View from the Bunker*, February 3, 2019 (https://www.vftb.net/?p=7604), retrieved 2/15/19.

501. Genesis 14:1–16.

502. Klaas Spronk, *Beatific Afterlife in Ancient Israel and in the Ancient Near East* (Kevelaer: Butzon & Bercker, 1986), 228.

503. "Discoveries." *Tall el-Hammam Excavation Project* (https://tallelhammam. com/discoveries), retrieved 2/15/19.

504. 1 Thessalonians 5:9.

505. Isaiah 14:10–11.

506. J. Daniel Hays, *The Message of the Prophets: A Survey of the Prophetic and Apocalyptic Books of the Old Testament* (Grand Rapids, Mich.: Zondervan, 2010), 56–57.

507. Christopher B. Hays, "An Egyptian Loanword in the Book of Isaiah and the Deir 'Alla Inscription: Heb. *nṣr*, Aram. *nqr*, and Eg. *nṯr* as "[Divinized] Corpse." *Journal of Ancient Egyptian Interconnections* Vol. 4:2 (2012), 18.

508. Ibid., 17.

509. 1 Enoch 16:1.

510. This leads to another line of speculation: If Seir—i.e., Petra—is the true origin of the Ka'ba, could this prophecy apply to Islam?

511. Amar Annus, "Sons of Seth and the South Wind," *Mesopotamian Medicine and Magic. Studies in Honor of Markham J. Geller*, edited by S. Panayotov and L. Vacin. *Ancient Magic and Divination*, Vol. 14 (Boston; Leiden: Brill, 2018), 11.

512. Amar Annus, "Are There Greek Rephaim? On the Etymology of Greek *Meropes* and *Titanes*." *Ugarit-Forschungen* 31 (1999), 19.

513. J. B. Pritchard, *Ancient Near Eastern Texts: Relating to the Old Testament* (Ann Arbor, Mich: Pro Quest, 2005), 329.

514. Ibid.

515. Genesis 14:5; Deuteronomy 2:10, 2:20–21.

516. Amar Annus, "Are There Greek Rephaim? On the Etymology of Greek *Meropes* and *Titanes*." *Ugarit-Forschungen* 31 (1999), 19. Annus cited Michael Heltzer, *The Suteans* (Naples: Istituto Universitario Orientale, 1981), 52.

517. 1 Corinthians 15:1–4.

518. Ezekiel 28:14.

519. Isaiah 14:9–21.

520. Isaiah 14:13 identified the sacred mountain of Baal, *yarkete* tsaphon (Mount Zaphon), as the mount of assembly of the divine rebel.

521. Jude 7.
522. Genesis 6:1–4.
523. 1 Enoch 16:1.
524. A theme explored in depth in my book *Last Clash of the Titans.*
525. Ugarit text KTU 1.161.
526. 1 Peter 3:19–20. Peter links the spirits in prison to the Flood.
527. The fifth trumpet during the Tribulation; Revelation 9:1–11.
528. Gilbert (2017), op.cit., 52–66.
529. Deuteronomy 32:8–9; 4:19.
530. 1 Corinthians 2:6–8.
531. 1 Peter 3:19.
532. Douglas Mangum, "Interpreting First Peter 3:18–22." *Faithlife Study Bible* (Bellingham, WA: Lexham Press, 2012).